Optimise

Student's Book

A2

macmillan education

UNIT	READING	GRAMMAR	VOCABULARY
1 Time out (HOBBIES) p 4–13	*How to find the right hobby* Finding words which mean the same Matching	Present simple, adverbs of frequency, imperatives Possessive *'s*, prepositions of time and place	Words connected with *hobbies* Nouns/verbs Phrasal verbs
2 That's entertainment! (LEISURE) p 14–23	*Gaming is big business* Understanding important words Right/Wrong/Doesn't say	Present simple and present continuous Present continuous for future use	Words connected with *entertainment* Words + prepositions Collocations with nouns
Progress check Units 1 and 2: Grammar and vocabulary / Exam skills p 24–25			
3 What's for dinner? (FOOD) p 26–35	*Kids in the kitchen* Identifying *'when'* and *'who'* Multiple-choice cloze	Past simple: regular verbs, *Wh-* words Past simple: irregular verbs	Words connected with *food* Verbs/adjectives Collocations with verbs
4 On your way (TRAVEL) p 36–45	*Useful travel tips* Deciding the general message Matching	Past continuous, linking words Past simple and past continuous	Words connected with *travel* Compound nouns Phrasal verbs
Progress check Units 3 and 4: Grammar and vocabulary / Exam skills p 46–47			
5 Technology talks (TECHNOLOGY) p 48–57	*Technology habits around the world* Understanding how often Right/Wrong/Doesn't say	Quantifiers with countable and uncountable nouns Comparatives and superlatives	Words connected with *communication and technology* Compound nouns Collocations with verbs
6 Teen fashion (CLOTHES) p 58–67	*Fashion changes* Choosing between similar answers Multiple-choice cloze	Present perfect simple with *ever* and *never* Present perfect simple and past simple	Words connected with *fashion, clothes and shopping* Verbs + prepositions Collocations with verbs
Progress check Units 5 and 6: Grammar and vocabulary / Exam skills p 68–69			
7 The future of learning (EDUCATION) p 70–79	*Technology for all* Understanding *this, that, these, it, them* Multiple-choice cloze	*going to* *will* and *going to*	Words connected with *school and studying* Words + prepositions Collocations with verbs
8 It's only a game (SPORT) p 80–89	*The way to win* Scanning Right/Wrong/Doesn't say	Modals (1): ability, necessity, obligation, possibility Modals (2): advice, permission, polite requests, prohibition	Words connected with *sport* Verbs/nouns Collocations with verbs
Progress check Units 7 and 8: Grammar and vocabulary / Exam skills p 90–91			
9 Whatever the weather (WEATHER) p 92–101	*The world's strangest weather* Skimming Multiple-choice cloze	Zero conditional, first conditional Second conditional	Words connected with *weather and nature* Words + prepositions Nouns/adjectives
10 Looking after yourself (HEALTH) p 102–111	*Doctors in the air* Guessing the meaning of new words Matching	Present perfect simple: *for, since, already, just, yet* Verb patterns: verb + infinitive / *-ing*	Words connected with *health* Words + prepositions Collocations with verbs
Progress check Units 9 and 10: Grammar and vocabulary / Exam skills p 112–113			
11 The world of work (JOBS) p 114–123	*All aboard the Children's Railway* Understanding the reasons for / purpose of a text Right/Wrong/Doesn't say	Indefinite pronouns Relative clauses : *who, which, that*	Words connected with *work and jobs* Words with *-ian / -ress / -ist / -er / -r* Words + prepositions
12 Home time (HOUSES) p 124–133	*Living with nature* Possessive adjectives Multiple-choice cloze	Present simple passive Past simple passive and *by*	Words connected with *houses and homes* Phrasal verbs Collocations with verbs
Progress check Units 11 and 12: Grammar and vocabulary / Exam skills p 134–135			

SPEAKING LESSON PROMPT CARDS p136–141 ► **OPTIMISE YOUR EXAMS** ► **READING AND WRITING** p 142–145

Grammar reference p150–161 Vocabulary reference p 162–168 Writing reference p 169–174 Irregular verbs reference p 175

LISTENING	SPEAKING	LANGUAGE IN USE	WRITING
Identifying factual information **Picture multiple choice**	Talking about yourself **Interview** Talk2Me	Focusing on the language **Multiple-matching dialogue**	Noting down key information **Information transfer**
Listening for words that mean the same **Multiple matching**	Talking about times **Collaborative task** Talk2Me	Thinking about context **Multiple-choice dialogue**	Using your own words **An email**
Predicting what the speaker will say **Multiple choice**	Explaining likes and dislikes **Interview** Talk2Me	Thinking about grammar (conjunctions, prepositions and pronouns) **Open cloze**	Use your vocabulary **A note**
Listening for important information **Gap fill**	Asking someone to repeat **Collaborative task** Talk2Me	Using linking words **Multiple choice**	Punctuation and spelling **A postcard**
Understanding when things happen **Picture multiple choice**	Making comparisons **Interview** Talk2Me	Pronouns **Multiple-choice dialogue**	Making notes: where and when **Information transfer**
Choosing the right answer **Multiple matching**	Giving details **Collaborative task** Talk2Me	Understanding functional language **Multiple-matching dialogue**	Giving your opinion **An online review**
Thinking about the missing information **Gap fill**	Talking about the future **Interview** Talk2Me	Learning word phrases **Multiple-choice cloze**	Understanding similar information **Information transfer**
Listening for important information **Multiple matching**	Asking questions **Collaborative task** Talk2Me	Modal verbs **Multiple-choice cloze**	Writing in an informal style **An email**
Understanding the speakers' questions **Picture multiple choice**	Talking about a topic **Interview** Talk2Me	Identifying key words **Multiple-choice dialogue**	Giving advice and instructions **A note**
Understanding when something happened **Multiple matching**	Giving yourself time to think **Collaborative task** Talk2Me	Giving short answers **Multiple-matching dialogue**	Giving advice **An online post**
Taking notes **Gap fill**	Talking about jobs **Interview** Talk2Me	Understanding the type of word that is missing **Open cloze**	Negative phrases and opposites **Information transfer**
Checking your answers **Multiple choice**	Talking about money **Collaborative task** Talk2Me	Learning vocabulary **Multiple-choice sentences**	Using adjectives **A postcard**

▶ LISTENING p 146–147 ▶ SPEAKING / SPEAKING TEST VIDEO p 148–149

Student's Resource Centre

- *Talk2Me* videos (flipped classroom)
- Speaking test videos
- *Optimise your grammar* worksheets
- *Optimise your vocabulary* worksheet
- *Say it right* pronunciation worksheets
- Culture and CLIL worksheets
- Class and Workbook audio

1 Time out

READING | Matching | Signs and notices

1 In pairs or as a group, answer the questions.

1 What are the most popular hobbies in your country at the moment?

2 Which of these hobbies do you do or would you like to do?

3 How do you usually choose your hobbies?

2 Read the online article on page 5 quickly. How many hobbies are mentioned?

____

3 1.01 **Read the article again and decide if the sentences (1–6) are true (T) or false (F).**

1 The writer suggests hobbies for different kinds of people. **T / F**

2 Kareem spends all his free time playing video games online. **T / F**

3 Amaya is a member of a club that meets once a week. **T / F**

4 Sometimes Amaya prints her favourite photos. **T / F**

5 Jake doesn't go skateboarding alone. **T / F**

6 It's never fun choosing a new hobby. **T / F**

4 In pairs, match the highlighted words in the article to a definition (1–8).

1 a machine for taking pictures ____________

2 easy ____________

3 an online diary ____________

4 magazines which tell stories through drawings ____________

5 not the same ____________

6 something you enjoy doing in your free time ____________

7 a person who belongs to a club ____________

8 to talk about ____________

EXAM SKILL

Finding words which mean the same

- Underline the most important words in the sentences.
- Now look for words in the signs and notices that mean the same as the underlined words, for example 'can't go into' = 'no entrance'.

How to find THE RIGHT HOBBY

Hobbies are a great way to learn something new. Hobbies help you to make friends or get fit. But how do you choose the right hobby for you? It's quite simple: first, think about what type of person you are and what you usually like doing, then choose an activity to try. Here are some suggestions.

Do you often spend time in your bedroom alone? Don't spend all week listening to music or playing games online. Try reading comics, writing a blog or drawing.

'I often play video games, but I don't spend all my free time playing online. I also write a blog about new video games every month.'
Kareem (*video game blogger*)

Do you prefer being with other people? Find a club to join that meets once or twice a week to do something you enjoy.

'I'm a member of a photography club and I always have my camera with me. We meet every Thursday evening to discuss ideas. We never print our photos, we post them online.'
Amaya (*photography club member*)

Do you like adventure? Try a new sport or an activity like skiing, skateboarding or climbing. These hobbies are fun, exciting and often they're free.

'My favourite hobby is skateboarding. I go skateboarding with my friends in the park. We sometimes skateboard to school!'
Jake (*skateboarder*)

Search online for more ideas or to find information about different clubs and activities in your area. People don't usually find the perfect hobby immediately. However, it's fun trying out new things and meeting people.

5 **Look at the sentences (1–5) and the signs and notices (A–H) in Exercise 6. Underline the important words in each one.**

OPTIMISE YOUR EXAM

Matching

- Read the signs and notices carefully and decide where they are from and who they are for.
- This will help you to understand the context of each sign or notice.

6 **Which notice (A–H) says this (1–5)? There are some extra letters you do not need.**

Example: You can't go into the room this way. _E_

1 This place opens again soon. ____
2 This place is open 24 hours a day. ____
3 You cannot do this activity in the rain. ____
4 You can try this activity twice a day, but don't forget a drink! ____
5 People can't use the room this afternoon. ____

A **Cycling classes**
mornings 10 am–11 am afternoons 2 pm–3 pm.
Remember to bring water!

B Turn off mobile phones in swimming pool area.

C NO TENNIS CLUB AGAIN BECAUSE OF BAD WEATHER TODAY!

D **COME AND TRY CLIMBING!**
Climbing wall open tomorrow 8 am.

E No entrance to photography studio. Please use other door.

F Art room closed for ten minutes – just gone for lunch!

G **SORRY!**
Computer room closed today 3 pm–5 pm.

H **Skateboarding park**
The park is always open!

THINK | RESEARCH | CULTURE | LEARN | ME

In pairs or groups, look at the notices in this lesson and say which activity you would like to do and why.

▶ **Workbook Unit 1:** Reading, pages 4–5, exercises 1, 2, 3

1 GRAMMAR 1 | Present simple, adverbs of frequency, imperatives

Grammar in context

Find and read these sentences in the text on page 5 and answer the questions.

1 *Hobbies **help** you to make friends* ... (Introduction)
2 *I often **play** video games,* ... (Kareem)

Which sentence uses the present simple for the following?

a) a habit ____
b) something that is usually true ____

Which word in sentence 2 is the adverb of frequency ____________

REMEMBER

- We use the present simple for:
  - habits or things we do often: ***Do** you **walk** to school? I **ride** my bike to school every day.*
  - things that are usually or always true: *We **live** in a small house. We **don't live** in a city.*
- We use adverbs of frequency with the present simple to say how often something happens:

  never sometimes often usually always
  0% ———————————— 100%

  They go before the main verb, (*I **never eat** cheese.*) or after the verb *to be* (*He is **often** late.*).
- We use time expressions to show when something happens:
  all/every day/week/month, once/twice a day/week/month / three times a day, etc.

▶ **See Grammar reference, Unit 1,** page 150

1 Complete the sentences with the verbs in the box.

go | goes | ~~has~~ | have | play | plays

1 She likes music. She ___*has*___ a guitar and a piano.
2 He usually ____________ to the park on his bike after school.
3 They ____________ English lessons on Mondays and Fridays.
4 She ____________ tennis and likes to go swimming.
5 I ____________ football in the park after school.
6 We ____________ swimming every Wednesday.

2 Choose the correct word or phrase to complete each question.

a) When **do / does** you **go** swimming? ____
b) Where **do / does** you play football? ____
c) What **do / does** she like? ____
d) When do they **have / has** English lessons? ____
e) What does he do when he **get / gets** home? ____
f) What sports does she **play / plays**? ____

3 Work in pairs. Match the answers in Exercise 1 to the questions in Exercise 2.

4 Rewrite the sentences including the words in bold.

1 It's very cold in the winter. **often**
____
2 I watch TV with my sister. **usually**
____
3 He goes to bed at 9 o'clock. **always**
____
4 I drink cola for breakfast. **never**
____

Grammar in context

Look at these sentences from the notices on page 5.

***Turn off** mobile phones in swimming pool area.*
***Please use** other door.*

REMEMBER

- We use imperative forms to give instructions or orders.
- We can use *please* with orders to be polite.

▶ **See Grammar reference, Unit 1,** page 150

5 Choose the correct words to complete the imperative sentences.

1 **Remember / Remembers** to do your homework.
2 **Don't / No** forget to bring your camera.
3 **Please open / Open please** the door.

6 Complete the text with the correct form of the verbs in the box.

be | have | hit | live
love | put | ride | watch

TWO HOBBIES IN ONE

Every weekend I go to the mountains with my bicycle. I go with my cousin. He (**1**) ____________ in a town near here. When we (**2**) ____________ our mountain bikes, we usually film the action. We have small cameras which we (**3**) ____________ on our helmets. It is really exciting. Mum always says, '(**4**) ____________ careful!'. But sometimes one of us (**5**) ____________ an accident. My cousin often (**6**) ____________ something and falls off his bike. When we get home we (**7**) ____________ our video on the laptop. We (**8**) ____________ it.

Words connected with *hobbies*

1 1.02 **Write the correct word for each picture. Use the words in the box. Listen and check.**

cycling | horse-riding
painting | playing computer games
reading | rock climbing
skateboarding | swimming

1 ______________

2 ______________

3 ______________

4 ______________

5 ______________

6 ______________

7 ______________

8 ______________

2 1.03 **Match the words in the box to the correct description. Listen and check.**

barbecue | beach | collect
magazine | photograph | tent

1 You can take one of these with a camera. ______________
2 People who like swimming in the sea often go here. ______________
3 A thin paper book with photographs, articles, stories, etc. ______________
4 When you buy and keep books or magazines, for example, you do this. ______________
5 A meal where you cook and eat food outdoors. ______________
6 You stay in this when you go camping. ______________

Nouns/verbs

3 1.04 **Complete the table. Listen and check.**

object	person	verb
painting	(1) ______________	to paint
photograph	(2) ______________	to photograph / take photographs
music	(3) ______________	to make/play music
guitar	guitarist	to (4) ______________ the guitar
(5) ______________	video (6) ______________	to play video games

4 **Complete the sentences with words from the table in Exercise 3.**

1 Anja loves ______________ and uses really bright colours.
2 I sometimes listen to ______________ in bed before I go to sleep.
3 He's a good guitarist. He ______________ every day.
4 The ______________ took lots of pictures of us climbing.
5 I want to be a ______________ one day and play the piano.
6 I like video games, but I'm not really a big ______________ .

SAY IT RIGHT

Resource centre: Unit 1
Word stress

Phrasal verbs

5 1.05 **Match the meanings (a–g) to the phrasal verbs (1–7). Listen and check.**

1 come in ___ **a)** to return after going somewhere
2 come round ___ **b)** to start a machine
3 get back ___ **c)** to stop a machine
4 get off ___ **d)** to leave a bus or train
5 look after ___ **e)** to enter
6 turn off ___ **f)** to take care of someone or something
7 turn on ___ **g)** to visit

6 **Choose the correct word to complete each sentence.**

1 Please turn **off** / **on** that loud music!
2 Welcome to 'Games Night'! Come **round** / **in** and join us.
3 Let's watch a film. Please turn **on** / **off** the TV.
4 Quick, we need to get **back** / **off** the bus here. The park's just over the road.
5 Alex is going to come **round** / **in** this afternoon. I want to play my new video game with him.
6 Can you look **under** / **after** my bag, please?
7 We won't get **back** / **off** until quite late after the football match.

▶ **Vocabulary reference,** page 163 ▶ **Workbook Unit 1:** Vocabulary, page 7, exercises 1, 2, 3

1 LISTENING | Picture multiple choice (short conversations)

1 **In pairs or as a group, look at the pictures in Exercise 4.**

1 What is the same about the pictures in each set?
2 What are the differences between the pictures?

EXAM SKILL

Identifying factual information

- Look at the pictures and make short notes on what you can see.
- In this part of the exam, you often hear information about prices, numbers, times and dates. Think of the different ways to say these, e.g. *half past four, four thirty*.
- You often hear about places and directions (e.g. *the place next to the hotel*). Note down any prepositions that give important information.

2 **Look at the set of pictures below (A–C) and match them to the notes (1–3).**

A

B

C

1 *camping, busy campsite, tents together* ____

2 *camping, campsite, tent on grass* ____

3 *camping, campsite, tent under tree* ____

3 1.06 **Listen to the conversation. Write a word or phrase in each gap.**

Girl: So, where is your cousin's tent?
Boy: It's in a good place. There aren't any other tents (1) ______________ it.
Girl: Is it (2) ______________ of that field?
Boy: No, it's (3) ______________ that big tree.

OPTIMISE YOUR EXAM

Picture multiple choice

- Read the questions carefully and underline the important words.
- When you listen, think about words with the same meaning as the words you underlined.

4 1.07 **Listen to the five conversations. There is one question for each conversation. For each conversation, choose the correct answer (A, B or C).**

1 What game do they play?

A ☐

B ☐

C ☐

2 What does Helen like to read?

A ☐

B ☐

C ☐

3 What time does football practice usually start?

A ☐

B ☐

C ☐

4 What do they have for dinner?

A ☐

B ☐

C ☐

5 When does the girl have an art lesson?

A ☐

B ☐

C ☐

5 1.07 **Listen again and check your answers.**

▶ **Workbook Unit 1:** Listening, page 8, exercises 1, 2

GRAMMAR 2 | Possessive *'s*, prepositions of time and place

Grammar in context

Look at these sentences from the audio in the listening lesson and answer the question.

1 *My brother**'s** new video game is good.*
2 *I sometimes look at my sister**'s** pop magazine.*
3 *Ryan**'s** dad brings us home.*

Which statement is true, a or b? ____

a) one of the sentences uses 's to replace *is*.
b) all of the sentences use 's to show possession.

REMEMBER

- We use ***'s*** to show possession: *It is the bag that Amy owns.* → *It is Amy**'s** bag.*
- We can use ***'s*** to show possession with plurals: *The children**'s** books are on their desks.*
- For plurals ending in **s**, we just add an apostrophe: *My parents' house is near here.*

Note: Apostrophes are also used in contractions to indicate missing letters, e.g. ***She's** my sister.* = ***She is** my sister. **He's** got a book.* = ***He has** got a book.*

▶ See Grammar reference, Unit 1, page 151

1 **Complete the second sentences using possessive *'s*.**

1 This book belongs to Anna.
This is __________ .
2 The bags that belong to the boys are all here.
The __________ are all here.
3 My parents own that red car.
That is __________ red car.
4 The desks for the children aren't very big.
The __________ aren't very big.

2 **Decide the use of *'s* in each sentence – possession (P) or the verb *to be* (B).**

1 Your mother's brother is your uncle. ____
2 That woman's married to Jim. ____
3 Your aunt's son is your cousin. ____
4 My sister's very good at English. ____

Grammar in context

Look at these sentences from the audio in the listening lesson. Match the words in bold to a function (a or b).

1 *It's **in** a good place. There aren't any other tents **near** it.*
2 *No, it's **under** that big tree.*
3 *It always begins **at** 9.30.*
4 *We had pizza **on** Monday.*

a) describing place __________ , __________ , __________

b) describing time __________ , __________

REMEMBER

- We use a variety of prepositions in time expressions:

at	in
6pm, midnight, New Year, the weekend, the moment	the morning/afternoon/ evening, June, summer, 2022, two weeks' time
on	**no preposition**
Saturday, Monday morning, New Year's Day, 22 June, holiday, my/your/ her, etc. birthday	today, yesterday, tomorrow, last night, two weeks ago, yesterday evening, tonight

- We use prepositions of place to show where things are:
*The book is **on** the table. My school is **next to** the library. There is a park **in front of** my house. We usually meet **at** the park.*

▶ See Grammar reference, Unit 1, page 151

3 **Choose the correct word or phrase to complete each sentence.**

1 We went to the cinema **in last week** / **last week**.
2 Our team plays football in the park next **to** / **of** the museum. We play **at** / **on** Saturday morning.
3 We usually go on holiday **in** / **at** August.
4 **In** / **On** two weeks' time I'm going to England.
5 We usually go to the pool every day **in** / **on** summer, but it's closed **today** / **at today**.
6 Do you usually have a party **at** / **on** your birthday?

4 **Complete the text with the words in the box.**

at	in	in front	near	next	on

Last year when we were **(1)** __________ holiday **(2)** __________ Greece, we stayed with my mum's best friend, Alexandra. She's Greek and she lives **(3)** __________ the sea. She's really good at painting and has a studio **(4)** __________ to the house with amazing sea views. **(5)** __________ the weekend, she paints beautiful pictures of the sea and of birds flying **(6)** __________ of her studio. This is one of her pictures.

1 SPEAKING | Interview

Talk2Me

My surname is ...

Flipped classroom

1 **Watch the *Talk2Me* video and answer the questions.**

1 Who are Jojo and Max? Who is Evie?
2 Which two days of the week are they all free to practise their dance?
3 When is the competition?

2 **Watch the video again. Underline the words and phrases in the *Phrase expert* box that you hear on the video.**

PHRASE EXPERT

My (sur)name is … | That's (S-M-I-T-H). | In my free time, I usually … | At lunchtime / After school / In the evenings / At the weekend / In the holidays … | I/We always/usually/often/sometimes/never …

3 1.08 **Listen and repeat the alphabet. Then in pairs, ask and answer the questions.**

Aa Bb Cc Dd Ee Ff Gg
Hh Ii Jj Kk Ll Mm Nn Oo Pp
Qq Rr Ss Tt Uu Vv
Ww Xx Yy Zz

What's your name?
What's your surname?
How do you spell it?

EXAM SKILL

Talking about yourself

- In the first part of the test, the examiner will ask you to spell your surname. Practise saying the alphabet and check that you know how to say the letters in your name.
- You also have to give information about yourself and what you like or dislike. Check that you can describe your hobbies and interests.

4 1.09 **Listen to a student talking to an examiner. Complete the table below.**

Surname:	
Hobbies:	
Evenings:	
Weekend:	
Holidays:	

5 1.09 **Listen again. Write down the questions the examiner asks.**

1 ______
2 ______
3 ______
4 ______
5 ______
6 ______

6 **Write down the phrase the student used to ask for the question to be repeated.**

______

______

OPTIMISE YOUR EXAM

Interview

- If you don't understand the examiner, ask them to repeat the question. Use phrases like *(Sorry,) could you repeat the question, please?*
- It is OK to give a short answer for your name. You should give a longer answer for everything else.

7 **Work in pairs. Use the prompts to take turns asking and answering the questions.**

- What's your surname?
- How do you spell it?
- What are your hobbies?
- What games do you like playing?
- How much free time do you have?
- What do you usually do in the evenings?
- What do you usually do at the weekend?

▶ **Workbook Unit 1:** Speaking, pages 8–9, exercises 1, 2, 3

1 Work in pairs. Read the text below and answer the questions.

1 What can you do at the club?
2 Can anyone use it?
3 How much is it to use the club?
4 Would you like to join the club? Why / Why not?

JOIN OUR CLUB!

Come and make new friends or try a new activity!

These are some of the fun things you can do at Eight-Mile Wood adventure club:

climb trees, ride your bike, build dens, join an art class, learn nature photography or cook wild food!

Every Friday we organise a barbecue. Every month there is a mini music festival. Bring your tent and camp between the trees.

It's free to join the club, but you pay £10 for special classes.

Children 11 years and over are welcome. You just need to fill in a form with your parents' contact details.

EXAM SKILL

Focusing on the language

- Read all the sentences carefully to understand the main ideas.
- Look at the language used in the sentences before and after the gap and choose the best answer.

2 Read the phone conversation below and number the sentences in the correct order.

a) Between the trees, but not too close to the musicians. ____
b) Yes, I study at a language school here. ____
c) Yes, please. I want to buy two tickets for the music festival. ____
d) Thanks, that's great. Goodbye. ____
e) OK, first of all, where would you like to camp? ____
f) Good morning. Can I help you? _1_
g) OK. Well, there's a student discount. Bring your ID on Friday. ____
h) Right, that's no problem. Are you a student? ____

3 Underline the words in Exercise 2 which helped you to put the conversation in order. Compare with a partner.

OPTIMISE YOUR EXAM

Multiple-matching dialogue

- Always read the instructions and example carefully.
- Cross out the example sentence so you don't try to use it again.

4 Complete the conversation about the sports club with sentences A–H. There are some extra letters you do not need.

Receptionist: Hello, Eight-Mile Wood, how can I help you?
Example:
Andy: _E_
Receptionist: Well, what kind of things do you like to do?
Andy: 1 ____
Receptionist: Well, it's certainly a great place to make new friends! How old are you?
Andy: 2 ____
Receptionist: I see. Well, there's a gaming club that meets here every month. I can ask a member to text you about it.
Andy: 3 ____
Receptionist: I think it's every Monday afternoon at 4. Then they go skateboarding together.
Andy: 4 ____
Receptionist: Yes. But you need to bring your own skateboard.
Andy: 5 ____ I'll ask him.
Receptionist: OK, great. I hope he says yes!

A I'm eleven. I start high school next week.
B I have lots of music, thanks.
C Really? That sounds good. Can I go too?
D My brother sometimes lets me borrow his.
E ~~Oh, hi. Can you tell me about your activities?~~
F It's on the 8th of September.
G Usually I play video games or listen to music at home. But I want to meet more people.
H That sounds great. When do they meet?

THINK | RESEARCH | **CULTURE** | LEARN | ME

Work in groups and answer the question.
Do you think there are enough places for young people to do activities outdoors in your country? Why / Why not?

▶ **Vocabulary reference,** page 163 ▶ **Workbook Unit 1:** Language in Use, page 9, exercises 1, 2

1 **In pairs or as a group, answer the questions.**

1 Do you go to any clubs or sports activities? Where? When?

2 Are after-school clubs popular with teenagers where you live? Why / Why not?

3 What kind of club would you like to go to? Why?

2 **Read and label the information about an activity course with the words in the box.**

booking form	email	poster

A ______________________

After-school Activities Plus

Basketball	Tuesday afternoon/evening
Football	Thursday evening
Photography	Wednesday afternoon
Skateboarding	Monday afternoon
Beginner Classes:	3.30–4.30 / 4.30–5.30 pm
Advanced Classes:	5.30–6.30 pm

Note: Always take Student ID to activities

B ______________________

To: After-school Activities Plus

Hello, my name is Paulo Verratti. I want to start a new hobby. I would like to learn how to play basketball. I am free after 4 pm on Monday and Tuesday.

Can I book a place on one of your courses? I'm almost 14 years old. Do I need to bring ID with a photograph?

Thanks,

Paulo

C ______________________

After-school Activities Plus

BOOKING FORM

Name:		*Paulo Verratti*
Age:	1	~~14~~ 13
Activity:	2	*basketbal*
Level:	3	*advanced*
Day:	4	*Thursday*
Start time:	5	*4.00 pm*

EXAM SKILL

Noting down key information

- Circle any dates, times, places and numbers in the poster and the email.
- Note down what they mean, e.g. *Is it when something starts or ends?*
- Look at the booking form for words with the same meaning as, or connected to, the words in the poster and email, e.g. *activity* → *course*; *level* → *beginner/advanced*.

3 **Look back at the information in A and B in Exercise 2 and underline all the days, times and numbers. Compare your answers with a partner and say what each one refers to.**

4 **Work in pairs. Look at Paulo's completed booking form in Exercise 2. Find the mistake in each piece of information (1–5) and correct it.**

OPTIMISE YOUR EXAM

Information transfer

- In this part of the exam you read two short texts, then write words or phrases to complete some notes.
- The two texts could be emails, advertisements, posters or notes.
- The notes you complete could be a diary or a form.

5 **Work in pairs or groups. Read texts A and B quickly and answer the questions.**

1 How many classes are there? ____________

2 What course did Simone do last year? ____________

Read the poster and the email. Fill in the information in the booking form.

A

Just do It!

Summer activities

Art classes	Monday morning/afternoon
Guitar lessons	Thursday evening
Horse-riding	Wednesday afternoon
Modern dance	Wednesday morning/afternoon
Photography	Tuesday morning/afternoon
Beginner Classes:	9.30–11.30 am 2.30–4.30 pm
Advanced Classes:	9.30–11.30 am 3.30–5.30 pm

Barbecue every Friday evening – ask for details

B

To: Just do It! Summer activities

Hi, my name is Simone Roca. I'm 14 years old. Last year I did the horse-riding course. This summer I want to do something different. I'm a member of a street-dance club and practise twice a week. Can I join your dance class too? I have a painting class on Wednesday mornings, but I'm free in the afternoon.

Thanks,

Simone

C

After-school Activities Plus

BOOKING FORM

Name:	*Simone Roca*
Age:	1
Activity:	2
Level:	3
Day:	4
Start time:	5

6 **Plan** **You are going to complete the booking form for Simone. Tick the things you need to do before you start writing.**

1 Read both texts, A and B. ____

2 Look for numbers, days and dates and find out what they mean. ____

3 Make sure I know exactly what information I need to complete the booking form. ____

7 **Write** **Write the information to complete Simone's booking form in Exercise 5. Check your spelling and use of capital letters.**

8 **Check** **Before you hand in your booking form, complete this checklist.**

Checklist

- ○ I've carefully read both texts.
- ○ I've completed all the answers on the form.
- ○ I've checked my spelling.
- ○ I've checked my use of capital letters.

Extra writing

9 **You are going to write an email asking about one of the activities in text A in Exercise 2. Choose a course you want to do, then answer questions 1–4.**

1 Who are you writing to?

____

2 What style should you write in?

____

3 What information can you give?

____

4 Which questions could you ask?

____

____

____

Now write your email in 25–35 words.

2 That's entertainment!

READING | Right/Wrong/Doesn't say | A magazine article

1 In pairs or as a group, answer the questions.

1. What do you like doing for entertainment on school days and at the weekend?
2. What do you like doing for entertainment with your friends and what do you like doing with your family?

2 Read the magazine article on page 15 quickly and find out who Florian is.

EXAM SKILL

Understanding important words

- Read the questions and underline the important words.
- Then read the text carefully and look for words with a similar meaning to the ones you underlined in the questions.
- Understanding these words will help you choose the correct answers.

OPTIMISE YOUR EXAM

Right/Wrong/Doesn't say

- Choose 'Right' if the sentence is true according to the information in the text.
- Choose 'Wrong' if the sentence is not true according to the information in the text.
- Choose 'Doesn't say' if the information is not in the text.

3 Read the sentences and underline the important words. Then read the first two paragraphs of the article again and label the sentences with the words in the box.

right	wrong	doesn't say

1. People play video games more now than they did in the past. ____________
2. New video games are very expensive. ____________
3. Video gaming is the world's most popular form of entertainment. ____________

GAMING IS BIG BUSINESS

1 **These days, more young people are playing video games. The world of video gaming entertainment is growing quickly. If you're a gaming fan, read this.**

2 Video gaming is now a very popular form of entertainment in the world (not quite as popular as listening to music and watching TV, though). Both girls and boys play video games regularly, mostly for fun. Some people play alone and others play in big competitions. There are places like the e-sports *Gfinity Arena* in London, where hundreds of people go to play online games with other fans around the world.

3 However, a small number of people make money from gaming. One person who does exactly that is teenager Brandon Relph. Brandon knows a lot about computer games. He started playing them when he was 10. He designed and built fantastic digital worlds using *Minecraft*. Now Brandon works on his business for a few hours every night, when he isn't doing his homework. Brandon still designs attractive worlds, but now people buy them and use them in adverts.

4 Brandon earned £10,000 from his business before he was 16! And he lives with his parents, so he doesn't need to spend money on an office.

5 Brandon works with a German teenager called Florian and they have friends in 13 different countries to help. At the moment they are making ads for YouTube, gaming channels and films.

6 Brandon and Florian are a good example of people who have made gaming a business. If you're a gamer, who knows – the next person to do this could be you!

4 1.10 **Read the article again. Are sentences 1–7 'Right' (A) or 'Wrong' (B)? If there is not enough information to answer 'Right' (A) or 'Wrong' (B), choose 'Doesn't say' (C).**

Example: Some people know more about video games than films.
A Right **B** Wrong (**C**) Doesn't say

1 Gamers can go to the *Gfinity Arena* to play online games.
A Right **B** Wrong **C** Doesn't say

2 Sometimes people make money from gaming.
A Right **B** Wrong **C** Doesn't say

3 Brandon doesn't live in the south of England now.
A Right **B** Wrong **C** Doesn't say

4 Brandon gets homework to do.
A Right **B** Wrong **C** Doesn't say

5 Brandon's company sells online games.
A Right **B** Wrong **C** Doesn't say

6 Brandon gives all the money he earns to his parents.
A Right **B** Wrong **C** Doesn't say

7 Brandon works on his own.
A Right **B** Wrong **C** Doesn't say

5 **Match the highlighted words in the article to a definition (1–8).**

1 on your own ____________
2 not many ____________
3 a word to describe something a lot of people like ____________
4 someone who likes a sport, game, etc. very much ____________
5 beautiful or pretty to look at ____________
6 another word for 'adverts' ____________
7 people can win prizes in these ____________
8 on the internet ____________

THINK | RESEARCH | **CULTURE** | LEARN | ME

In pairs, discuss the questions.

- Which types of entertainment are most popular in your country?
- Why do you think this is?

▶ **Workbook Unit 2:** Reading, pages 12–13, exercises 1, 2, 3, 4

GRAMMAR 1 | Present simple and present continuous

Grammar in context

Find the sentences in the text on page 15 then answer the questions.

1 *These days, more young people* ***are playing*** *video games.* (paragraph 1)

2 *Both girls and boys* ***play*** *video games regularly, …* (paragraph 2)

3 *Brandon* ***knows*** *a lot about computer games.* (paragraph 3)

Which sentence:

a) talks about a habit or routine? ____

b) uses a stative verb? ____

c) talks about something happening around now? ____

REMEMBER

- We use the present simple to talk about habits, routines, facts and permanent situations.
- We use the present continuous to talk about things that are happening at this moment. We use it to describe what is happening in pictures or photos, actions happening around now and temporary or changing situations.
- There are some verbs called stative verbs, e.g. *like, agree, know, understand* that are usually only used in the present simple to express states, not actions.

▶ **See Grammar reference, Unit 2,** page 151

1 Choose the correct form of the verb to complete each sentence.

1 I**'m learning** / **learn** to play the piano at the moment.

2 She **goes** / **'s going** to the art gallery almost every weekend.

3 Sam **plays** / **is playing** video games every weekend.

4 We**'re doing** / **do** our homework now, so we can't go out.

5 I**'m usually spending** / **usually spend** my money on clothes.

6 He**'s wearing** / **wears** his new trainers today.

7 They**'re never reading** / **never read** fashion magazines.

8 Amy**'s not liking** / **doesn't like** loud music.

2 Use the prompts to write sentences using the present simple or the present continuous.

1 every week / Dad / read / an online newspaper

____

2 at moment / I / play / a video game

____

3 Mum / not work / this week

____

4 Chris / come from / Slovenia / and / speak / three languages

____

5 I / usually / like / his books / but / I / not enjoy / this one

____

6 I / like / fruit / but / I / not eat / it / every day

____

SAY IT RIGHT

Resource centre: Unit 2
Pronunciation of *-ing*

3 Complete the paragraph using the correct present simple or present continuous form of the verbs in brackets.

Karl **(1)** ________ **(love)** being with his family and he **(2)** ________ **(spend)** a lot of his free time watching his children do their hobbies. His son, Marc, **(3)** ________ **(play)** the violin in a youth orchestra and Karl **(4)** ________ **(go)** to see Marc play whenever he can. But today is a special day for Megan, Karl's daughter. Her hobby is hip-hop dance and today she **(5)** ________ **(dance)** in a musical show. Karl **(6)** ________ **(prefer)** rock to hip-hop, but he **(7)** ________ **(enjoy)** the show and Megan **(8)** ________ **(do)** really well. Karl feels happy and he **(9)** ________ **(smile)**. Karl's father is at the show too, but he **(10)** ________ **(not watch)** the dancing. In fact, he **(11)** ________ **(sleep)**!

THINK | RESEARCH | CULTURE | LEARN | **ME**

Work in pairs. What's your favourite type of entertainment? Tell your partner about it.

▶ **Workbook Unit 2:** Grammar 1, page 14, exercises 1, 2

VOCABULARY | Topic vocabulary | Word patterns | Collocations

Words connected with *entertainment*

1 1.11 **Match the places (A–F) to the entertainment (1–6). Listen and check.**

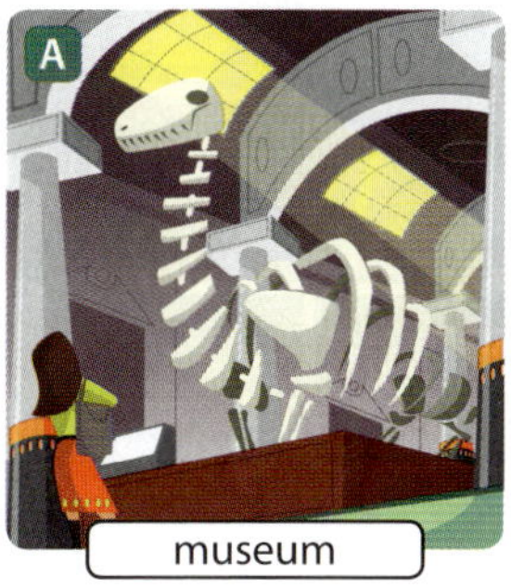

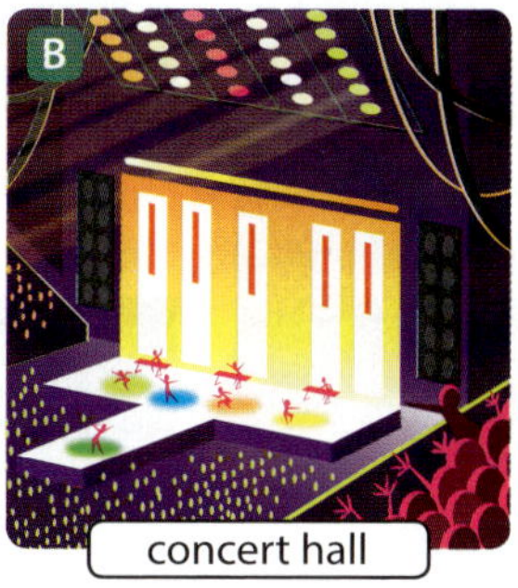

1 see an exhibition of famous paintings ____
2 see a play ____
3 learn about a period in history ____
4 listen to a famous classical singer ____
5 download a game ____
6 see a well-known band ____

2 **Complete the sentences using words from Exercise 1.**

1 We saw a really cool exhibition of fashion photography at the ______________ .
2 His brother's playing the violin at a ______________ in London. They are showing it on TV!
3 My parents are going to the ______________ to listen to some world-famous singers.
4 Joe's playing a game online at the ______________ . He's playing with people from all over the world.
5 You can see lots of interesting things from hundreds of years ago at the ______________ .
6 We saw a great play at the ______________ last Saturday.

Words + prepositions

3 1.12 **Read the descriptions of what different people do for entertainment. Choose the correct preposition to complete each sentence. Listen and check.**

1 On Friday nights I stay **in** / **out** and listen **at** / **to** music. Every Saturday evening I go **in** / **out** with my friends.

2 We like looking **at** / **with** the new fashions. Sometimes we try **on** / **out** different clothes.

3 I really like the theatre. I go to an after-school drama club. I want to act **in** / **out** a play.

4 I love street dancing. Most kids I know prefer to play video games, but they thought it was cool when I danced **on** / **with** my club in a competition. And we won!

Collocations with nouns

4 1.13 **Complete the phrases in bold with the words in the box. Listen and check.**

article | game | player programme | screen

1 Chess is a well-known **board** ___________ . I love playing it.
2 Did you read the **newspaper** ___________ ? There are some good photographs in it.
3 I'm watching a great **TV** ___________ about the history of rock music.
4 I'm getting a new **MP3** ___________ soon – I want one I can record films on, too.
5 I'm going to watch a film on the big new 3-D **cinema** ___________ in town.

2

1 **In pairs or as a group, look at the photo and answer the questions.**

1 How much television do you watch each day?
2 How do you prefer to watch programmes – on TV or online?
3 What do you prefer to do – play video games or watch films?

EXAM SKILL

Listening for words that mean the same

- In multiple-matching tasks, the speakers sometimes use different words to say the same thing.
- It's important to read all the answer options carefully and think of different words the speakers might use to say the same thing.

2 **Read the sentences below. Think of different ways to say the underlined words.**

1 I don't want to play this game anymore. It's not very interesting and it's too hard. ____
2 I'm listening to a new song by Jane's favourite band. It's really nice but a bit slow. ____
3 He told me the book was excellent, but it's not. The story is too unusual. ____

3 **Read the sentences (a–c) then match them to the sentences (1–3) in Exercise 2 which have the same meaning.**

a) It's pleasant but not very fast.
b) It's really terrible and quite strange.
c) It's a bit boring and really difficult.

4 **Work in pairs. Discuss which words helped you to match the sentences in exercises 2 and 3.**

OPTIMISE YOUR EXAM

Multiple matching

- Before you listen, make notes on the different ways you can say the words (A–H).
- When you listen the first time, check your notes before you choose the answers.
- The second time you listen, check your answers carefully.

5 **Look at the 'opinion/feeling' words (A–H) in Exercise 6. For each one, think of another word that has the same meaning. Compare your ideas with a partner.**

6 1.14 **Listen to Paul talking to his cousin Kacey about what he watches on TV. For each programme/channel (1–5), choose an opinion/feeling (A–H). There are some extra letters you do not need.**

TV programme/channel	opinion/feeling
Example: sport _H_	
1 cartoons ____	**A** clever
2 action films ____	**B** excellent
3 the news ____	**C** exciting
4 video gaming channel ____	**D** funny
5 music videos ____	**E** terrible
	F noisy
	G unhappy
	~~**H** interesting~~

7 1.14 **Listen again and check your answers.**

THINK | RESEARCH | CULTURE | LEARN | ME

In pairs or groups, discuss the questions.

- How is the internet changing the entertainment industry? Are these changes good or bad?

 ▶ **Workbook Unit 2:** Listening, page 16, exercises 1, 2, 3

GRAMMAR 2 | Present continuous for future use

Grammar in context

Match these sentences from the audio in the listening lesson to the descriptions.

1 *I'm **doing** a school project on entertainment.*

2 *We're **watching** a new one tonight.*

a) describe an action happening around now. ____

b) talk about future plans and arrangements. ____

REMEMBER

- When we use the present continuous to talk about future plans and arrangements, we usually give a future time (e.g. *tomorrow*):

  *He's **taking** me to watch a football game **on Saturday**.*
  *They **aren't coming** to the theatre with us **tonight**.*
  ***Are** you **seeing** your friends **this weekend**?*

- We can also use the present simple to talk about the future, when we're talking about timetables or programmed events:

  *The train **leaves** at 11:15.*

▶ **See Grammar reference, Unit 2,** page 152

1 **Complete the questions with the correct form of the verbs in the box. Use one verb in each set of questions (1–6).**

cook	do	~~go~~	meet	study	play

1 ___Are___ you ___going___ anywhere this weekend?
Where _are you going_ ? Who _are you going_ with?

2 __________ you __________ anything special for dinner tonight?
What ______________________________________ ?

3 __________ you __________ anything exciting next week?
What ______________________________________ ?

4 __________ you __________ anyone after this lesson?
Who ______________________________________ ?

5 __________ you __________ this evening?
What subjects ______________________________ ?

6 What video games __________ at the weekend?
Who ____________________________ them with?

2 **In pairs or groups, take turns asking and answering the questions from Exercise 1.**

Example:

A: Are you going anywhere this weekend?

B: Yes, I am.

A: Really? Where are you going?

3 **Complete the texts with the correct present simple or continuous form of the verbs in brackets.**

ENTERTAINMENT!

We continue our series about entertainment by talking to three teenagers from around the world. We asked them about their favourite forms of entertainment.

A I'm really into fashion and I **(1)** __________ (**follow**) a few different fashion vloggers online. At the moment I **(2)** __________ (**learn**) all about different ways to dress, and what the latest styles are. Next week I **(3)** __________ (**start**) a course on clothes design. For the first few weeks of the course, the students **(4)** __________ (**have**) lessons in college. But in March we **(5)** __________ (**go**) on a trip to Paris! I can't wait. The only problem is that the plane **(6)** __________ (**leave**) at 6 in the morning, so it's a very early start!

Alexandra, Moscow

B This week I **(1)** __________ (**listen**) to a lot of new hip hop music. It's a useful way to learn new English words. Next weekend, I **(2)** __________ (**make**) playlists for my friends to listen to. Our exams **(3)** __________ (**start**) soon so next week we **(4)** __________ (**go**) to the library every day to study. I **(5)** __________ (**spend**) my evenings studying at home, too. If I do well in my exams, I **(6)** __________ (**get**) a new smartphone. Then I can download more music.

Piotr, Krakow

C Later this evening my brother and I **(1)** __________ (**play**) a game called *Carcassonne*. In this game, you **(2)** __________ (**live**) in the past, and **(3)** __________ (**build**) a city. It's lots of fun, and makes you think a lot. A few of my friends also play board games. They usually **(4)** __________ (**play**) online, but next week they **(5)** __________ (**meet**) at my house so we can all play face to face. Next month my brother Josh and I **(6)** __________ (**design**) a board game about the music business. I'll let you know what happens!

Johnny, Manchester

2 SPEAKING | Collaborative task

Talk2Me

It starts at ...

Flipped classroom

1 **Watch the *Talk2Me* video and answer the questions.**

1 Who has piano lessons on Mondays?
2 When do they decide to go to the cinema?
3 What are they doing after the cinema?

2 **Watch the video again. Underline the phrases in the *Phrase expert* box that you hear on the video.**

> **PHRASE EXPERT**
> It starts at (six) o'clock and finishes at (eight) o'clock. | It's every (Thursday) from (eight) until (ten) pm. | They meet on (Fridays) at (seven) in the evening.

3 **In pairs or as a group, look at the poster and answer the questions.**

1 What does the poster advertise?
2 What time does the concert start?
3 How long is the concert on for?

> **EXAM SKILL**
> ### Talking about times
> - For this part of the Speaking test, you need to practise asking and answering questions and talking about times.
> - Learn the correct prepositions to use with time phrases: ***from*** *9* ***to*** *12;* ***at*** *6.30;* ***on*** *Sunday morning,* etc.

4 1.15 **Work in pairs. Look at the prompts and pictures then take turns to ask and answer questions. Listen and check.**

1 what time / concert / start

Example:
What time does the concert start?
It starts at 8:00 pm.

2 what / be / opening hours / museum

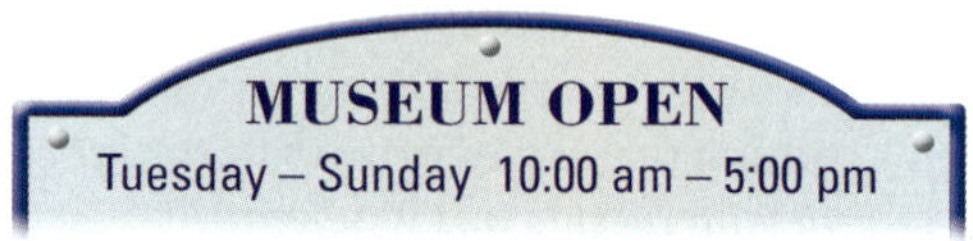

3 how long / film / last

4 when / be / football training

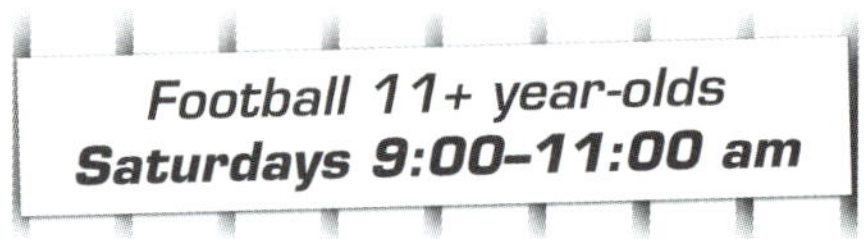

5 what time / concert / finish

> **OPTIMISE YOUR EXAM**
> ### Collaborative task
> - Use phrases like *Let me see,* or *Hang on, just let me check that* to give you more time to think and check information before answering.

5 **In pairs (Student A and Student B), do the exam task.**

> Student A: turn to page 136 and look at the information about *Big beats disco*. Answer Student B's questions about it.
>
> Student B: look at the question prompts on page 139. Ask Student A your questions.
>
> Student B: turn to page 139 and look at the information about the *Student Film Festival*. Answer Student A's questions about it.
>
> Student A: look at the question prompts on page 136. Ask Student B your questions.

LANGUAGE IN USE | Multiple-choice dialogue

1 **Work in pairs or groups. Read the text and answer the questions below.**

There are lots of ways to find out what is happening in the world. A lot of people read the news by looking at online newspaper websites and social media. This is now more popular than TV. A study showed that over 60% of young people read news online. Fewer young people are listening to the radio or reading a newspaper to find out about the news. Only 6% buy or read a newspaper every day.

1 Where do most people get their news from in your country, the TV, newspapers, the internet or somewhere else?
2 Which is best? Why?

EXAM SKILL

Thinking about context

- In this part of the exam you need to understand everyday functional language.
- Think about the context – who is speaking, who they are speaking to, where they are and what they are doing.
- Before you look at the possible answers, decide on the context for each conversation.

2 **Match the contexts in the box to the situations in sentences 1–6.**

at a ticket office | at home | in a shop
in school | on the phone | on the street

1 Hello, this is the information line, how can I help you? ________
2 What page are we on? ________
3 Why don't we watch some TV? ________
4 Excuse me, where's the art gallery? ________
5 Where can I find the board games? ________
6 How much is it for an adult and a child? ________

3 **Write answers for the questions in Exercise 2. Compare with a partner.**

OPTIMISE YOUR EXAM

Multiple-choice dialogue

- Think of your own ideas before you look at the possible answers. This will help you focus on the correct grammar.
- Then look at options A–C. If an option is similar to your ideas, it may be correct.

4 **Complete the five conversations. For questions 1–5, choose the best answer (A, B or C).**

Example:

What are you doing?

A I'm feeling terrible today.
(B) I'm watching the news on TV.
C I love watching films on TV.

1 What are we doing tomorrow?
A We're very sad.
B We're listening to it.
C We're visiting a museum.

2 Where is the concert?
A It's in the theatre.
B It's very loud.
C Here's a ticket.

3 What do you do?
A I'm drawing a picture.
B I'm going there tomorrow.
C I'm a student.

4 Did you read this article?
A Yes, it was very interesting.
B I'm not interesting.
C I like reading books.

5 What are you playing?
A I don't know why.
B It's the news.
C It's a new video game.

THINK | RESEARCH | CULTURE | LEARN | ME

Work in groups. Answer the question.

- What do people in your country usually talk about when they meet?

2 WRITING | An email

1 In pairs or groups, answer the questions.

1 How often do you send emails?
2 Who do you usually email?

EXAM SKILL

Using your own words

- You will need to use ideas from the instructions and texts, but it is important to use your own words, too.
- Underline the key words and phrases in the exam task, then think of different ways to say the same thing before you start writing.

2 Read the exam task below. Underline the questions in the email.

Read the email from your English friend, Julia.

From: Julia

Hi,

What are you doing this afternoon? Can you come to the art gallery? There's a fantastic photography exhibition on. It's going to be fun. I'm meeting Jessica outside the art gallery at 4 pm. Are you free?

Write an email to Julia and answer the questions. Write **25–35** words.

3 Work in pairs. Look at these two answers to Julia's email. Which answer best completes the exam task? Why?

A

Hi Julia,

I'm visiting the art gallery. I <u>really like</u> photographs. Tell Jessica I'm meeting you <u>later today</u> too.

<u>See you later</u>

B

Hi Julia,

Sorry, <u>I'm busy</u> this afternoon because I'm practising for a concert. So, I'm not free to <u>go to</u> the art gallery with you and Jessica.

<u>Have fun!</u>

The Art Gallery of South Australia

4 Work in pairs. Discuss different ways to say the underlined words and phrases in the students' answers in Exercise 3.

OPTIMISE YOUR EXAM

An email

If the exam task asks you to write an email, read the instructions carefully and think about:

- who you are emailing.
- why you are emailing.
- how you will include all the information the question asks for.

5 Work in pairs. Write your own reply to the email from Julia in Exercise 2.

6 Look at this writing task and answer the questions.

From: Sara

What are you doing tonight? There is a new adventure film on at the cinema at 6.30. Do you want to see it? Holly and I are going for a pizza after. Do you want to come?

Write an email to Sara and answer the questions. Write **25–35** words.

1 What does Sara ask? Underline the questions.
2 What is Sara going to do after watching the film?

____

7 **Work in pairs or groups. Decide which plan (A or B) is better for your email to Sara. Say why.**

A

	Detail	My notes
Question 1	*Explain what you are doing*	*I'm doing my homework – I have a project on classical music.*
Question 2	*Make suggestion*	*I want to see the film. How about watching it on Saturday?*
Question 3	*Arrange to see her at school*	*See you tomorrow at school.*

B

	Detail	My notes
Question 1	*Say sorry for not coming*	*I'm sorry I can't come to the cinema.*
Question 2	*Explain reason / what I'm doing*	*I'm not going out tonight because I'm studying for a test.*
Question 3	*Suggest meeting another time*	*I really want to see the film – it looks great. How about watching it and then having pizza on Saturday?*

8 **Plan** **Now plan your email. Use the chart to help you.**

	Detail	My notes
Question 1		
Question 2		
Question 3		

9 **Write** **Write your email in an appropriate style. Write 25–35 words.**

10 **Check** **Before you hand in your email, complete this checklist.**

Checklist

- ◯ I've followed my writing plan.
- ◯ I've started and ended the email in the right way.
- ◯ I've answered the three questions.
- ◯ I've used some of my own words.
- ◯ I've written 25–35 words.
- ◯ I've checked my spelling and grammar.

PROGRESS CHECK UNITS 1–2

GRAMMAR AND VOCABULARY

1 Choose the correct word to complete each sentence.

1 Do you stay in a **tent** / **beach** when you go camping?
2 I really love that **painting** / **painter**, the colours in it are beautiful.
3 He's really famous. I read a newspaper **article** / **programme** about him.
4 I like going **swimming** / **cycling** in the sea when I'm on holiday.
5 William goes **in** / **out** with his friends on Saturdays.
6 She's a very good **music** / **musician**. She plays the violin and piano.
7 What's your favourite board **game** / **player**?
8 Mum and Dad are at **a classical** / **an opera** concert this evening.
9 My sister is a **gamer** / **game** and she plays on her computer most days.
10 Adam usually meets his friends at the internet **house** / **café** at the weekend.

__/10

2 Complete the sentences using the correct form of the verbs in brackets.

1 Let's go and see my cousin. He usually ______________ (**play**) football in the park on a Saturday morning.
2 I ______________ (**look**) for a book about rock music. Have you got one?
3 Let's hurry. The film ______________ (**start**) in ten minutes.
4 Don't be late for class! We ______________ (**practise**) a new dance this afternoon.
5 Oliver is at home this evening. He ______________ (**watch**) something on TV.
6 The boys are upstairs. They ______________ (**do**) their homework at the moment.
7 Does your grandmother ______________ (**live**) near you?
8 Amy always ______________ (**try**) to climb higher than anyone else.

__/8

3 Choose the correct word to fill each gap.

I love using my digital camera and I (**1**) ____ make short films with it. My brother, Samuel, likes writing stories, and sometimes we act (**2**) ____ one of (**3**) ____ stories in a film. We design our own costumes, too! Some of our films are terrible, but (**4**) ____ learning a lot (**5**) ____ how to make good films. There's a film club at our school and Samuel and I go there (**6**) ____ Wednesday. It's a great place to share ideas. Mr Watson, our teacher, gives us tips on how to use our digital cameras. I always listen (**7**) ____ him very carefully because he knows a lot about cameras! Sometimes my classmates come (**8**) ____ to my house and we all make a film together. That's usually a lot of fun!

	A	B	C
1	**A** often	**B** am	**C** never
2	**A** at	**B** out	**C** in
3	**A** their	**B** its	**C** his
4	**A** it's	**B** he's	**C** we're
5	**A** about	**B** from	**C** for
6	**A** a	**B** the	**C** every
7	**A** at	**B** to	**C** for
8	**A** round	**B** off	**C** after

__/8

4 Complete the sentences with the verbs in the box.

come	get	go	look	stay	turn

1 The bus goes past the park, and then into town. We __________ off at the museum.
2 Hello, nice to see you. Please __________ in.
3 I like to __________ out with my friends at the weekend.
4 My grandparents are going to __________ after me and my brother during the school holiday.
5 Please can you __________ off the television and come and speak to your auntie?
6 I have to __________ in and do my homework this evening. Tomorrow I'm going to the cinema.

__/6

5 Complete the text with one word in each gap.

My name is Pablo Riva. I'm 14 and I live **(1)** __________ Turin. I **(2)** __________ two sisters, Laura and Anna. Both of **(3)** __________ are younger than me. **(4)** __________ live with our parents, and grandmother in a big house. Next **(5)** __________ the house is a park. I always **(6)** __________ skateboarding there with my friends. We like to go in **(7)** __________ afternoon, when school is over. My sisters don't like skateboarding at all, so they **(8)** __________ come with me. They like riding their bikes. At the moment, I **(9)** __________ studying English. **(10)** __________ is my favourite subject.

__/10

6 Read the descriptions. What is the word for each one? The first letter is given.

1 When people stay in a tent on holiday they are doing this. c_ _ _ _ _ _ _
2 If you are in this you could win a prize. c_ _ _ _ _ _ _ _ _ _ _
3 People use this to take photographs. c_ _ _ _ _
4 This is what we call a person who plays the guitar. g_ _ _ _ _ _ _ _ _
5 This describes something beautiful or pretty to look at. a_ _ _ _ _ _ _ _ _ _
6 This word describes a person who is part of a group or club. m_ _ _ _ _
7 Something that is shown on television to make people buy things. a_ _ _ _ _
8 This describes something that is liked by many people. p_ _ _ _ _ _

__/8

Total score __/50

EXAM SKILLS

Tick the statements that are true for you. Review the skills in the unit if you need more help.

I can …	Unit/page
☐ find words which mean the same.	Unit 1 p4
☐ listen to short conversations to answer picture multiple-choice questions.	Unit 1 p8
☐ answer questions about myself.	Unit 1 p10
☐ focus on a listening task.	Unit 1 p11
☐ note down key information.	Unit 1 p12
☐ understand important words.	Unit 2 p14
☐ listen for words that mean the same.	Unit 2 p18
☐ work with a partner.	Unit 2 p20
☐ think about context.	Unit 2 p21
☐ use my own words in an email.	Unit 2 p22

3 What's for dinner?

READING | Multiple-choice cloze | A magazine article

1 In pairs or as a group, answer the questions.

1 Describe the food in your country. What's your favourite national dish?

2 What type of food do you like cooking?

EXAM SKILL

Identifying '*when*' and '*who*'

- Identifying if a sentence is about the present, past or future can help you understand a text.
- In the reading exam you often need to understand when something happens and who is doing it.

2 Read the sentences (1–3) and decide when they refer to. Write *past*, *present* or *future*.

1 Many people prefer eating in restaurants to eating at home. ____________

2 Matt worked as a waiter in the UK over 10 years ago. ____________

3 She is planning to be the head chef of a famous hotel one day. ____________

3 Work in pairs. Say which words or phrases helped you to choose your answers in Exercise 2.

4 Read the sentences. Match the people in the box to the words in bold.

busy people | everybody people who don't eat fish the person reading the article

1 **We** all know it's important to eat healthy food. ____________

2 Some people don't cook because **they** don't have free time. ____________

3 Some people don't eat fish because **they** don't like it. ____________

4 So, how can **you** learn how to cook? ____________

5 Read the magazine article on page 27 quickly. Which purpose (A, B or C) best explains why the article was written?

A to advertise a new cookery show

B to make teenagers want to learn to cook

C to share different recipes

Kids in the kitchen

In the UK, 60% of 18-year-olds can't cook five easy meals. There are, however, many different ways young people can learn to cook.

1 Some people learn **Example:** _B_ watching TV cooking competitions like *Junior MasterChef*. **(1)** ____ programme started in the UK 20 years ago. The idea for the programme **(2)** ____ simple – to help people think about the food they eat. In the show, young people prepare different delicious dishes every week. The one who **(3)** ____ the best food is the winner. And some of the food is amazing. Everyone remembers the famous alligator chilli one junior chef made!

2 *Junior MasterChef* winners **(4)** ____ help other people learn to cook by sharing their recipes online. One winner said she actually learnt to cook by watching YouTube videos. However, many winners learnt to cook when they helped their parents **(5)** ____ home.

3 There are also cooking courses for teenagers in the UK. At **(6)** ____ school, the teacher, Ben Coyle-Larner, isn't a chef. He's a successful rapper called Loyle Carner. When Ben was a teenager, he found it difficult to study. Ben says, 'My brain is always busy, but with cooking there is no time to think about other things.' In 2016, Ben opened his cooking school to help teenagers like him.

4 So, next time you're online, why not look up the recipe of your favourite dish or watch a video about how to cook **(7)** ____ ? Or watch the latest cookery show to get **(8)** ____ great ideas. Then start cooking!

OPTIMISE YOUR EXAM

Multiple-choice cloze

- In this part of the exam you read a short text with eight gaps.
- Read the words before and after the gap. This can help you decide which type of word you need.
- Choose the answer which fits the grammar and the meaning.

6 1.16 **Read the magazine article about a TV cooking competition. For questions 1–7, choose the best word (A, B or C) for each space.**

Example:

	A	with	**(B)**	by	**C**	at
1	**A**	One	**B**	A	**C**	The
2	**A**	be	**B**	were	**C**	was
3	**A**	cooking	**B**	cooks	**C**	to cook
4	**A**	has	**B**	can	**C**	are
5	**A**	on	**B**	at	**C**	from
6	**A**	one	**B**	each	**C**	every
7	**A**	them	**B**	her	**C**	it
8	**A**	each	**B**	both	**C**	some

7 Match the highlighted words in the article to a definition (1–8).

1 a cook in a restaurant ____________
2 to make food ready for eating ____________
3 something or someone a lot of people know about ____________
4 suggestion or plan ____________
5 to learn by reading or doing homework ____________
6 lunch is an example of one of these ____________
7 instructions on how to make different dishes ____________
8 another word for 'programme' ____________

THINK | RESEARCH | **CULTURE** | LEARN | ME

In pairs or groups, choose a dish from your country and write the recipe. Compare your ideas with other students.

3 GRAMMAR 1 | Past simple: regular verbs, *Wh-* words

Grammar in context

Choose the correct word or phrase to complete each sentence. Then find them in the text on page 27 and check your answers.

1 *The programme* ***starts / started*** *in the UK 20 years ago.* (paragraph 1)

2 *However, many winners learnt to cook when they* ***help / helped*** *their parents at home.* (paragraph 2)

3 *In 2016, Ben* ***opened / was opening*** *his cooking school to help teenagers like him.* (paragraph 3)

REMEMBER

- We use the past simple to talk about:
  - something that happened once in the past.
  - something that happened again and again in the past.
  - something that was true for a period of time in the past.
- We often use time expressions with the past simple, e.g. *in 2014, last year, last month, yesterday, this morning.*

▶ **See Grammar reference, Unit 3,** page 152

1 Complete the text with the past simple of the verbs in the box.

ask	bake	practise	prefer
start	use	want	watch

Sweet dreams

Amy-Beth Ellice (**1**) __________ baking at the age of three. As a child she (**2**) __________ her mother carefully when she was cooking. That's how she learnt to cook.

Amy-Beth quickly became very good at cooking because she worked hard and (**3**) __________ baking skills every day. Many of her friends (**4**) __________ spending their time chatting on social media, but Amy-Beth (**5**) __________ her free time to bake.

Amy (**6**) __________ cakes for friends and family, and put pictures of them online. People saw the pictures and (**7**) __________ Amy to make cakes for them too. Now Amy bakes cakes for celebrity parties and weddings.

Amy always (**8**) __________ to be a good chef, but now she is a famous one too!

SAY IT RIGHT

Resource centre: Unit 3
Pronunciation of *-ed*

Grammar in context

Read this question: ***When did you learn to cook?***

a) Is the question about the present or the past? ______

b) Is the question asking about a time or a place? ______

REMEMBER

- We use *wh-* words at the beginning of questions that are asking for information. You can't answer a *wh-* question with *yes* or *no*: ***Where*** *did you live?* ***Who*** *did you live with?*

▶ **See Grammar reference, Unit 3,** page 152

2 Match the things they usually ask about (a–f) to the *Wh-* words (1–6).

	We use	To ask about
1	What/Which _f_	**a)** a person
2	Where ____	**b)** a possession
3	Why ____	**c)** a place
4	Who ____	**d)** a reason
5	When ____	**e)** a time
6	Whose ____	~~**f)** a thing~~

3 Choose the correct words to complete the interview.

Young start-ups

article rating ★★☆

Today we're (**1**) **talking** / **talked** to Leo and Izzy, two teenagers who started an ice-cream business in London.

Q: (**2**) **When** / **Who** did you decide that ice cream was a good idea for a food business?

A: A few years ago we (**3**) **travelling** / **travelled** to Ireland. We saw lots of young people eating ice cream although it wasn't hot. We (**4**) **decided** / **decide** it was one of the most popular snacks available.

Q: (**5**) **Who** / **Why** did you talk to to find out more?

A: We (**6**) **talk** / **talked** to other young people and we learnt that teens want ice cream to be fun, fashionable and healthy.

Q: (**7**) **When** / **Where** do you make your ice cream?

A: We make it in the kitchen of a café and our customers test our new flavours.

Q: (**8**) **What** / **Which** do you make it with?

A: We use coconut milk because it's sweet but healthy.

Q: (**9**) **Why** / **Which** ice cream do you sell the most?

A: Chocolate is the most popular.

Q: (**10**) **What** / **When** can you tell other young people who want to start a food business, Leo?

A: Find a food people like, and make it in a new or exciting way!

Words connected with *food*

1 1.17 **Complete the food lists with the words in the box. Listen and check.**

~~apple~~ | banana | ~~beans~~ | ~~beef~~ | ~~bread~~ carrots | cereal | ~~cheese~~ | chicken | ~~honey~~ lettuce | milk | oil | onions | oranges pasta | potatoes | rice | salt | steak strawberries | tomatoes | vinegar | yoghurt

Vegetables	Fruit	Carbohydrates
beans	*apple*	*bread*
______	______	______
______	______	______
______	______	______
______		
______		

Meat	Dairy	Other
beef	*cheese*	*honey*
______	______	______
______	______	______
		______

2 **Complete the text using words from Exercise 1.**

MY FAVOURITE SNACK

What's my favourite breakfast snack? Well, if I'm feeling lazy, I have a bowl of (**1**) ______ – usually with milk, but sometimes (**2**) ______. Or a slice of (**3**) ______ with some (**4**) ______ on it.

But if I'm feeling hungry, I often go into the kitchen and make something a bit more interesting. Sometimes I make a burger – not like the ones you get at fast-food places, but a really good one. It's quite easy. You take some good meat, like (**5**) ______ and make it into flat circles. You put a little (**6**) ______ on it, then you cook it under the grill for about eight minutes on each side. I always add a slice of (**7**) ______, too, to make it a cheeseburger, and some fried (**8**) ______. I usually have a salad with tomatoes and (**9**) ______ as well, and then some fruit – a bowl of lovely red (**10**) ______ or a banana.

Verbs/adjectives

3 1.18 **Complete the table. Listen and check.**

verb	adjective
bake	(**1**) ______
boil	(**2**) ______
(**3**) ______	fried
grill	(**4**) ______
roast	(**5**) ______

4 1.19 **Choose the correct word to complete each sentence. Listen and check.**

1 I ate some delicious **fried** / **fry** fish at the new Thai restaurant.
2 He **boiled** / **boil** the pasta for a long time. It tasted terrible.
3 We need to **grilled** / **grill** this chicken for 20 minutes.
4 I like **baked** / **bake** potatoes with cheese and beans.

5 **Look at the meal review. Underline the adjectives.**

I ate some delicious fried fish at the new Thai restaurant. Then I had some cold coconut ice cream with fresh green grapes.

REMEMBER

- In English, we usually put adjectives of opinion before adjectives describing qualities.
- The usual order for adjectives is: opinion, size, shape, age, colour, nationality, material. We don't often use all the types of adjective in one sentence.

6 **Tick the correct sentence, A or B.**

1 **A** I love eating big red apples. ____
B I love eating red big apples. ____
2 **A** That's a lovely mountain bike. ____
B That's a mountain lovely bike. ____
3 **A** Mum bought a round, big French cheese. ____
B Mum bought a big, round French cheese. ____

Collocations with verbs

7 1.20 **Complete the phrases with the words in the box. Listen and check.**

bake | do | have | make | take

1 ______ lunch / a drink / a good time
2 ______ an exam / a train / a photo
3 ______ homework / the washing-up / sports
4 ______ breakfast / a picnic / a mistake
5 ______ bread / a cake / a potato

8 **Tick the correct sentences. Underline the mistake in the incorrect sentences and write the correct word.**

1 Make sure you <u>have</u> the washing-up. *do*
2 We bake lunch at 12. ______
3 Ask Mia to take a photo of us. ______
4 I'm going to bake Mum a cake for her birthday. ______
5 Let's do sandwiches and go to the park. ______

3 LISTENING | Multiple choice

1 **In pairs or as a group, answer the questions.**

1 How often do you go to cafés and restaurants?
2 What kind of café is popular where you live? Why?

EXAM SKILL

Predicting what the speaker will say

- You can often use the questions and options to predict what the speaker is going to say.
- Read the instructions, questions and options carefully to help you understand what you will hear.

2 **Read the exam question below and underline any important words.**

> **Listen to Kay telling a friend about a new café.**
> **1** The reason Kay likes the café is
> **A** the cheap cake.
> **B** the good coffee.
> **C** the friendly staff.

3 **Read the students' notes, A and B. Which do you think are better? Why?**

A

Lion Street café
1. Kay likes the café because ____________
A cake is free
B coffee is good
C staff are friendly

B

Lion Street café
1. Like / because
A not expensive / doesn't cost much
B coffee great/amazing/fantastic, etc.
C helpful/friendly / waiter/waitress

4 1.21 **Listen to part of a conversation and choose the correct answer in Exercise 2. You can use the notes in Exercise 3 to help you.**

1 ____

OPTIMISE YOUR EXAM

Multiple choice

- In this part of the exam one speaker in the conversation gives all the answers.
- Listen carefully to both speakers, but remember that one person will ask the questions and one will give the answers.

5 **Read the questions and the options in Exercise 6. Underline key words. Write short notes predicting what you will hear.**

6 1.22 **Listen to Clare talking to her friend Simon about a trip to a café and choose the correct answers.**

1 Clare went to the music café on
A Friday evening.
B Saturday afternoon.
C Saturday evening.

2 The café had
A three tables.
B four tables.
C five tables.

3 Clare thought the food was
A enjoyable.
B not fresh.
C not good.

4 Clare decided to eat
A an omelette.
B a fish main course.
C a curry.

5 Clare finished her meal with
A a cold drink.
B some fruit.
C a dessert.

7 1.22 **Listen again and check your answers.**

THINK | **RESEARCH** | CULTURE | LEARN | ME

Work in pairs or groups and answer the questions.

- Find out about interesting cafés or places to eat near you.
- Choose your favourite, and tell the class.

▶ **Workbook Unit 3:** Listening, page 24, exercises 1, 2, 3, 4

GRAMMAR 2 | Past simple: irregular verbs

Grammar in context

Look at these sentences from the audio in the listening lesson. Choose the correct word to complete each sentence.

1 *It was a bit smaller than I **think** / **thought**.*
2 *Did you **eat** / **ate** a main course, or just a snack?*
3 *I **have** / **had** grilled fish for my main, …*
4 *… so I **chose** / **choose** a cold glass of lemonade.*
5 *But the best thing was that I didn't **paid** / **pay**.*

Note: Irregular verbs (*get, have, say, teach, go*, etc.) don't follow a pattern. You need to learn the past simple of these verbs. See the *Irregular verbs reference* on page 175.

REMEMBER

- To make negatives, you put *didn't* before both regular and irregular verbs:
  *She **didn't order** a drink.*
  *I **didn't eat** anything.*
- In questions, you use *Did/Didn't* + the infinitive of regular and irregular verbs:
  ***Did** you **like** the café?*
  *What **did** they have to eat?*

▶ See Grammar reference, Unit 3, page 153

1 Write the sentences in the past simple. Use the words in brackets.

1 Alana eats lunch in the café next door. (**yesterday**)
Alana ate lunch in the café next door yesterday.
2 Helen doesn't go to the restaurant. (**last week**)
______
3 Paul gets up early. (**this morning**)
______
4 He sees his friends after school. (**last night**)
______
5 Rob can't come for dinner. (**last Monday**)
______
6 She buys a sandwich at the local shop. (**this morning**)
______
7 We meet in the park. (**in 2014**)
______
8 I have a lot of comics. (**as a child**)
______

2 Use the prompts to write past simple sentences that are true for you.

1 you / eat / for breakfast / this morning
I ate cereals and milk for breakfast this morning.
2 the teacher / teach / you / English / last year
______
3 the best programme / you / see / on TV / yesterday
______
4 you / go / with your friends / at the weekend
______
5 you / do / before bed / last night
______
6 the best meal / you / have / last week
______

3 Work in pairs. Ask and answer the questions from Exercise 2.

What did you eat for breakfast this morning?

I ate cereal and milk for breakfast this morning. How about you?

4 Complete the text using the correct past simple form of the verbs in brackets.

The emoji menu

On Monday I (1) ______ (go) to an interesting café with my grandparents. When they (2) (see) the menu they (3) ______ (get) a bit of a surprise – it (4) ______ (not have) any words on it! When I first (5) ______ (hear) about the way the Little Yellow Door café was using emojis on menus, I (6) ______ (think) it sounded difficult to understand. But actually it worked well. Customers (7) ______ (say) that they (8) ______ (understand) exactly what all the pictures were.
I ordered a big salad with potatoes and fish. It was delicious and I (9) ______ (eat) it all. My grandma was pleased because I (10) ______ (not leave) anything on my plate.

THINK | RESEARCH | CULTURE | LEARN | **ME**

Work in pairs and take turns to tell your partner about an interesting restaurant you visited with your family.

▶ **Workbook Unit 3:** Grammar 2, page 23, exercises 1, 2, 3

3 SPEAKING | Interview

Talk2Me

It's my favourite because…

Flipped classroom

1 **Watch the *Talk2Me* video and answer the questions.**

1 What did the twins make for their mum last week?
2 What type of cake did Evie make?
3 What did Evie's dad buy in the supermarket?

2 **Watch the video again. Underline the phrases in the *Phrase expert* box that you hear on the video.**

> **PHRASE EXPERT**
> I love/hate … because it's (delicious) …
> I prefer … | It's my (least) favourite because …
> The reason I (prefer) … is …

EXAM SKILL

Explaining likes and dislikes

- Listen very carefully to the examiner. Answer exactly the question he or she asks.
- When the examiner asks about what you like, dislike or like doing, remember to give a reason for your opinion if possible.

3 **In pairs or as a group, answer the questions. Use phrases from the *Phrase expert* box.**

1 Which is your favourite meal of the day? Why?
2 Do you prefer healthy food or fast food? Why?

4 1.23 **Listen to a student answering these questions. Write the foods.**

1 What's your favourite type of food? ______________
2 What's your least favourite type of food?
____
3 What food do you like to eat at festivals and celebrations? ______________

5 1.23 **Listen again and note down the reasons the student gives for their answers.**

1 ______________________________
2 ______________________________
3 ______________________________

OPTIMISE YOUR EXAM

Interview

- In the first part of the test, the examiner may ask about your likes and dislikes. You can prepare and practise for this, but don't learn long sections by memory because it won't sound natural.
- The examiner won't always ask the same questions, so you need to think of different questions and answers for each topic.
- Noting down possible questions, useful vocabulary and ideas for answers can help.

6 **Complete the mind map with your own answers to the questions in Exercise 4. Write the food and the reason.**

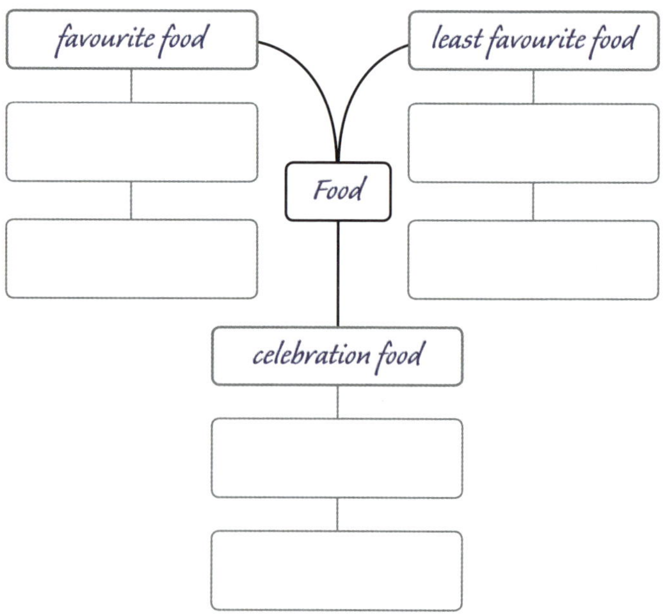

7 **Work in pairs. Take turns asking and answering the questions in Exercise 4. Use your notes in the mind map to give examples and reasons.**

LANGUAGE IN USE | Open cloze

1 **What is the most important thing about where you choose to eat? Order the points from 1 (most important) to 6 (least important).**

- The food is good. ____
- The food is cheap. ____
- The waiters and waitresses are friendly. ____
- It's clean. ____
- It's a cool place to go. ____
- There's a lot to choose from on the menu. ____

2 **Work in pairs or groups. Compare your ideas in Exercise 1 and give reasons for your choices.**

3 **In your pairs or groups, agree on a final order for the points in Exercise 1. Tell the class. Think of examples of places you know.**

EXAM SKILL

Thinking about grammar (conjunctions, prepositions and pronouns)

❍ Look for grammar patterns in the sentences:

– If the missing word is in the middle of two sentence parts, you may need a linking word (*and, but, or*).

– If the missing word is before a noun or pronoun or after a verb, it could be a preposition (e.g. *at, about, for, in, on, to*).

❍ If you think the missing word is a pronoun (e.g. *I, he, she*), read the sentences before and after to check which one you need.

4 **Work in pairs. Decide which word completes each sentence. Say why.**

and	because	but	from	in	we

1 I really enjoyed the fruit that we bought ____________ the man in the market.

2 I've got an old recipe book ____________ I always use it when I make cakes.

3 My brother and I cooked dinner. ____________ made steak and chips.

4 This is too sweet! I think there's sugar ____________ my drink.

5 I didn't bake you a cake ____________ the cooker doesn't work.

6 She's very interested in food, ____________ she's not a very good cook.

OPTIMISE YOUR EXAM

Open cloze

- Read the whole text to make sure you understand it.
- Complete the easy gaps first, then look again at the more difficult ones.
- Make sure you only write one word in each gap, and always write an answer for every gap.

5 **Complete the post on a food blog. Write one word in each gap.**

Hi, my name is Samuel, I'm from the Netherlands. The best meal I ever **Example:** ___*ate*___ was in Italy. I went there **(1)** ____________ holiday with my parents last year. **(2)** ____________ visited Florence and Bologna. One evening we **(3)** ____________ to an old restaurant in the train station. I thought it looked strange. It looked too old **(4)** ____________ it was a bit small – **(5)** ____________ when I saw the food, I changed my mind. They cooked **(6)** ____________ most fantastic food. I chose a local dish **(7)** ____________ my main meal. It was delicious. They also baked bread **(8)** ____________ the restaurant. I ate a few slices with olive oil. For dessert, I had strawberry ice cream. I ate **(9)** ____________ lot, so when I got back to our hotel I needed to lie down and rest **(10)** ____________ an hour!

THINK | RESEARCH | CULTURE | LEARN | ME

Work in groups and answer the questions.

- Think of at least three sentences to describe a favourite food. Write them down. Do not name the food you're describing.
- Say your sentences to your group. Ask them to guess the food.

3 WRITING | A note

1 In pairs or groups, answer the questions.

1 Who writes notes to you? Why?
2 When did you last write a note to somebody? What was it about?

2 Read the exam task below. How many questions does Tom ask? Underline the important word(s) in each question.

Read the note from your brother, Tom.

> *Mum said you went shopping for food for dinner.*
> *What did you buy?*
> *What are we eating?*
> *Can my friend come for dinner?*
> *Tom*

Write a note to Tom. Answer his questions.
Write **25–35** words.

EXAM SKILL

Using your vocabulary

- The examiners will look for a good range of vocabulary in your answer.
- Don't use exactly the same words that are in the exam instructions and note. Show the examiner your ideas.
- Before you start writing, think of different ways to say the same thing and choose the best idea.

3 In pairs, read the examples below. Do they complete the task in Exercise 2? Why / Why not?

A

Hi Tom,
I got cheese, eggs, peppers and potatoes at the market. I'm making a cheese omelette with chips and peppers. Bring your friend. I asked Mum and she said it was fine for your friend to come too.
Dan

B

Hi Tom,
I like fish and chips. They are great.
Let's eat some.
Your friend can come too.
Zoltan

4 Rewrite the example below. Use the correct form of the verbs in the box to replace the underlined words.

buy	invite	prepare	tell

Hi Tom,
I (1) got some tomatoes, pasta and some vegetables at the market. I'm (2) making a pasta dish with a nice sauce. I (3) said to Mum that you (4) asked a friend. She said it's fine.
Jenna

OPTIMISE YOUR **EXAM**

A note

- When the writing task is a note, you have to answer three questions.
- Before writing:
  - make sure you understand what each question is asking about.
  - circle important words and note down useful vocabulary.
  - plan how you will answer each question.

5 **Look at this writing task and make notes to answer questions 1–6.**

Read the note from your friend, Ella.

I missed the cookery class today!
What did you make?
What are we making next week?
Do I need to bring anything?
Ella

Write a note to Ella and answer the questions.
Write **25–35** words.

1 Who are you writing to?
______
2 How many words do you need to write?
______
3 How many questions do you have to answer?
______
4 What do you have to explain?
______
5 Which tenses should you use?
______
6 Which words or phrases from this unit could you use?
______
______

6 **Plan** **Plan your note. Use the chart to help you.**

	Detail	My notes	Useful language
Question 1			
Question 2			
Question 3			

7 **Write** **Write your note in an appropriate style. Write 25–35 words.**

8 **Check** **Before you hand in your note, complete this checklist.**

Checklist ✓

- ○ I've followed my writing plan.
- ○ I've answered the three questions.
- ○ I've used the correct tenses.
- ○ I've used a good range of vocabulary.
- ○ I've written 25–35 words.
- ○ I've checked my spelling and grammar.

▶ **Writing reference,** page 169 ▶ **Workbook Unit 3:** Writing, page 26, exercises 1, 2, 3, 4 and Progress check 3, page 27

4 On your way

READING | Matching | Signs and notices

1 **In pairs or as a group, answer the questions.**

1 When did you last go to these places?
- airport
- bus station
- campsite
- petrol station
- train station
- city centre

2 Why did you go there?

Example: *I went to a train station at the weekend to catch a train to Nottingham.*

2 1.24 **Read the blog posts on page 37 quickly. Match each paragraph (A–C) to the tips (1–3).**

1 **TIP**: Wear comfortable shoes for walking tours. ____

2 **TIP**: Always take a good book with you when you travel. ____

3 **TIP**: For outdoor events, go prepared for the weather. ____

3 **Read the blog posts again. Match the highlighted words in the text to a definition (1–8).**

1 travelling round a place to see interesting things ____________
2 to put things in a bag to take with you ____________
3 the act of going somewhere for a time and then returning ____________
4 the acts of travelling from one place to another ____________
5 weather with lots of rain and strong wind ____________
6 the opposite of dry ____________
7 a journey through the air in a plane ____________
8 lots of films, music, etc. happening in one place ____________

EXAM SKILL

Deciding the general message

- Decide the general message, e.g. does the sign/notice tell you what (not) to do?
- Often the sentence will say the same thing but in the opposite way.

4 **Read the signs and notices A–H and decide which tell you to do something (✔), which tell you NOT to do something (✘) and which give information only (*i*).**

USEFUL TRAVEL TIPS

Readers share their experiences

A I hate long journeys. Last winter I went to Mexico City with my family. When we arrived at the airport in London, our flight was delayed because there was a terrible storm. Luckily, I had my tablet with me, so I downloaded an eBook. We were waiting there for five hours but I was reading an exciting story, so the time went quickly.

Kat

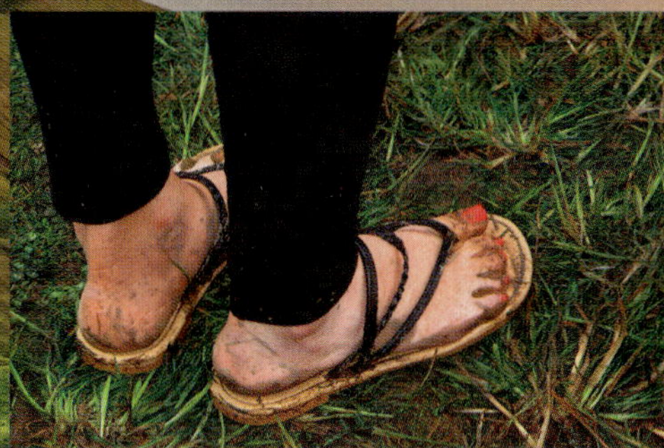

B Last July, I went to a language school in the UK. I made some new friends and when I wasn't studying, we spent time together. One weekend we went to a music festival for teenagers. It was raining all day, but we had a lot of fun. Most people were wearing boots, but I didn't pack any, so my new sandals got really wet and muddy. The music was brilliant, and I kept my dirty sandals as a souvenir!

Jess

C Last summer I went on a school trip to Edinburgh. On the first day we went sightseeing – my favourite place was Edinburgh Castle. However, I was walking all day in uncomfortable shoes, so by late afternoon my feet were hurting. That evening I decided to stay in the hotel to rest. What were my friends doing while I was in the hotel? A tour guide took them on an exciting night tour of the city – by bus!

Allisa

OPTIMISE YOUR EXAM

Matching

- Don't worry about words you don't know.
- Try to understand the general message of the sign or notice.

5 **Which sign or notice (A–H) says this (1–5)? There are some extra letters you do not need.**

Example: **Close your tents to keep your food safe.** C

1 You need to wait longer to travel. ____
2 You mustn't drive here. ____
3 Don't use your phone on this plane. ____
4 You must stay on the left. ____
5 This is the way to the trains. ____

A Please turn off mobile phones during flight ____

B No driving on the right! ____

C *Do not leave tents open. Animals may steal your food!* ____

D Please turn off your car engine. ____

E No concert tonight. ____

F Flights delayed by six hours. ____

G *Come sightseeing. Bus every 30 minutes. Last bus leaves 5 pm.* ____

H Walk across the bridge to Platforms 4 and 5. ____

4 GRAMMAR 1 | Past continuous, linking words

Grammar in context

Choose the correct verb form to complete each sentence. Then find them in the texts on page 37 and check your answers.

1 *We were waiting there for five hours, but I* ***was reading / read*** *an exciting story, ...* (paragraph A)

2 *I made some new friends and when I* ***wasn't studying / didn't study****, we spent time together.* (paragraph B)

3 *What* ***did my friends do / were my friends doing*** *while I was in the hotel?* (paragraph C)

REMEMBER

- We use the past continuous to talk about something that was happening over a period of time in the past:
  I ***was watching*** *TV all yesterday afternoon.*

▶ **See Grammar reference, Unit 4,** page 153

Grammar in context

Complete the sentences with a linking word in the box. Then find them in the texts on page 37 and check your answers.

because | but | when

1 *... our flight was delayed ___________ there was a terrible storm.*

2 *I made some new friends and ___________ I wasn't studying, we spent time together.*

3 *It was raining all day ___________ we had a lot of fun.*

REMEMBER

- We use linking words (*and, because, but, or, when*) to connect one phrase, clause or sentence with another.
- We can use the linking word at the beginning or the middle of the sentence:
  When *we arrived at the airport, there was a terrible storm.*

▶ **See Grammar reference, Unit 4,** page 153

1 Complete the conversation using the past continuous form of the verbs in brackets.

Ben: I think I saw you yesterday when I (**1**) ___________ (**walk**) into town. Were you in a black car with your dad and your brother?

Joe: Yes, I was.

Ben: I'm sure there were bikes in the car, too. Where (**2**) ___________ (**you go**)?

Joe: Dad (**3**) ___________ (**drive**) to Sanders Hill. We've both got new mud bikes and Dad (**4**) ___________ (**take**) us out to ride them on a hill for the first time.

Ben: Great! How was it?

Joe: I (**5**) ___________ (**do**) well until my bike went over a stone.

Ben: Were you riding too fast?

Joe: Well, we (**6**) ___________ (**both cycle**) quite fast but we (**7**) ___________ (**be**) careful. Anyway, I (**8**) ___________ (**not look**) in the right place so I didn't see the stone. I hit it and fell off my bike.

Ben: So that's why you've got a bandage on your arm today, then.

Joe: Exactly!

2 Use the prompts in brackets to answer the questions.

1 What were you doing yesterday? (ride bike)
I was riding my bike yesterday.

2 When was she playing music? (last night)
____

3 Who was studying in London last year? (James)
____

4 Were you studying in Scotland last summer? (no / sightseeing)
____

3 Complete the text using the past continuous of the verbs in brackets or a word from the box.

and | because | but | when

AROUND THE WORLD IN 80 WAYS

Posts from teen travellers, telling us their experiences.

I love going to South America. Last year I went to Peru with my parents. One day, my dad (1) ___________ (**feel**) tired, so he stayed in the hotel, (**2**) ___________ Mum and I decided to go on a bus trip to Lake Titicaca. We left the city and we (**3**) ___________ (**travel**) through the countryside (**4**) ___________ the bus suddenly stopped. The driver told us there was a problem with the engine. Luckily there was a café nearby where we could wait. Mum (**5**) ___________ (**speak**) to Dad on the phone when a mechanic arrived. While he (**6**) ___________ (**work**) on the engine, I talked to his son, Roberto. He's a football fan, and I am too, so we had lots to talk about!

I gave him my contact details (**7**) ___________ I really liked him. The mechanic fixed the engine, so we all got back on the bus. As we (**8**) ___________ (**leave**), I waved goodbye to Roberto. When I got home, Roberto messaged me straight away. A year later and we're still in touch.

Jordan

SAY IT RIGHT

Resource centre: Unit 4
/ə/

Words connected with *travel*

1 1.25 **Complete Jo's message about how to get to school with the words in the box. Listen and check.**

bridge | bus stop | delayed | miss railway station | roundabout | traffic traffic lights

Hi Amelie,

Here is the information about getting to school tomorrow. We can catch the bus at the **(1)** ______________ outside my house at 7.40 am.

We arrive at school at about 8.15, unless the bus is **(2)** ______________ or we **(3)** ______________ it. ☹ We don't need tickets because we have student ID cards. We cross the **(4)** ______________ over the river, then Kelly gets on the bus in town. We go through three **(5)** ______________ , then arrive at Jamie's stop. Then we go past the **(6)** ______________ , where we pick up passengers from the train – so, Yasmin and Leo get on the bus there. Next, the bus goes round a **(7)** ______________ and then after a few more stops we arrive at school. Sometimes there's a lot of **(8)** ______________ and the journey's slow – but then we get more time to chat! ☺

2 **Read the travel and transport descriptions and complete the words.**

1 A big circle where roads meet and cars go around: r_ _ _ _ _ _ _ _ _
2 The cars and other vehicles that use a road: t_ _ _ _ _ _
3 A way over a river, road or railway, to help people cross: b_ _ _ _ _
4 The place to wait for a bus: b_ _ s_ _ _
5 Lights used to make cars and other vehicles stop and start: t_ _ _ _ _ _ l_ _ _ _ _

Compound nouns

3 1.26 **Match the words (a–h) to (1–8) to make compound nouns. Listen and check.**

1 car ____ a) ride
2 driving ____ b) boat
3 helicopter ____ c) station
4 petrol ____ d) park
5 sailing ____ e) licence
6 ticket ____ f) guide
7 tour ____ g) machine
8 traffic ____ h) news

4 **Complete the sentences with the compound nouns from Exercise 3.**

1 We checked the ______________ online before starting our journey.
2 We looked round the city centre with a ______________ and she showed us the sights.
3 When we were in New Zealand, we went on a ______________ over the mountains. It was incredible!
4 We wanted to hire a car, but nobody had a ______________ .
5 You can book your train journey online or use a ______________ at the station.
6 When we arrived at the concert hall, the ______________ was full, so we had to leave the car somewhere else.
7 Before going on a long journey, you should fill up the car at a ______________ .
8 I'd love to go around the Mediterranean islands on a ______________ .

Phrasal verbs

5 1.27 **Complete the definitions with the phrasal verbs in the box. Listen and check.**

come in | go in | pick up | set off take off | turn off

1 to enter a place ______________
2 to leave the ground and go into the sky ______________
3 to start a journey ______________
4 what somebody says to invite you into a place ______________
5 to collect something or somebody, often in a car ______________
6 to leave a main road ______________

6 **Complete the message with the phrasal verbs from Exercise 5. There is one phrasal verb you do not need.**

Posts Comments

School Skiing trip – update…

Dear parents,

As you know, the weather in Geneva is very bad and the plane did not **(1)** ______________ at 10:30. It is going to be two hours late. The bus that is going to **(2)** ______________ the children will **(3)** ______________ to the airport this afternoon. You are welcome to **(4)** ______________ to school this evening and wait for the bus to arrive. Don't forget you need to leave your car behind the school – you need to **(5)** ______________ the road after the petrol station to get into the car park.

▶ **Vocabulary reference,** page 164 ▶ **Workbook Unit 4:** Vocabulary, pages 30–31, exercises 1, 2, 3

4 LISTENING | Gap fill

1 **In pairs or as a group, look at the photo and plan a holiday together. Think about:**

- what kind of holiday you will go on (beach, walking, adventure, etc.).
- how you will travel.
- what you need to take with you.

EXAM SKILL

Listening for important information

- In this part of the exam you often need to listen for prices, numbers, times and dates.
- Listen carefully because you might hear more than one of them.
- Also listen for words that can sound like numbers: *free – three, for – four, ate – eight.*

2 1.28 **Listen to the conversations. Write the numbers. Compare your answers with a partner.**

1 Where the boy lives ______
2 Biscuits eaten ______
3 The phone number the caller wanted ______
4 The birthday ______
5 The train time ______

OPTIMISE YOUR EXAM

Gap fill

- Sometimes the answer is a name. The speaker often spells this out.
- Write each letter carefully as the speaker says it.
- Remember that speakers sometimes make mistakes and change the spelling. Listen for phrases like *No, it's …*

3 1.29 **Listen and write the words the speakers spell out.**

1 *Jeremiah Gayle*
2 ______
3 ______
4 ______
5 ______
6 ______
7 ______
8 ______

4 1.30 **Listen to the phone conversation between a customer and a travel company and complete questions 1–5. Listen and check.**

Flight Time	
Name:	1 *Ms Amanda*
Booking reference number:	2
Travelling to:	3
Will leave on:	4
Cost of change to flights:	5

5 1.31 **You will hear some information about a sailing trip. Listen and complete questions 1–5.**

SAILING TRIP	
Meet in front of the building:	1
Meet:	2 .... *am*
Return:	3 .... *pm*
Lunch:	4 *Outdoor*....................
Take	5 .... *and a towel*

6 1.31 **Listen again and check your answers.**

THINK | RESEARCH | CULTURE | **LEARN** | ME

Work in pairs. Discuss the question.

- What different ways can you think of for checking the spelling of new vocabulary in listening texts?

▶ **Workbook Unit 4:** Listening, page 32, exercises 1, 2, 3

Grammar in context

Look at this sentence from the audio in the listening lesson and answer the questions.

Last week when we ***were sailing****, one person* ***fell*** *into the water.*

a) What are the two action verbs in the sentence? ______________ and ______________

b) Which action was the longest? ______________

c) Which action happened in the middle of another action? ______________

REMEMBER

- We use the past simple to say what we did and when:
  I ***played*** *a video game* ***last night****.*
- We use the past continuous to describe continuous actions that were happening before and after a particular time in the past:
  What ***were*** *you* ***doing*** *at 8 o'clock last night?*
  I ***was watching*** *a film.*
- We use the past continuous to talk about what was happening when another action happened. We use the past simple for the other action:
  I ***was listening*** *to music* ***when*** *my mobile phone* ***rang****.*
- In stories, we use the past continuous to describe the situation and the past simple for the main things that happened:
  The sun ***was shining****, so we* ***decided*** *to go for a long walk.*

▶ **See Grammar reference, Unit 4,** page 154

1 Choose the correct verb form to complete each sentence.

1. When I **arrived** / **was arriving** at the barbecue, everyone **had** / **was having** a good time.
2. I **was listening** / **listened** to my favourite song when you **called** / **were calling**.
3. How **did you break** / **were you breaking** your arm? **Were** you **running** / **Did** you **run** at the time?
4. I **rode** / **was riding** my bike very fast and I **fell** / **was falling** off.
5. Last week the police **stopped** / **were stopping** a man because he **was driving** / **drove** his car at 135 kilometres an hour.
6. While I **shopped** / **was shopping** this afternoon, I **lost** / **was losing** my backpack.

2 Complete the sentences using the past simple or past continuous form of the verbs in brackets.

1. I ______________ (**say**) hello to the tourists, but they didn't answer me because they ______________ (**look**) at the sights.
2. When we ______________ (**walk**), we ______________ (**see**) Maria. She ______________ (**shop**).
3. I ______________ (**not want**) to get up today. It ______________ (**rain**) outside.
4. They ______________ (**drive**) through the countryside when the car suddenly ______________ (**stop**).
5. The traffic lights ______________ (**change**) when we ______________ (**chat**) to each other.

3 Complete the travel blog using the past simple or past continuous of the verbs in brackets.

Sorry I (**1**) ______________ (**not post**) any blogs last week while Mum, Dad and I (**2**) ______________ (**stay**) on the Uyuni Salt Flats in Bolivia. There were beautiful night skies – but there wasn't any wi-fi! I (**3**) ______________ (**not stream**) any video either, so I'm sending you these pictures instead. We (**4**) ______________ (**not camp**) – we stayed in an old-fashioned caravan, in the middle of the salt flats. Our guide, Arturo, (**5**) ______________ (**take**) us outside when it (**6**) ______________ (**begin**) to get dark, so we could see the stars. I (**7**) ______________ (**look**) up at the sky when at least 20 shooting stars (**8**) ______________ (**fly**) past. When we (**9**) ______________ (**take**) lots of photos, Arturo (**10**) ______________ (**start**) a fire. Soon there was hot chocolate for everyone, which (**11**) ______________ (**keep**) us warm. We stayed up all night. I (**12**) ______________ (**stand**) looking at the sky when the sun came up. It was amazing!

THINK | RESEARCH | CULTURE | LEARN | ME

Work with a partner. Take turns to tell each other about the things you and your family were doing:

- last Friday evening / Saturday morning / Sunday

4 SPEAKING | Collaborative task

Flipped classroom

1 **Watch the Talk2Me video and answer the questions.**

1 What does Evie think about running?
2 Why does Jojo think it's a good idea to buy bikes?
3 Where did they get the bikes from?

2 **Watch the video again. Underline the questions in the *Phrase expert* box that you hear on the video.**

> **PHRASE EXPERT**
> Did you say …? | I'm sorry, could you repeat that? | Pardon? | Please could you say that again?

3 **In pairs or as a group, answer the questions.**

1 What is your favourite form of transport? Why?
2 What's the best way to travel around the place where you live? Why?

4 **Work in pairs. Look at the information about the car museum and discuss what questions you may ask and answer.**

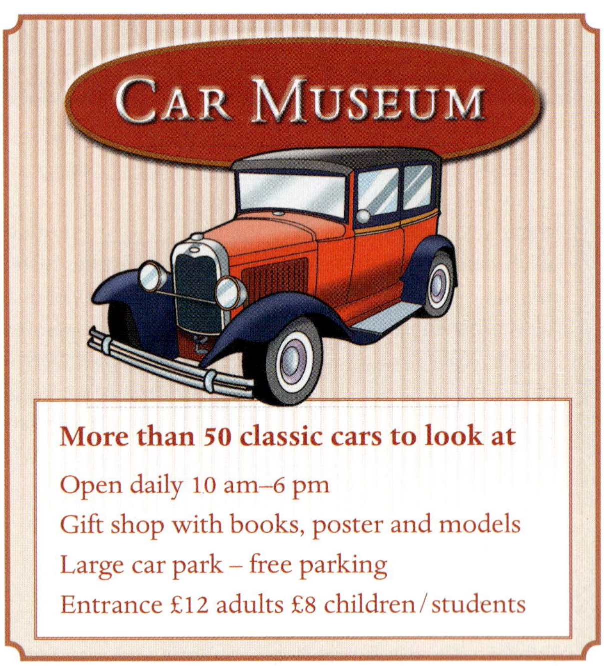

5 1.32 **Listen and check. Write the questions you hear.**

1 ______________________
2 ______________________
3 ______________________
4 ______________________
5 ______________________

6 1.32 **Listen again. Correct any answers which are incorrect.**

____

____

EXAM SKILL

Asking someone to repeat

- Sometimes you might not clearly hear or understand what your partner says.
- Use phrases like *I'm sorry, could you repeat that?* or *Did you say …?* to hear the question again or to check what was said.

7 1.33 **Listen to another student answering three more questions. Write the phrases that ask the speaker to repeat.**

1 ______________________
2 ______________________
3 ______________________

OPTIMISE YOUR EXAM

Collaborative task

- In the collaborative task, you need to answer your partner's questions about information you have.
- Read the information quickly and use it to predict the kind of question you might hear, e.g. if your information has dates, you might be asked *When is … on?*
- Remember you need to put the information you have into full sentences.

8 **In pairs (Student A and Student B), do the exam task.**

> **Student A:** turn to page 136 and look at the information about a *Travel Photography Competition*. Answer Student B's questions about it.
>
> **Student B:** look at the question prompts on page 139. Ask Student A your questions.
>
> **Student B:** turn to page 139 and look at the information about the *Arden Motor Show*. Answer Student A's questions about it.
>
> **Student A:** look at the question prompts on page 136. Ask Student B your questions.

▶ **Workbook Unit 4:** Speaking, pages 32–33, exercises 1, 2

LANGUAGE IN USE | Multiple choice

4

1 Choose the best answer.

1 We were on a ____ of the city when it started to rain.
A tour **B** journey **C** explore

2 Excuse me. I think that's my ____ . My ticket says 17B.
A engine **B** seat **C** luggage

3 While we were checking in our ____ , we remembered our passports were in the car!
A luggage **B** tickets **C** seat

4 Our train stopped but the ____ came and fixed it.
A tourist **B** explorer **C** mechanic

5 The ____ from London to Paris took 3 hours by train.
A travel **B** sailing **C** journey

6 We took three ____ with us when we went on holiday last summer.
A suitcases **B** luggage **C** tickets

7 We want to see all the famous sights, so we plan to ____ the city with a tour guide.
A trip **B** travel **C** explore

8 There are lots of things for ____ to see in this city.
A tourists **B** journeys **C** transport

EXAM SKILL

Using linking words

- We use *and, or* and *but* to join two parts of a sentence together.
- We use *before, after, when* and *until* to say when something happens.
- We use *because* to say why something happens.

2 Complete the sentences with a linking word from the box.

because	before	but	until	when

1 I feel ill when I travel by car, so I never have a big meal ____________ I go on a long car journey.

2 We waited at the railway station ____________ Aunt Ruby's train arrived.

3 Mum loves beach holidays ____________ Dad prefers going to the mountains.

4 What time was it ____________ you arrived at your hotel?

5 We aren't going on holiday this year ____________ I'm working all summer.

OPTIMISE YOUR EXAM

Multiple choice

- Read each sentence carefully and look at the words before and after the gap.
- Think about the different meanings of the possible answers.
- Read the sentences with each possible answer to make sure you choose the correct one.

3 Read the article about travel writer Réka Kaponay. For questions 1–8, choose the best answer (A, B or C) to fill each gap.

In 2012 Australian teenager Réka Kaponay was **Example:** _B_ in Melbourne and doing the things most ten-year-old girls do. (**1**) ____ parents enjoyed travelling all over Australia, and they (**2**) ____ Réka a lot of famous sights. Then (**3**) ____ day they decided to sell everything. They went on a long journey (**4**) ____ only two suitcases. Their journey started in America, then in the (**5**) ____ four years they travelled to 32 countries and six continents.

Réka posts pictures of her travel experiences (**6**) ____ days on her blog. (**7**) ____ she travels, she studies and finds out about the people and places she visits. In 2016, she (**8**) ____ a book about her travels.

Example:

	A	B	C
	A lives	**(B)** living	**C** lived
1	**A** She	**B** Hers	**C** Her
2	**A** showing	**B** showed	**C** show
3	**A** the	**B** one	**C** a
4	**A** with	**B** for	**C** and
5	**A** more	**B** after	**C** next
6	**A** every	**B** all	**C** most
7	**A** During	**B** While	**C** Where
8	**A** wrote	**B** writing	**C** writes

4 WRITING | A postcard

1 In pairs or groups, answer the questions.

1 When did you last buy, send or receive a postcard? Where was it from? What was the picture on it?

2 What do you think is the best picture for a postcard showing where **you** come from? Why?

2 Read the exam task below and answer the questions.

- What does Agnes want you to send?
- What are the three questions Agnes asks?

Read this postcard from your friend, Agnes.

Post Car

Here is a postcard of my town.
Please send me a postcard of yours.
Why do people visit your town?
How do people get to your town?
What's the best way to get around it?

Write a postcard to Agnes and answer her questions. Write **25–35** words.

EXAM SKILL

Punctuation and spelling

- The examiners will look for correct punctuation and spelling in your answer. Check your postcard for capital letters, commas and full stops.
- Check the spelling of topic vocabulary and remember spelling patterns with past tense verbs, e.g. *travel* → *travelled*.

3 Read the example below. There are five mistakes. Correct them.

Dear Agnes,
My town is near the sea. most visitors come by ship. Their are lots of ships ariving every day. A taxi can take you to the hotel, because you can walk. Its not far.
Maria

4 Work in pairs or groups. Decide which answer to Agnes's postcard is better, A or B. Use the questions below to help you.

- Are the three questions answered clearly?
- Is it easy to understand what the writer means?
- Does the answer start and end in a good way?
- Does the writer use interesting words and phrases?

Post Ca

A

Hello Agnes,
We get lots of visitors to my town because it's interesting. There is a castle and a museum. People usually use the bus or the tram to get around.
Julia

Post Ca

B

Dear Agnes,
People visit my town to see the beautiful old buildings. Most people come here by plane. The airport is large and very busy. The best way to get around is by walking.
Jordi

OPTIMISE YOUR **EXAM**

A postcard

- In this exam task, you may need to write a postcard in reply to a friend.
- Read your friend's postcard carefully and underline the three questions before you start writing.
- Your postcard should be friendly and interesting to read.

5 **Look at this writing task and make notes to answer questions 1–6.**

Read the postcard from your friend, Felix.

Post Ca

I'm on holiday. We're travelling on a ship. Yesterday I visited Barcelona. We went sightseeing. We used the underground, buses and taxis. Where did you last travel to? What did you see? How did you travel?

Felix

Write a postcard to Felix and answer the questions.
Write **25–35** words.

1 Who are you writing to?

______

2 How many words should you write?

______

3 How many questions should you answer?

______

4 What information are you going to tell Felix?

______

5 Which tenses should you use?

______

6 Which words or phrases from this unit could you use?

______

6 **Plan** **Plan your postcard. Use the chart to help you.**

	Detail	Useful language	My notes
First line			
Question 1			
Question 2			
Question 3			
Last line			

7 **Write** **Write your postcard in an appropriate style. Write 25–35 words.**

8 **Check** **Before you hand in your postcard, complete this checklist.**

Checklist

- ◯ I've followed my writing plan.
- ◯ I've answered the three questions.
- ◯ I've used the correct tenses.
- ◯ I've used a good range of vocabulary.
- ◯ I've written 25–35 words.
- ◯ I've checked my spelling and grammar.

▶ **Writing reference,** page 169 ▶ **Workbook Unit 4:** Writing, page 34, exercises 1, 2, 3, 4 and Progress check 4, page 35

PROGRESS CHECK UNITS 3–4

GRAMMAR AND VOCABULARY

1 Complete the sentences with the words in the box.

in	near	off	on	outside	ride	stop	there

1 Where's the bus ___________ for the number 22 bus?
2 Excuse me, is the station ___________ here?
3 That restaurant looks nice. Let's go ___________ and have something to eat.
4 We can sit ___________ the grass and wait for the bus.
5 Come in and get warm – but leave your wet boots ___________ , please
6 They all went on a helicopter ___________ over the city.
7 To get to the park, turn ___________ this road at the traffic lights.
8 That Turkish restaurant is very good. Shall we go ___________ tomorrow?

__/8

2 Choose the correct word to complete each sentence.

1 Clare phoned earlier. She'll pick me **off / up** at 8 o'clock.
2 Don't stand outside in the cold. Come **in / on** and get warm.
3 We were waiting for ages before the plane took **on / off**.
4 This place looks nice. Shall we go **in / out** and order something to eat?
5 We're going the wrong way. Let's turn **over / off** this road, park the car and look at the map.
6 Did you **do / bake** this bread? It's delicious.
7 Let's ask the waiter to **make / take** our photo.
8 What time do you usually **have / take** lunch?

__/8

3 Choose the correct word to fill each gap.

Last month, Jessica (**1**) ____ everything she had because she (**2**) ____ to travel around the world. But (**3**) ____ not just a tourist. In 2016, Jessica (**4**) ____ a food blog where people can share information (**5**) ____ their favourite meals. She (**6**) ____ a lot of time in Greece, taking photos of local food, and learning family recipes. While she was (**7**) ____ there, she (**8**) ____ an article about eating in Athens.

1 **A** sell **B** sells **C** sold
2 **A** wanted **B** wants **C** 's wanting
3 **A** she's **B** she **C** her
4 **A** starts **B** started **C** starting
5 **A** about **B** of **C** in
6 **A** spend **B** spends **C** spent
7 **A** stay **B** staying **C** stayed
8 **A** was posting **B** posted **C** post

__/8

4 Complete the sentences using the correct form of the verbs in brackets.

1 I _______________ (**ask**) the waiter for some water, but he didn't hear because the chef _______________ (**shout**).
2 While I _______________ (**travel**) in Vietnam, I _______________ (**eat**) some amazing street food.
3 We _______________ (**decide**) to have a picnic because the sun _______________ (**shine**) this morning.
4 Last weekend, I _______________ (**buy**) some Chinese food from the supermarket because we _______________ (**cook**) a special meal for Mum's birthday.

__/8

5 **Complete the email with the words in the box.**

did | was | weren't | what | when | where | which | who | whose | why

Hi Lily,

How was your weekend? (**1**) ____________ did you do? (**2**) ____________ you go out at all?

I had a great time at the school disco, and do you know (**3**) ____________ was there? The boy (**4**) ____________ mother works in the school library! He's really nice. I (**5**) ____________ talking to him for a long time. He asked me (**6**) ____________ you weren't there, so I think he likes you!

(**7**) ____________ were you yesterday morning? I didn't see you at the football game. I hope you (**8**) ____________ feeling ill.

I want to ask you about homework. Do you know (**9**) ____________ maths exercises we've got to do? And, (**10**) ____________ does the teacher want us to give her our projects? Does she want them tomorrow?

Thanks.

Kirsty

__/10

6 **Read the descriptions. What is the word for each one? The first letter is given.**

1 Instructions on how to make different dishes are r__ __ __ __ __ __ .
2 When food is cooked in oil or hot fat, it is f__ __ __ __ .
3 To make food ready to eat, is to pr__ __ __ __ __ it.
4 A long trip somewhere is sometimes called a j__ __ __ __ __ __ .
5 Cars must stop when there is a red t__ __ __ __ __ __ l__ __ __ __ .
6 People fill up their car at the p__ __ __ __ __ s__ __ __ __ __ __ .
7 The place where you get on and off trains is the r__ __ __ __ __ __ s__ __ __ __ __ __ .
8 The person who gives you information about a place you visit is a t__ __ __ g__ __ __ __ .

__/8

Total score __/50

EXAM SKILLS

Tick the statements that are true for you. Review the skills in the unit if you need more help.

I can ...	**Unit/page**
☐ identify *when* something happens and *who* is doing it.	Unit 3 p26
☐ predict what the speaker will say.	Unit 3 p30
☐ answer about likes, dislikes and daily life.	Unit 3 p32
☐ think about grammar.	Unit 3 p33
☐ use my vocabulary.	Unit 3 p34
☐ decide what the general message is.	Unit 4 p36
☐ listen for important information.	Unit 4 p40
☐ respond to questions.	Unit 4 p42
☐ focus on vocabulary.	Unit 4 p43
☐ use correct punctuation and spelling.	Unit 4 p44

5 Technology talks

READING | Right/Wrong/Doesn't say | An online article

1 In pairs or as a group, answer the questions.

1 Do you think most people have a mobile phone or a landline phone or both in your country?
2 What do people use their landline/mobile phones for? Why?
3 Do you think people spend too much time on their landline/mobile phones? Why / Why not?

EXAM SKILL

Understanding how often

- It is sometimes important to understand how often something happens.
- Remember that adverbs like *always*, *often* and *usually* can change the meaning of sentences.

2 Read sentences 1–3 and select the sentence with the same meaning, A or B. Then read the online article on page 49 quickly to check your answers.

1 People in China often shop online.
A It is unusual for people in China to shop online.
B People in China shop online regularly.

2 Venezuelans use their mobile phones to take photos a lot, but not always.
A Venezuelans often use their mobiles to take photos.
B Venezuelans almost never take photos with their mobiles.

3 It is unusual for people in Nigeria to use a landline phone.
A People in Nigeria usually use a landline phone.
B People in Nigeria almost never use a landline phone.

3 Read the article quickly again and find out what the following numbers are about.

1 37 ______
2 17 ______
3 1% ______

4 Work in pairs. Compare your answers. Say which number(s) you found most surprising, and why.

SAY IT RIGHT

Resource centre: Unit 5
Missing vowel sounds in questions

TECHNOLOGY HABITS AROUND THE WORLD

1 How much time do people spend on social networking sites? How many people take selfies? What do most people use their smartphones for? The answers to these questions are different in every country. Here are a few interesting facts about the use of technology around the world.

2 Does your family shop online? Many people around the world do. It's now very popular with lots of people in China, where 52% of the population regularly do their shopping online. There are now some important online stores in China, such as Alibaba and Baidu.

2 What do people usually use their smartphones for? A lot of young people like streaming music, chatting on social networks and taking selfies. In fact, 60% of Chileans, Argentinians and Brazilians regularly take photos with their phones. However, mobile photography is most popular in Venezuela, where 88% of Venezuelans often use their mobiles to take photos, sometimes with a little help from a selfie stick.

4 In the Philippines, people spend about 37 hours a week using social networking sites. That's more hours than in the USA, where the people spend 17 hours a week. What do they chat online about? Well, 70% of Filipinos talk about music and films, and over 50% chat about sport.

5 In Nigeria, a lot of people own a mobile phone – nearly 90% of the population. They almost never use a landline phone because only 1% of Nigerians have them in their homes. Things are different in the UK. Only 15% of the British population live in a 'mobile-only' home.

OPTIMISE YOUR EXAM

Right/Wrong/Doesn't say

- Read the text quickly first. Remember that the questions are in the same order as the text.
- Look for the answer to question 1 at the start of the text and look for the answer to question 7 near the end of the text.

5 2.01 **Read the article again. Are sentences 1–7 'Right' (A) or 'Wrong' (B)? If there is not enough information to answer 'Right' (A) or 'Wrong' (B), choose 'Doesn't say' (C).**

Example: Technology is the same in every country.
A Right B Wrong C Doesn't say

1 Online shopping is popular in many countries.
A Right B Wrong C Doesn't say

2 Many people from the UK shop online at Alibaba.
A Right B Wrong C Doesn't say

3 Less than 50% of people in Brazil take photos with their mobiles.
A Right B Wrong C Doesn't say

4 People spend more time on social networking sites in the USA than in the Philippines.
A Right B Wrong C Doesn't say

5 Filipinos never chat online about video games.
A Right B Wrong C Doesn't say

6 Mobile phones are very popular in Nigeria.
A Right B Wrong C Doesn't say

7 Only 15% of the people in Britain have a landline phone.
A Right B Wrong C Doesn't say

6 Match the highlighted words in the article to a definition (1–8).

1 buying things over the internet ______
2 all the people who live in a particular place ______
3 the American word for 'shops' ______
4 to do something for a period of time ______
5 pieces of true information ______
6 photos you take of yourself ______
7 another word for 'talk' ______
8 places on the internet with information about different subjects ______

THINK | RESEARCH | CULTURE | LEARN | ME

Work in pairs or in groups and answer the question.

- What are the good and bad things about owning a mobile phone?

5 GRAMMAR 1 | Quantifiers with countable and uncountable nouns

Grammar in context

Choose the correct word or phrase to complete the sentence. Then find them in the text on page 49 and check your answers.

1 *How* ***much*** */* ***many*** *time do people spend on social networking sites?* (paragraph 1)
2 *How* ***lot*** */* ***many*** *people take selfies?* (paragraph 1)
3 *Here are* ***a few*** */* ***a little*** *interesting facts ...* (paragraph 1)
4 *There are now* ***lots*** */* ***some*** *important online stores in China, ...* (paragraph 2)
5 *... with* ***many*** */* ***a little*** *help from a selfie stick.* (paragraph 3)
6 *In Nigeria, a* ***lot*** */* ***many*** *of people own a mobile phone ...* (paragraph 5)

REMEMBER

We use quantifiers to talk about quantities and amounts.

- We use *some* with countable and uncountable nouns, in positive sentences:
  I have ***some*** *photos from the trip.*
- We use *any* with countable and uncountable nouns, in negative sentences and questions:
  *There is****n't any*** *information on this site. Are there* ***any*** *apps you use every day?*
- We use *(not) much* with uncountable nouns and *(not) many* with countable nouns, in negative sentences and questions:
  I ***don't*** *listen to* ***much*** *music online.*
  Are there ***many*** *landlines in your country?*
- We use *a lot of / lots of* to talk about a large quantity:
  I have ***a lot of*** *apps on my phone.*
- We also use *a few* or *a little* to talk about a small number or quantity:
  We have ***a few*** *computers in our classroom. (= not many)*
  She has ***a little*** *free time later. (= not much)*

▶ **See Grammar reference, Unit 5,** page 154

1 Choose the correct words to complete each sentence.

1 I think I need **much** / **a little** help with my IT project.
2 I downloaded **a lot of** / **many** songs. I don't have time to listen to them all!
3 **A lot** / **A few** people in my town don't own a mobile phone.
4 Do you need **any** / **many** help downloading the information?
5 There are **a little** / **a lot of** people here today.
6 I don't know how to use this app, and there's not **a few** / **much** information about it online.

2 Complete the text about a school project. Choose the best answer (A, B or C).

(**1**) _____ of teachers think that speaking to students in different countries is important, so (**2**) _____ young people have pen friends in other countries. It's a great way to learn about how other people live. Our teacher wanted our class to speak online to children in Ghana. (**3**) _____ of students said 'yes' to the idea. We don't know (**4**) _____ children in Africa, so It's very interesting.

Now we regularly speak to students in Ghana online. Once every two weeks, we turn on the screen in our classroom and have a video chat with a school in Accra.

At first, it was a bit difficult because (**5**) _____ students were speaking at the same time. But after (**6**) _____ conversations, we decided to write down (**7**) _____ questions in class before chatting. Now different students ask (**8**) _____ questions every week and everyone can hear them. It's interesting talking to our friends in Accra, and it's (**9**) _____ fun, too.

	A	B	C
1	**A** Many	**B** Lots	**C** Little
2	**A** some	**B** few	**C** any
3	**A** Lot	**B** A lot	**C** A little
4	**A** much	**B** many	**C** few
5	**A** much	**B** few	**C** a lot of
6	**A** a little	**B** a lot	**C** a few
7	**A** few	**B** some	**C** much
8	**A** a little	**B** lot	**C** a few
9	**A** a lot of	**B** a little	**C** many

3 Use the words in the box to write six sentences about modern technology. Use a quantifier in every sentence.

emails | mobile phone | music | photos
social networking | video games

Example: *I don't send many emails.*

Words connected with *communication and technology*

1 2.02 **Complete the names for the things in the picture with the words in the box. Listen and check.**

camera | keyboard | laptop
mouse | printer | screen

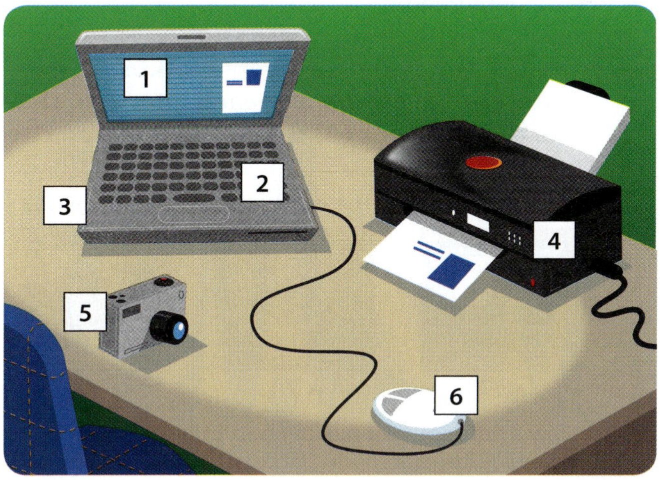

1 _ _ _ _ _ _
2 _ _ _ _ _ _ _ _
3 _ _ _ _ _ _
4 _ _ _ _ _ _ _
5 _ _ _ _ _ _
6 _ _ _ _ _

2 2.03 **Complete the text with the words in the box. Listen and check.**

blogging | camera | download | graphics
keyboard | laptop | mouse | ~~online~~
printer | screen | software | stream

Hi everyone! Sorry I've been quiet! I've just moved house. It's good to get (1) *online* again – I missed (2) __________ ! I have a lovely big desk for my (3) __________ in the new house. So, I can use that when I'm at home. It's got a really big (4) __________ , which is perfect for watching videos. I decided to get a (5) __________ as well, so I can print the photos I like. The laptop is good for gaming too. The (6) __________ in the games look much better. The (7) __________ is a bit different from my last one, so sorry if I make any spelling mistakes! The wireless (8) __________ is great and isn't noisy when you click it. I still need to (9) __________ my files from the old computer. And I need some new (10) __________ so that I can (11) __________ music faster. Tomorrow, I'll use the (12) __________ and upload some photos of me at my new desk!

Share Like Comment

Compound nouns

3 2.04 **Write the words in the box on the correct line to make technology words. Listen and check.**

computer | phone | player | web

CD / DVD / MP3 **(1)** __________

camera / cell / mobile **(2)** __________

(3) __________ address / page / site

laptop / personal / **(4)** __________ /
(4) __________ file / software

4 **Choose the correct word to complete each sentence.**

1 Let's listen to music on the **DVD** / **MP3** player.
2 This **website** / **address** is full of adverts.
3 The new information is on their web **address** / **page**.
4 I bought some computer **files** / **software** to help me change the way photographs look.

Collocations with verbs

5 2.05 **Complete the phrases with the words in the box. Sometimes there may be more than one answer. Listen and check.**

download | make | open
send | start | take

1 __________ a phone call
2 __________ a piece of software
3 __________ a file
4 __________ a photograph
5 __________ a text message
6 __________ a conversation

6 **Complete the sentences using the correct form of the collocations from Exercise 5.**

1 I met her on the train and she __________ with me. We talked about social networking sites.
2 Lola can't come out because she's __________ to her brother in Canada. They talk every week.
3 Can I use your laptop? I need to __________ that has my school project in it.
4 You need to __________ so your computer works faster. It's getting old.
5 Would you __________ of me and my cat, please? I want to post it on Instagram.
6 If you can't come to the barbecue, __________ to Mum so she knows.

1 **In pairs or as a group, look at the photo and answer the questions.**

1 What is happening in the picture?
2 Have you ever made anything like this? If so, where and when? If not, would you like to, and why?
3 How do you think we will use robots in the future?

EXAM SKILL

Understanding when things happen

- It is important to understand if someone is talking about the past, the present or the future.
- The tense and words like *first*, *next* and *later* can help you decide when different things happen.

2 **Read the conversation. Match the underlined phrases to the tenses.**

Boy: Oh, no! My new printer doesn't work.
Girl: Look at this information. There's a number to phone for help. Why not call it?
Boy: No, <u>I looked</u> on their website. <u>It says</u> to send them an email, so <u>I'm writing</u> one now.
Girl: It might be quicker to phone …

1 past simple ______________________
2 present continuous ______________________
3 present simple ______________________

3 **Put the events (a–d) in the order they happened (1–4) in Exercise 2.**

a) The girl read the information. ____
b) The boy wrote an email. ____
c) The boy looked at the website. ____
d) The boy tried the printer. ____

OPTIMISE YOUR EXAM

Picture multiple choice

- In short conversations, you often hear someone asking for and giving opinions.
- Listen carefully to the questions. *What's it like?* and *Do you like it?* don't mean the same thing.
- Listen carefully to the opinions. *I don't really like it.* and *It's not what I like.* means the speaker doesn't like something.

4 2.06 **You will hear people talking in five different situations. For each question, choose the right answer (A, B or C). Listen and check.**

Example: What is the boy having a problem with?

A ☐ B ☐ C ☑

1 How does Sarah contact her pen friends in other countries?

A ☐ B ☐ C ☐

2 What are Kirsty and her brother doing later?

A ☐ B ☐ C ☐

3 What is the man going to buy his son?

A ☐ B ☐ C ☐

4 How many people were in the chat room?

A ☐ B ☐ C ☐

5 Which app is Mum going to download?

A ☐ B ☐ C ☐

▶ **Workbook Unit 5:** Listening, page 40, exercises 1, 2

GRAMMAR 2 | Comparatives and superlatives

Grammar in context

Look at these sentences from the audio in the listening lesson. Choose the correct word to complete each sentence.

1 *Dan says it's the **best** / **better** game he's ever played.*

2 *... I hope it's **good** / **better** than the football game we played!*

3 *It's **most** / **more** exciting than the football game.*

REMEMBER

- We use the comparative form of adjectives + *than* to compare two people/things: *My laptop is **bigger than** yours. Maths is **more difficult than** English.*
- We use *the* + the superlative form of adjectives to compare more than two people/things: *Vikki is **the oldest** girl in the class. This is **the most interesting** website of all.*

▶ **See Grammar reference, Unit 5,** page 155

1 **Write sentences using the comparative form of the adjectives in the box + *than*.**

big | expensive | interesting | long modern | ~~old~~ | popular | strange

1 I bought the football game in 2012. I bought the adventure game in 2010.
The adventure game is older than the football game.

2 The PC is £499 and the laptop is £359.
______

3 Lots of my friends like rock music, but more of my friends like rap.
______

4 Your blog has lots of good things to read. Her blog has more good things to read.
______

5 The video of the skateboarder is a bit unusual. The video of the surfer is very unusual!
______

6 There are 30 people in my computing class, and 10 in the photography class.
______

7 Her email was 150 words. His email was 250 words.
______

8 The design of the PC is not new. The design of the laptop is very new.
______

2 **Choose the correct comparative or superlative form to complete each sentence.**

1 My smartphone is **the newest** / **newer than** my laptop.

2 Her new laptop is **the biggest** / **bigger than** her old one.

3 Phones in this shop are **more expensive** / **most expensive** than ones anywhere else.

4 Ida's technology project was **the best** / **better than** in the class.

5 His idea is **more** / **the most** interesting than the one we heard yesterday.

6 This old phone is **the heaviest** / **heavier than** my new one.

7 Online gaming is **the most popular** / **more popular than** hobby for teenage boys.

3 **Complete the extract from a blog using the comparative or superlative form of the adjectives in brackets.**

Last month, my class did a project on technology. It was a (**1**) ______ (**exciting**) project than the one we did last year. The teacher said it was for a competition. He told us, 'The group with (**2**) ______ (**interesting**) idea will go to London!'

We had to think of a (**3**) ______ (**good**) idea. One group tried to build a 3-D printer, but it didn't work. Lots of students worked quickly but we were (**4**) ______ (**careful**) than them. We talked about it a lot and decided to make an electronic drum machine. It was (**5**) ______ (**difficult**) than we thought, and the others finished before us. But we didn't care because we knew our project was (**6**) ______ (**good**) in the class!

We won a school prize for our project ... and we went to the competition in London. London is very big and it's (**7**) ______ (**busy**) than my town, but I loved it.

The judges really liked our drum machine and said it was (**8**) ______ (**unusual**) project. We didn't win first prize, but we had a great time in London.

THINK | RESEARCH | CULTURE | LEARN | **ME**

In your opinion, what's the most useful piece of technology? Why? Discuss your ideas with a partner.

▶ **Workbook Unit 5:** Grammar 2, page 39, exercises 1, 2

5 SPEAKING | Interview

Talk 2 Me
It's better to…

Flipped classroom

1 **Watch the *Talk2Me* video and answer the questions.**

1 Why does Evie like shopping online?
2 Name four things that they buy online.
3 What did the cat do?

2 **Watch the video again. Underline the phrases in the *Phrase expert* box that you hear on the video.**

> **PHRASE EXPERT**
> I like … more than anything else/the best.
> … is better than … | It's better to (go) …
> It's better for (shopping) … | It's my favourite way to (relax). | The best thing is …
> The most difficult thing is …

A

B

3 **In pairs or as a group, look at the photos and answer the questions.**

1 Which way of communicating is the best? Why?
2 How do you usually talk to your family and friends?

> **EXAM SKILL**
> ### Making comparisons
> - In Speaking exams, you are often asked about daily experiences, the past and future plans.
> - When you talk about these details, you can compare more than one.
> - Using phrases which compare things shows the examiner your range of vocabulary and grammar.

4 2.07 **Listen to four students answering personal questions. Choose the correct answer.**

1 What do you like doing in your free time?
hanging out with friends / chatting online
2 What did you do yesterday?
watched a film / relaxed on the beach
3 What are you doing on Saturday?
shopping with friends / sightseeing in London
4 What do you like doing on your computer?
chatting online / playing games online

5 2.07 **Listen again and number the comparison phrases (A–D) in the order that you hear them.**

A more than anything else ____
B it's better for shopping ____
C It's my favourite way to relax ____
D I like … the best. ____

> **OPTIMISE YOUR EXAM**
> ### Interview
> - During the Speaking test, the examiner will ask personal questions.
> - Be ready to talk in the present, the past and the future tense.
> - Listen carefully to the question so you know what tense to use.

6 **Work in pairs. Take turns asking and answering the questions from Exercise 4. Use phrases from the Phrase expert box in your answers.**

▶ **Workbook Unit 5:** Speaking, pages 40–41, exercises 1, 2, 3

LANGUAGE IN USE | Multiple-choice dialogue

1 2.08 **Listen to the teenagers talking about technology. Match the ways of communicating (A–C) to the speakers.**

A instant messaging
B video chat
C video sharing

It's good to talk

How do you keep in touch with people?

1 Peter 2 Chloe 3 Sam

___ ___ ___

2 **In pairs or as a group, answer the questions.**

1 Which ways of communicating in Exercise 1 do you use?
2 Which way do you think is best? Why?
3 Do you communicate with different people in different ways? Why? How?

EXAM SKILL

Pronouns

- Pronouns are words like *it, you, them, these, something, anything.*
- Make sure the pronoun in the answer matches the subject or object in the first sentence.
- However, don't just choose the answer because the pronoun matches, it must be the correct response to the sentence.

3 **Choose the correct pronoun to complete each conversation.**

1 A: This is my new laptop.
B: **It's** / **He's** got a really big screen.
2 A: Do you like this website?
B: Yes, **they** / **I** do.
3 A: Is your brother going to call later?
B: Yes, **he** / **she** is.
4 A: Can you all hear me?
B: Yes, **I** / **we** can.
5 A: They are my favourite band.
B: I've never heard of **them** / **her**.
6 A: Who took these pictures?
B: John took **him** / **them** with his digital camera.

OPTIMISE YOUR EXAM

Multiple-choice dialogue

- Read each question and think of an answer of your own before you look at the three answer options.
- Check your answers by reading the question and answer together to make sure they make sense.

4 **Complete the sentences with one pronoun in each gap.**

1 'Do you enjoy taking photos, Jade?' 'Yes, ___________ do.'
2 'What are they doing?' '___________ 're instant messaging their friends.'
3 'Alex, can you help me find my phone?' 'Yes, of course ___________ can.'
4 'Why are you and Milly laughing?' 'Because Izabel told ___________ a joke.'

5 **Complete the five conversations. For questions 1–5, choose the best answer (A, B or C).**

Example:

Who are you talking to?

A They are on the desk.
(B) I'm talking to my cousin.
C She's speaking English.

1	What are you downloading?	**A** Fine, thanks. **B** It's a new film. **C** On the internet.
2	Which website is it on?	**A** The new music one. **B** There are too many. **C** It's really busy.
3	Did you talk to them on the phone?	**A** Yes, please. **B** No. I sent a text. **C** She's on the phone.
4	Please could you answer the phone?	**A** Why did she call? **B** Why can't I? **C** Why can't you?
5	Who called just now?	**A** It's Kate speaking. **B** I forgot to ask. **C** I know his name.

THINK | RESEARCH | CULTURE | LEARN | ME

Work in groups and answer the questions.

- Why do you think it is important to communicate with people from other countries?
- What are the best ways to communicate with people?

5 WRITING | Information transfer

1 **In pairs or groups, answer the questions.**

1 How do you use technology at home?
2 How do you use technology at school?

EXAM SKILL

Making notes: when and where

- Remember that there are different ways to talk about time, e.g. *am/pm, in the morning*, etc.
- Look for times in the texts and think of different ways to say them.
- Sometimes there are prepositions in the notes. Always read them carefully. You may need to write a time or place after *at*. After *in* you usually write a place, and *on* usually comes before a day or date.

2 **Read the texts A and B, below. Underline the times in text A. Match the words or phrases in text B that also talk about time.**

A

WANT TO MEET NEW FRIENDS FROM AROUND THE WORLD?

Come to our international club and chat online with students from four other countries.

Every Wednesday (Room 11a)
2.30–4.30pm

Special online games activities!
Saturday morning
10.00am–12.00pm

B

Hi Toni,
I might go to the international group this week. I'm busy until half past three on Wednesday, but I could go for the last hour. Will you be able to stay at school until half past four? Saturday morning looks OK. But I need to leave before twelve to get my bus home.
Adele

3 **Match the sentences (a–f) to the notes (1–6) with the same meaning.**

1 Online chat starts at 2:30pm. ____
2 She can stay until half past four. ____
3 The club ends at 4:30pm. ____
4 The online gaming ends at 12. ____
5 The bus leaves at 11:55am. ____
6 She's busy until 3:30pm. ____

a) It ends at noon.
b) She's doing something until half past three.
c) She doesn't need to go before 4:30pm.
d) It starts at half past two.
e) It finishes at half past four in the afternoon.
f) It goes just before 12.

4 **Read Toni's notes below. Then look at the texts in Exercise 2 again and choose the correct answers.**

TONI'S NOTES – INTERNATIONAL CLUB

Go with:	*Adele*
Meet in:	1 *Wednesday / Room 11a*
Chat with students from:	2 *4 / 5 countries*
Start times	
Wednesday:	3 *3.30 pm / 4.30 pm*
Saturday:	4 *10 am / 10 pm*
Game activity ends:	5 *11.55 / 12*

5 **Work in pairs and do the following:**

1 Compare your answers in Exercise 4 and say where you found the answers in the texts in Exercise 2.
Text A says the group meets in Room 11a.
2 Find the wrong answers in the texts in Exercise 4 and say why they are wrong.
Wednesday is in Text A but it is the wrong answer. It's wrong because the notes say 'Meet in' so the answer is a place, not a day.

OPTIMISE YOUR EXAM

Information transfer

- Remember to read both texts carefully.
- You will need to use information from both texts to complete the notes.

6 Plan You are going to complete Ollie's notes. Complete these steps:

1 Read both texts carefully.
2 Underline the prepositions in the booking form so you know what you are looking for (a time, a day/date or a place).
3 Look through both texts for the information.

Read the poster and the message. Fill in the information in Ollie's notes.

Online Gaming Club

All-day gaming event (9:30–17:30)

25 October under 12s • 26 October 12+

The event starts at 9.30 in the school hall.
Arrive 9.15.
Contact club secretary (931844) by 10 October to enter.
Each game lasts one hour. Eight games played.
Bring your own food.

All welcome

Hi Ollie,

My new mobile number is 079226. What's yours? We're too old for the event on the 25th, but the other one is OK. You bring the snacks. Is that OK? It's only a 10-minute cycle to the school hall, so I'm going by bike. Can you meet me outside main door at 9 am?

Serge

OLLIE'S NOTES

Online Gaming Club – all-day event

Event on:	1
Meet Serge at:	2 am
Number of games:	3
Take:	4
OGC phone number:	5

7 Write Write the information to complete Ollie's notes. Check your spelling and the use of capital letters.

8 Check Before you hand in your booking form, complete this checklist.

Checklist

- ○ I've carefully read both texts.
- ○ I've looked carefully at prepositions to see what word can follow them.
- ○ I've completed all the answers on the form.
- ○ I've checked my spelling.
- ○ I've checked my use of capital letters.

Extra writing

9 You are going to reply to Serge's message from Exercise 6. Read the message again and answer questions 1–4.

1 What style should you write in?

____

2 What three questions does Serge ask?

____

____

____

3 Which words or phrases from this unit could you use?

____

Now write your message in 25–35 words.

6 Teen fashion

READING | Multiple-choice cloze | An online article

1 In pairs or as a group, answer the questions.

1 What kind of clothes do you usually wear / do you like wearing?
2 Where do you buy your clothes?
3 Do you wear different clothes on school days and at the weekend?

EXAM SKILL

Choosing between similar answers

- The possible answers often look similar, e.g. auxiliary verbs (*be, do, have*) or prepositions (*in, on, at*).
- Choose the best answer, then read the whole sentence again to check it fits.

2 Choose the correct preposition to complete each sentence.

1 Did you see Olga **for** / **at** school today?
2 The designer is **from** / **to** Italy.
3 She bought her new jacket **on** / **in** Saturday.
4 Laurel is studying fashion **to** / **in** France.

3 Complete the sentences with the auxiliary verbs in the box.

are	did	do	does	is	was

1 She ____________ buying some new clothes now.
2 ____________ students at your school wear school uniforms?
3 Zara and I ____________ shopping in town at the moment.
4 The jumper ____________ too small so I took it back to the shop.
5 ____________ you buy that T-shirt when you were on holiday?
6 ____________ she spend a lot of money on clothes?

OPTIMISE YOUR EXAM

Multiple-choice cloze

Before you read the text, ask yourself these questions:

- What is it about? Is it about people or places?
- Does it tell a story or give information?
- Remember that the title and pictures can give you more information about a text.

fashion changes

1 Online shopping has changed the world **Example:** _B_ fashion. We can buy clothes from all over the world, compare prices and find the best places to shop. What other things have changed the fashion world?

2 There are a (1) ____ of new people starting new trends, especially teenagers. Some of them are famous, like Romeo Beckham, but many are normal teenagers who use social media (2) ____ show people how to dress well. A lot of people follow them on social media, so clothing companies now look at their ideas. These teens (3) ____ just follow fashion, they make it. To them, it (4) ____ matter if something is old or new. The most important thing is that it looks good.

3 Clothes are made from different things these days, too. Have you ever worn (5) ____ T-shirt made from old plastic bottles? Many people are interested (6) ____ looking after the world, and some customers think carefully about this when buying fashion. They choose clothes made of different plants, like bamboo, coconut and banana, or from recycled materials like bottles, tyres and coffee. And now you can even buy shoes that make electricity (7) ____ you walk. They're amazing!

4 Many people buy (8) ____ clothes online, but shopping centres are still very busy. There are lots of clothes shops to choose from. Some shops use unusual ideas to try and get more customers. For example, many shoppers have been to visit Johnny Cupcakes … and it's an experience they won't forget. It's a clothes shop that smells of cakes and sugar! The shop assistant puts your clothes in cake boxes, not bags. I've never visited the store, but it must make you hungry!

4 **Work in pairs. Read the online article above quickly and find six 'different' materials that clothes can be made of.**

____________ ____________
____________ ____________
____________ ____________

5 2.09 **Read the online article about fashion. For questions 1–8, choose the best answer (A, B or C) to fill each gap.**

Example:

	A	B	C
	A in	(B) of	C at
1	A much	B lot	C many
2	A to	B and	C for
3	A not	B are	C don't
4	A hasn't	B doesn't	C isn't
5	A any	B the	C a
6	A in	B at	C from
7	A why	B what	C when
8	A your	B their	C our

6 **Match the highlighted words in the article to a definition (1–8).**

1 feeling that you want food ____________
2 not unusual or special in any way ____________
3 the cost of different things ____________
4 to be interested in someone online and regularly look at their social media sites ____________
5 full of people ____________
6 a person who works in a shop ____________
7 not normal ____________
8 another word for 'businesses' ____________

THINK | RESEARCH | **CULTURE** | LEARN | ME

Work in pairs or groups and answer the questions.

- What kinds of clothes are in fashion at the moment?
- Look at the list below. Who changes fashion the most, and how?
  - newspapers and magazines
  - celebrities (actors, sports stars, etc.)
  - vloggers and bloggers

▶ **Workbook Unit 6:** Reading, pages 44–55, exercises 1, 2, 3

6 GRAMMAR 1 | Present perfect simple with *ever* and *never*

Grammar in context

Find these sentences in the text on page 59 and fill in the missing words.

1 *Online shopping* ___________ ***changed*** *the world of fashion.* (paragraph 1)
2 *What other things* **have** ___________ *the fashion world?* (paragraph 1)
3 ___________ *you* ***ever worn*** *a T-shirt made from old plastic bottles?* (paragraph 3)
4 *I've* ___________ ***visited*** *the store, ...* (paragraph 4)

REMEMBER

- We use the present perfect simple to talk about past actions when the time they happened isn't important or isn't known:
  *I've **bought** lots of pairs of shoes.*
- We use the present perfect to talk about experiences: *He's **been** to lots of fashion shows.*
- *Ever* and *never* are often used with the present perfect simple, in questions and negative sentences: *Have you **ever** seen one of these? I've **never** worn a tie.*

▶ **See Grammar reference, Unit 6,** page 155

1 Use the prompts to write questions using *Have you ever ...?*

1 have you / make / a meal for your family __d__
Have you ever made a meal for your family?
2 you / travel / by train alone ____
____
3 you / see / the Eiffel Tower ____
____
4 you / wear / socks in bed ____
____
5 you and your friends / eat together in a restaurant ____
____
6 you and your family / move / house ____
____

2 Match the answers (a–f) to the questions in Exercise 1.

a No, we haven't. We've always lived in the same house.
b Yes, we have. We've been to all the fast-food restaurants in our city together.
c No, I haven't. But I have worn a hat!
d Yes, I have. I've made pizza and salad for my mum a few times.
e Yes, I have. I've travelled to Wales alone to visit my grandparents.
f No, I haven't. I've never been to Paris.

3 Work in pairs. Take turns asking and answering your questions from Exercise 1.

Have you ever made a meal for your family?

No, I haven't. But I help Mum make meals sometimes.

4 Complete the conversation.

A: Have you ever **(1)** ___________ to France?
B: No, I **(2)** ___________ , but my sister has.
A: Really. Which cities **(3)** ___________ she been to?
B: Only Paris, I think. She loves fashion and art.
A: Right. Has she **(4)** ___________ visited London? There are so many great shops and galleries there.
B: No, she **(5)** ___________ . But she's planning to go there for a short holiday.
A: **(6)** ___________ you been to the UK?
B: No, I've **(7)** ___________ been there. Have you?
A: Yes, I **(8)** ___________ . I've been to Cambridge. I went to a summer language school there.

5 Complete the text using the present perfect form of the verbs in brackets.

Hi guys! Well, I **(1)** ___________ (**have**) a great week! We've been in the UAE – sightseeing and shopping. Today we went to the most amazing place. **(2)** ___________ (**you / ever / hear**) of Mall of the Emirates? I think it's the coolest place to shop in Dubai. I **(3)** ___________ (**never / see**) such a huge building! There are more than 700 different stores, and over 100 different places to eat. This week, my parents and I **(4)** ___________ (**eat**) a lot of delicious food. Inside the mall is a theme park called Magic Planet. It has got a 4-D cinema and a huge roller coaster, which I **(5)** ___________ (**ride**) on three times so far. It's fantastic! But the best thing is the ski slope. I **(6)** ___________ (**never / try**) skiing, but Dad and I are going tomorrow!

Sorry that I **(7)** ___________ (**not / write**) to some of you who sent comments and messages last month. And I **(8)** ___________ (**not / forget**) that I promised to post some new photos – I'll post some soon!

SAY IT RIGHT

Resource centre: Unit 6
Pronunciation of *have*

Words connected with *fashion, clothes and shopping*

1 2.10 **Complete the lists with the words in the box. Listen and check.**

bill | buy | cash | change (×2) | cheque | cost | credit card | ~~customer~~ | department store | market | receipt | shop assistant | shopper | shopping centre | spend | supermarket

people	places	money (verbs)	money (nouns)
customer	______	______	______
______	______	______	______
______	______	______	______
	______	______	______
			______
			______

2 **Complete the sentences using the correct form of the words from Exercise 1.**

1 People often don't carry a lot of ______ these days because they prefer using their ______ to pay for things.

2 Take a list when you go shopping, so that you only ______ the things you need and don't ______ too much.

3 In ______ you can find everything you need in one big shop. But ______ are still popular, because all the different shops are in the same place.

4 There are lots of ______ out on the streets today but the book shop doesn't look very popular – there aren't many ______ inside.

5 After the meal, we paid the ______ and the waiter brought our ______.

6 In most shops, you get a ______ for the things you bought – it shows how much everything ______.

Verbs + prepositions

3 2.11 **Choose the correct word to complete the phrases in bold in each sentence. Listen and check.**

1 When I go shopping, I always **pay for / in** cash.
2 **Write up / down** what you want and I'll go to the supermarket for you.
3 Please **take on / off** your wet boots before you go into the house.
4 It's raining so **put on / back** your raincoat before you go out.
5 Did you **pay back / for** the online shopping by credit card?
6 Most shops give you 30 days to **take on / back** anything you don't want.

4 **Complete the sentences with some of the phrases you made in Exercise 3.**

1 Excuse me, did you ______ that drink? Can you show me your receipt?
2 I need to ______ these shoes. They are hurting my feet.
3 Here's the bill. Would you like to ______ cash or by credit card?
4 I always ______ what I want to buy before I go to the supermarket.

Collocations with verbs

5 2.12 **Complete the sentences with the words in the box. Listen and check.**

do | catch | for | go | keep | save

1 Do you prefer to ______ shopping with your friends or with your mum?
2 You can ______ money for a new computer game if you stop buying chocolate and cakes!
3 We usually ______ the bus when we want to go to the shopping centre.
4 The bill was nine pounds and 20 pence, so Dad gave the waiter £10 and told him to ______ the change.
5 'Mum, there's no milk left.' 'It's OK – I'm going to ______ the shopping later.'
6 There are some lovely clothes ______ sale in that shop.

▶ Vocabulary reference, page 165 ▶ Workbook Unit 6: Vocabulary, page 41, exercises 1, 2, 3

6 LISTENING | Multiple matching

1 **In pairs or as a group, look at the photo above and answer the questions.**

1 Have you got any clothes that are really important to you? Why are they important?
2 Who usually pays for your clothes, you or your parents?
3 Have you ever saved your money to buy something special? What was it?
4 What kind of things have you bought in the last month? Where? Why?

EXAM SKILL

Choosing the right answer

- In this part of the exam you often hear all the words or phrases in A–H.
- Be careful. Just because you hear one of the words, it doesn't mean it is a correct answer.

2 2.13 **Listen to four people talking about shopping and choose the correct answers.**

1 This week, the speaker has been to …
  A the market. **B** the shopping centre.
2 The speaker's friend contacted her …
  A at the shops. **B** at home.
3 The speaker watched the football match …
  A in his house. **B** at the stadium.
4 The person who pays for the clothes now is …
  A the speaker. **B** the speaker's mother.

OPTIMISE YOUR EXAM

Multiple matching

- Listen carefully to all the information before you choose an answer.
- Put a line through each answer you choose so that you know you can't use it again.

3 2.14 **Listen to Hannah talking to a friend about some of her clothes. For each item of clothing (1–5), choose the place she got it from (A–H). There are some extra letters you do not need.**

Clothes		**Places**
Example:		**A** the airport
jeans	*E*	**B** summer school
1 T-shirt	____	**C** department store
2 necklace	____	**D** museum shop
3 sunglasses	____	~~**E** London~~
4 cap	____	**F** supermarket
5 trainers	____	**G** music festival
		H the beach

4 2.14 **Listen again and check your answers.**

THINK | RESEARCH | CULTURE | LEARN | ME

Work in pairs or groups and answer the questions.

- Do you think people buy more or less than in the past?
- Is this a good or bad thing? Why?

▶ **Workbook Unit 6:** Listening, page 48, exercises 1, 2, 3

GRAMMAR 2 | Present perfect simple and past simple

Grammar in context

Read these sentences from the audio in the listening lesson. Then answer the questions.

1 *I've **had** these for years.*
2 *I **found** them on the beach.*

a) Which sentence tells us about a past action that is linked to the present? ____
b) Which tells us about a completed action in the past? ____

REMEMBER

- We use the present perfect to talk about an action which happened in the past and is linked to the present:
  *Katie **has put** her clothes in the suitcase.* (Her clothes are in the suitcase now. We don't know when she put them in.)
- We use the past simple to talk about a finished action:
  *Katie **put** her clothes in her suitcase last night.* (We know when she did it.)
- We use the present perfect to report information or news:
  *I**'ve bought** some new shoes.*
- We use the past simple to give details or explanations:
  *I **bought** some shoes at the new department store last Saturday.*

▶ **See Grammar reference, Unit 6,** page 156

1 Choose the correct verb form to complete each sentence.

1 You don't need to buy anything for the barbecue. **I've done** / **did** all the shopping already.
2 I'm sorry, we don't have that necklace anymore. A customer **has bought** / **bought** the last one this morning.
3 Oh, no! **I've lost** / **lost** my credit card. I can't find it anywhere.
4 The department store sale **has started** / **started** last week. It's been really popular with shoppers.
5 **Have you sold** / **Did you sell** many of those bags yesterday?
6 'Is that jacket new?' 'No, I **had** / **'ve had** it for years!'

2 Write pairs of sentences using the prompts. Use the present perfect in one sentence and the past simple in the other sentence.

1 I / spend / my money. I / buy / a pair of shoes.
I've spent my money. I bought a pair of shoes.
2 The boys / walk / into town. They / leave / at 2 o'clock.
____
3 I / get / Mum / a present for her birthday. I / pay / 10 euros for it.
____
4 He / not like / his old flat. He / live / in three different flats this year.
____
5 She / lose / an earring. She / drop / it in the street.
____
6 I / not wear / these boots before. My / old ones / be / very comfortable.
____

3 Complete the text using the correct form of the verbs in brackets.

YOUNG DESIGNER

(**1**) ______________ (**you ever** / **make**) your own clothes – perhaps with your mum, grandma or at school? I (**2**) ______________ (**start**) to design my own clothes when I was 13. At first, I (**3**) ______________ (**look**) at lots of different fashion magazines to see what people were wearing. But quite quickly I (**4**) ______________ (**decide**) to try to make my own designs. When I (**5**) ______________ (**tell**) my parents that I (**6**) ______________ (**want**) to be a designer, they (**7**) ______________ (**think**) it was a great idea, and they (**8**) ______________ (**help**) me to make my dream come true.

I (**9**) ______________ (**begin**) making my own clothes in 2015, and I (**10**) ______________ (**learn**) a lot in the last few years. Last year, I (**11**) ______________ (**meet**) some other young clothes designers. We (**12**) ______________ (**share**) a lot of ideas together online, and now we are planning to have a pop-up shop near the beach next summer.

THINK | RESEARCH | CULTURE | LEARN | **ME**

Work in pairs. Take turns to give your partner some news about something that has happened to you recently. Ask for some extra information about your partner's news.
I've bought some new jeans. *Where did you get them?*

▶ **Workbook Unit 6:** Grammar 2, page 47, exercises 1, 2

6 SPEAKING | Collaborative task

Flipped classroom

1 **Watch the *Talk2Me* video and answer the questions.**

1 What do Evie and Jojo decide to do to get some money?
2 What does Jojo learn when she calls the community centre?
3 How much money do they make? Why?

2 **Watch the video again. Underline the phrases in the *Phrase expert* box that you hear on the video.**

> **PHRASE EXPERT**
> It's at (465 Main Street). | The address is … | The (presentation) is in (room 12). | The (sale) is on (day) at (time). | The web page / email address is … | You can call (020 667 5858) for more information.

3 **Work in pairs and answer the questions.**

1 How often do you go shopping?
2 Where do you usually go shopping?
3 Who do you usually go shopping with?

EXAM SKILL

Giving details

- Learn how to say addresses, phone numbers, webpages, dates and times.
- Use prepositions and determiners (<u>the</u> sixth <u>of</u> February); learn how to say unusual characters (/ = forward slash, @ = at, . = dot) and numbers (0 = zero or oh, 77 = double seven).

4 2.15 **Listen, repeat and write down what you hear.**

1 ______________________
2 ______________________
3 ______________________
4 ______________________
5 ______________________
6 ______________________

5 2.16 **Listen to two students discussing the new shopping centre and complete the details.**

BLUELAKE SHOPPING CENTRE

Grand Opening (**1**) ________ October (**2**) ________
Visit new shops, restaurants and cinemas
Wi-Fi and free parking
Address: (**3**) ________ North Gate (**4**) ________
Phone number: 024 771 (**5**) ________

OPTIMISE YOUR EXAM

Collaborative task

- It is important to show that you are interested in the conversation.
- As well as looking at your partner and nodding your head when you agree with them, use phrases like *thanks*, *I see*, *great* and *OK* to show that you are really listening to your partner.

6 **In pairs (Student A and Student B), do the exam task.**

> **Student A:** turn to page 137 and look at the information about *A Book for All* Bookshop. Answer Student B's questions about it.
>
> **Student B**: look at the question prompts on page 140. Ask Student A your questions.
>
> **Student B:** turn to page 140 and look at the information about *A1 Fashion Store*. Answer Student A's questions about it.
>
> **Student A:** look at the question prompts on page 137. Ask Student B your questions.

THINK | **RESEARCH** | CULTURE | LEARN | ME

Work in pairs or groups.

1 Go online and find out the name of an interesting place to shop where you live, or in a place that you know well.
2 Note down the opening hours, address, phone number and website details. Find an interesting fact about the shop or what they sell.
3 Report back to the class.

 ▶ **Workbook Unit 6:** Speaking, page 48, exercises 1, 2

1 **Work in pairs. Read each sentence and decide together who said it, and where they said it.**

1 That's £9.99, please.

2 Did you understand what the teacher said in that lesson?

3 Can I try this jacket on, please?

4 I'm sorry I'm late for dinner, Mum. I missed my bus.

EXAM SKILL

Understanding functional language

- It is important to understand *why* someone says something as well as *what* they say.
- Think about what the speakers are doing. For example, are they describing something, explaining something or inviting someone?

2 **Read the questions (1–6) and choose the best word to describe the function. Underline the words that helped you identify the function each time.**

1 Do you like this T-shirt? _d_
This question is asking for **an opinion** / **a description**.

2 Hi Jade. How are you? ____
This question is **a choice** / **a greeting**.

3 I don't understand this – can you help me please? ____
This question is asking for **a description** / **an explanation**.

4 Would you like to come to my party? ____
This question is **inviting** / **explaining**.

5 What's your new jacket like? ____
This question is asking for **a choice** / **a description.**

6 What are you doing tomorrow? ____
This is a question about **future plans** / **opinions**.

3 **Match the responses (a–f) to the questions in Exercise 2.**

a) Hi. I'm fine thanks. And you?
b) I'm meeting Ben and Anna in town.
c) It's black with a guitar on the front.
~~**d)** Yes, I like it a lot.~~
e) Yes, of course I can.
f) Yes, please.

OPTIMISE YOUR EXAM

Multiple-matching dialogue

- Read the dialogue carefully so you understand what it is about.
- Read all the options before choosing an answer.
- Think about the function of each sentence. For example, do they show agreement or disagreement?

4 **Complete the conversation about plans with sentences A–H. There are some extra letters you do not need.**

Robbie: Hi, it's Robbie. How are you?
Fiona: Example: _E_
Robbie: Yes, I'm OK thanks.
Fiona: What are your plans today?
Robbie: I was going to stay at home today, but I've changed my mind.
Fiona: (1) ____
Robbie: Well how about going to the new shopping centre in town together?
Fiona: (2) ____
Robbie: Ah, maybe that's not a good idea, then. Can you think of anything we can do?
Fiona: (3) ____
Robbie: That sounds interesting. When is it open?
Fiona: (4) ____
Robbie: OK. Do you want to meet at the café and get something to eat first?
Fiona: (5) ____
Robbie: OK, see you soon!

A Well, I've seen an advert for a fashion exhibition.
B Only on Friday.
C I'm not very thirsty.
D All day today. We could go this afternoon.
~~**E** Oh, hi! I'm fine, thanks. How about you?~~
F Yes, OK. Let's meet there at 12.
G I've heard it's really busy, and very expensive.
H Really? Where would you like to go?

THINK | RESEARCH | CULTURE | LEARN | ME

Work with a partner. Make a list of the people you usually speak to each day. Take turns to ask your partner what they usually talk to the people about.

What do you talk to your mum about?

I talk to her about food. I tell her what time I'll be home. I ask her ...

WRITING | An online review

1 In pairs or groups, answer the questions.

1 What kind of things do people buy online?

2 When you buy things online, do you read or write reviews? Why / Why not?

OPTIMISE YOUR EXAM

An online review

- Use your own experiences to help you to complete the writing task.
- Before writing:
  - decide what product you want to review.
  - remember what makes a good review (giving opinions and reasons).
  - think about the order of information you give.

2 Read the exam task below, and the students' answers. Which is better, A or B? Why?

You recently went shopping and bought something, but there is a problem with it.

Write an online review. Say:
- **what you bought.**
- **why you bought it.**
- **what the problem is.**

Write **25–35** words.

A

I bought a pair of these trainers last week. They are really bad. There is a problem with them. I want my money back.

B

I've bought shoes like these before. Unfortunately, this pair has a problem. When I run in them, they hurt my feet. They don't fit. I think they've put the wrong size on them.

3 Work in pairs. Compare your answers to Exercise 2. Decide if the texts in A and B answer all the points in the exam task.

4 Match the texts (A–B) in Exercise 2 to the examiner's comments below.

1 ___

This is quite a good answer.

The writer doesn't use a variety of tenses.

Two points are answered, but one point is not answered.

The reason why the student bought the item is not included.

2 ___

This is not a good answer.

The writer uses a variety of tenses, including the present perfect.

There is not enough information. The student has not said why they bought the item and what the problem is.

The answer is not long enough – it needs to be 25–35 words.

EXAM SKILL

Giving your opinion

- Some exam writing tasks ask you to give your opinion.
- Think of different ways to express your opinion.Use words and phrases like *In my opinion, I think that, I believe ...*

5 **Read another student's answer to the task in Exercise 2. Choose the best words or phrases to complete the text.**

(1) The last week / A week ago, I bought some new trainers (2) because / when I've had my old ones a long time. (3) However / Because they aren't very comfortable. (4) In my opinion / My opinion the size is wrong. They say size 39, but I (5) believe / sure they are 38.

6 **Look at this writing task and make notes to answer questions 1–6.**

You went shopping last week and bought something you really like.

Write an online review. Say:
- **what you bought.**
- **why you bought it.**
- **why you like it.**

Write your online review. Make sure you write about the three points in the task.

Write **25–35** words.

1 What product did you buy?

______

2 How many points should you answer?

______

3 What other information or opinions can you include?

______

4 Which tenses should you use?

______

5 Which words or phrases from this unit could you use?

______

______

6 How many words should you write?

______

7 **Plan** **Plan your review. Use the chart to help you.**

	Detail	Useful language	My notes
Point 1	*The thing I bought*		
Point 2			
Point 3			

8 **Write** **Write your review in an appropriate style. Write 25–35 words.**

9 **Check** **Before you hand in your review, complete this checklist.**

Checklist

- ◯ I've followed my writing plan.
- ◯ I've explained what I bought.
- ◯ I've explained why I bought it.
- ◯ I've said why I like it.
- ◯ I've used the correct tenses.
- ◯ I've used a good range of vocabulary.
- ◯ I've written 25–35 words.
- ◯ I've checked my spelling and grammar.

▶ **Writing reference,** page 169 ▶ **Workbook Unit 6:** Writing, page 50, exercises 1, 2, 3, 4 and Progress check 6, page 51

PROGRESS CHECK UNITS 5–6

GRAMMAR AND VOCABULARY

1 Complete the sentences using the correct form of the verbs in brackets.

1 Pria ____________ (**walk**) to school yesterday. She's never done that before!
2 ____________ you ____________ (**work**) in a shop before or is this the first time?
3 I ________________ (**buy**) a few things there last week, but there isn't much choice.
4 ____________ you ____________ (**wear**) a school uniform when you were younger?
5 I think I ________________ (**lose**) my watch. I can't find it anywhere.
6 We ________________ (**never shop**) in any of the big clothes shops in London.
7 Are those new jeans? I ________________ (**not see**) them before.
8 Alfie ____________ (**not like**) his birthday present so Mum took it back to the shop.

__/8

2 Choose the correct word to complete each sentence.

1 I sometimes find it difficult to **say** / **start** a conversation with new people.
2 Can you help me download this new **mouse** / **software**, please.
3 Do you want to try **out** / **on** this shirt? It's a really nice colour.
4 I couldn't **open** / **start** the file you sent me. Was there a problem with it?
5 How much did you pay **for** / **with** those trainers? I think they are cheaper online.
6 We haven't decided where to go this weekend. I'll **make** / **send** a text when I know the plan.
7 I'm sorry, we don't take credit cards. We only take **cash** / **change**.
8 Their new laptop has a really big **camera** / **screen** – it's great for online gaming.

__/8

3 Choose the correct word or phrase to fill each gap.

Fashion designer Dhillan Bhardwaj (**1**) ____ his first shop at the age of 18. A few months later he was a millionaire. He (**2**) ____ making clothes at home after he left school. (**3**) ____ friends saw his first designs and they asked him to make clothes for them. He put photos on social media and suddenly lots of people (**4**) ____ him to make (**5**) ____ clothes. The clothes were (**6**) ____ popular than he expected and (**7**) ____ of people bought them. Dhillan soon needed help making the clothes. Now his brand, Ratchet, is the (**8**) ____ independent clothing company in the UK.

	A	B	C
1	**A** opened	**B** opens	**C** has opened
2	**A** begin	**B** began	C has begun
3	**A** Much	**B** Few	**C** Some
4	**A** wanted	**B** want	**C** have wanted
5	**A** their	**B** your	**C** her
6	**A** more	**B** many	**C** most
7	**A** lots	**B** any	**C** many
8	**A** large	**B** larger	**C** largest

__/8

4 Complete the paragraph with the words in the box.

biggest	ever	has	in	lots	much	never	older	some	than

How are you? School (**1**) ___________ finished here for the holidays. We're visiting my cousin (**2**) ___________ Denmark. Have you (**3**) ___________ been there? I don't know (**4**) ___________ about the place, but I've looked at (**5**) ___________ of pictures online. They live in Copenhagen, which is bigger (**6**) ___________ my town. I think it's the (**7**) ___________ city in Denmark. My cousin is (**8**) ___________ than me. I've (**9**) ___________ met her. I'll send you (**10**) ___________ photos.

__/10

5 Choose the correct word or phrase to complete each sentence.

1 I didn't work very hard today. I sent **a few** / **much** emails, then read a magazine.
2 Not **much** / **many** people buy things in that shop – it's very expensive.
3 I'm going on holiday next week. I need to get **lots** / **any** of new clothes before I go.
4 There were too **many** / **much** people in the shopping centre, so we left.
5 **Some** / **A little** people say that this is the best computer game ever.
6 I could only understand a **few** / **little** of what he was saying. He speaks really quickly.
7 How **many** / **much** money do you usually spend on clothes in a year?
8 Excuse me, do you have **any** / **much** of these trainers in a size 10?

__/8

6 Read the descriptions. What is the word for each one? The first letter is given.

1 A large shop where people buy food is a s_ _ _ _ _ _ _ _ _ _ .
2 A program that makes computers do different things is a piece of s_ _ _ _ _ _ _ .
3 When you use the internet you are o_ _ _ _ _ .
4 The people who buy things in a shop are called c_ _ _ _ _ _ _ _ .
5 You can use this to pay for things you buy: c_ _ _ _ _ c_ _ _ .
6 Pictures made by computers are called g_ _ _ _ _ _ _ .
7 When you write on a computer, you use a k_ _ _ _ _ _ _ .
8 You do this when you copy programs or music from the internet: d_ _ _ _ _ _ _ .

__/8

Total score __/50

EXAM SKILLS

Tick the statements that are true for you. Review the skills in the unit if you need more help.

I can …	Unit/page
☐ understand how often something happens.	Unit 5 p48
☐ understand when things happen.	Unit 5 p52
☐ compare things.	Unit 5 p54
☐ identify pronouns and people.	Unit 5 p55
☐ note down important information about when and where.	Unit 5 p56
☐ choose between similar answers.	Unit 6 p58
☐ choose the right answer.	Unit 6 p62
☐ exchange information.	Unit 6 p64
☐ understand functional language.	Unit 6 p65
☐ give my opinion.	Unit 6 p66

7 The future of learning

READING | Multiple-choice cloze | A news article

1 In pairs or as a group, answer the questions.

1 Do you use technology in your classroom? What do you use it for?

2 What do you think the students in the pictures on page 71 are using the laptops for?

2 Choose the correct word to complete each sentence.

1 We have technology lessons in my new school. We didn't have **it** / **them** in my old school.

2 My laptop has stopped working. I'm going to ask our technology teacher to look at **this** / **it**.

3 The maths teacher isn't well today. **These** / **That** means we won't have a lesson this afternoon.

4 Our technology lessons are really interesting. I think I learn more in **these** / **them** lessons than in any others.

5 The gaming café is closed today. My friends aren't happy about **them** / **this**.

EXAM SKILL

Understanding *this, that, these, it, them*

- We use words like *this*, *that*, *these*, *it* and *them* to talk about things we mentioned earlier. We use these words so we don't need to repeat something.
- We can use them to talk about a word, a phrase or even a sentence.

3 Read the news article on page 71 quickly and answer the questions.

1 How many cars carry the mobile computer classroom equipment?

2 How many people a day can have lessons from the mobile computer classrooms?

3 How many schools in Uganda are going to have computer classrooms?

OPTIMISE YOUR EXAM

Multiple-choice cloze

- Think about the different meanings of the possible answers.
- After choosing your answers, read the whole sentence with the two answers you didn't choose, to check they don't fit.

TECHNOLOGY FOR ALL

1 In classrooms around the world, **Example:** _B_ students now have computers or tablets (**1**) ____ their desks instead of books. Technology is helping young people to learn about the world, and preparing (**2**) ____ for work. But in poorer countries, there (**3**) ____ any computers available for students.

2 That was a problem for schools in the countryside in Uganda, in East Africa. But since 2007, the Mobile Solar Computer Classroom (**4**) ____ helped many classes of children and adults at schools and libraries to use computers. There are two mobile computer classrooms, and they travel all over the country in two large cars, going to schools to (**5**) ____ computer lessons. Later today, one of them is going to visit a village in the west of the country. It's a long way down a difficult road, but the drivers are lucky because it isn't going to rain, and that helps. (**6**) ____ the car, there are 15 laptop computers, desks and chairs, two ICT teachers and a large battery. This produces solar energy for the computers, (**7**) ____ many of the villages don't have electricity.

3 More than 200 people a day can have computer lessons from the two mobile classrooms. This means over 5,000 people have these lessons each year! What are they going to do next? Well, over the next few years, they are going to build computer classrooms in 55 Ugandan schools. Teachers and students know how important computers will be in the future and (**8**) ____ classrooms will really help students prepare for a job in tomorrow's world.

4 🔊 2.17 Read the article about mobile classrooms. For questions 1–8, choose the best answer (A, B or C) to fill each gap.

Example:	A much	(B) many	C lot
1	A on	B over	C inside
2	A their	B they	C them
3	A isn't	B aren't	C are
4	A has	B have	C is
5	A giving	B give	C gives
6	A On	B To	C In
7	A because	B but	C so
8	A this	B these	C its

5 Match the highlighted words in the article to a definition (1–8).

1 older people, not children ____________
2 an object in a car, radio, etc. that gives it electricity ____________
3 small, mobile computers that are bigger than mobile phones but smaller than laptops ____________
4 work that you do to make money ____________
5 places where you can borrow books ____________
6 when something good happens as a result of good luck ____________
7 the people who drive vehicles like trains, buses and cars ____________
8 the area outside towns and cities ____________

THINK | RESEARCH | CULTURE | LEARN | ME

Work in pairs. Make a list of the different ways you can use computers to help you learn.

▶ **Workbook Unit 7:** Reading, pages 52–53, exercises 1, 2, 3, 4

Grammar in context

Find these sentences in the text on page 71 then answer the question.

1 Later today, one of them ***is going to visit*** a village in the west of the country. (paragraph 2)

2 ... but the drivers are lucky because it ***isn't going to rain***, and that helps. (paragraph 2)

3 What ***are they going to do*** next? (paragraph 3)

What are these sentences about? Choose the correct answer.

a) the present ____

b) the past ____

c) the future ____

REMEMBER

- We use *going to* to talk about future plans: *I'm* ***going to buy*** *a new bike next week.*
- We also use *going to* when we predict something because of what we see now: *She's playing very well. I think she'****s going to win****.*

▶ **See Grammar reference, Unit 7,** page 156

1 Complete the conversation with the correct form of *going to*.

Teacher: You need to finish your project about the town by Friday. What are your plans?

Alicia: Well, I **(1)** ___am going to___ write the introduction today and then Demir **(2)** ______________ check it tomorrow.

Demir: After I've checked it, Alicia and I **(3)** ______________ take some pictures for the cover.

Teacher: But you can't do that tomorrow, because Alicia **(4)** ______________ be at school. She **(5)** ______________ go on a school trip.

Demir: Yes, I know. We **(6)** ______________ do it on Wednesday.

Alicia: Then on Thursday, Demir **(7)** ______________ write about the history of the town.

Teacher: **(8)** ______________ use the internet, Demir?

Demir: Yes, I am, because I need to get some more information.

Alicia: I **(9)** ______________ use the internet. I don't need it for my part of the project.

Teacher: Well, you seem to have everything organised. I think your project **(10)** ______________ be really good!

2 Complete the sentences using the correct form of *going to* and the verbs in brackets.

1 Giulio ______________ (**study**) English in London next summer. He's very excited.

2 Maria and Marco ______________ (**not win**) the race – they're right at the back.

3 What ______________ she ______________ (**do**) next year?

4 I ______________ (**not go**) to school tomorrow because it's a holiday.

5 My sister ______________ (**be**) a doctor when she finishes university.

6 It's very cold today. I think it ______________ (**snow**).

3 Complete the text with the verbs in the box and the correct form of *going to*.

be (× 3)	have	meet
not go	not use	study

BIG School

I'm a student at City Montessori School in Lucknow, the largest school in the world. There are over 50,000 students at the school. At the moment, there are 45 students in my class, but next term there **(1)** ______________ more because it's very popular. This morning we have maths. We often use computers in class, but today we **(2)** ______________ them because we **(3)** ______________ a test. After that, I **(4)** ______________ in one of the libraries. I love the libraries here. They're always quiet and there are thousands of books to read.

There are also lots of events at my school. Next month, there **(5)** ______________ a children's film festival here. Unfortunately, I have exams so I **(6)** ______________, but my friends are. They **(7)** ______________ children from all over the world at the festival. It **(8)** ______________ great.

SAY IT RIGHT

Resource centre: Unit 7
Pronunciation of *going to*

▶ **Workbook Unit 7:** Grammar 1, page 54, exercises 1, 2

Words connected with *school and studying*

1 2.18 **Put the words in the box into the correct category. Listen and check.**

biology | ~~board~~ | bookshelf | desk
dictionary | eraser | geography | history
learn | maths | music | physics
practise | remember | study | teach

things in the classroom	school subjects	verbs for things people do at school
board	______	______
______	______	______
______	______	______
______	______	______
______	______	______
	______	

2 **Read the sentences. Which subject from Exercise 1 is each one about?**

1 Today we're going to learn about the kings and queens of France.

______

2 The longest river in Europe is the Volga.

______

3 All animals need water to live.

______

4 What is 12 × 6?

______

5 In today's lesson, we're going to look at how aeroplanes fly.

______

6 Now, let's sing that again.

______

Words + prepositions

3 2.19 **Choose the best word (A, B or C) for each gap. Listen and check.**

1 You can learn a lot ____ books.
A on **B** for **C** from

2 You need to use technology when you study or are ____ work.
A at **B** to **C** for

3 Today we're going to learn ____ how the stomach works.
A for **B** on **C** about

4 Do you need any help ____ your homework?
A to **B** with **C** at

5 I usually arrive ____ school just before 9am.
A to **B** for **C** at

6 You can borrow three books ____ the library at one time.
A from **B** to **C** for

Collocations with verbs

4 2.20 **Match the nouns (a–f) to the verbs (1–6) to make phrases. Listen and check.**

1 do *d*
2 draw ____
3 take ____
4 leave ____
5 go ____
6 learn ____

a) a course
b) to university
c) school
~~**d)** homework~~
e) a foreign language
f) a picture

5 **Complete the sentences using phrases from Exercise 4.**

1 In our art lesson today we're going to ______ of these flowers.
2 Jess is going to live in a different country for the summer so that she can ______ .
3 I'm going to ______ in photography.
4 Would you like to ______ when you finish school?
5 The students have to ______ every evening.
6 Most students in the UK ______ when they're 18.

THINK | RESEARCH | CULTURE | LEARN | ME

Work in pairs and answer the questions.

- What do you like most about school? Why?
- What are your favourite subjects? Why?
- How much time do you spend doing homework every day?

▶ Vocabulary reference, page 166 ▶ Workbook Unit 7: Vocabulary, pages 54–55, exercises 1, 2, 3

7 LISTENING | Gap fill

1 **Work in pairs and answer the questions.**

1 Who do you ask when you need help with your homework?

2 Would you like to have someone to talk to about it online? Why / Why not?

EXAM SKILL

Thinking about the missing information

- Look carefully at the words before the gaps.
- If there is a preposition before the gap, think about which words can and can't follow it.
- For example, in Exercise 4, question 3, you need to listen for a period of time – probably a month or year.

2 **Complete the table with the words in the box.**

afternoon | Amsterdam | Halloween
March | night | Paris | Wednesday
2018 | 3:20

in	months and years, e.g. in September, in 2012, ________ , ________ towns and countries, e.g. in Manchester, Spain, ________ , ________ time of the day, e.g. in the morning, in the ________
on	days of the week, e.g. on Tuesday, on your birthday, ________
at	time of the day, e.g. at 10:30am, at midday, ________ , ________ holiday time, e.g. at New Year, at half term, ________

3 **Delete the word or phrase that CANNOT complete the sentence.**

1 Alice lives in:
Scotland | a city | a village | a computer

2 She teaches on Mondays and:
Tuesdays | Thursdays | evenings | Fridays

3 She started teaching online in:
April | Monday | 2017 | London

4 The subjects she helps with are:
maths | geography | study | English

5 She has photos of:
online | flowers | the countryside | her family

OPTIMISE YOUR EXAM

Gap fill

- Before you listen, read the information carefully and decide what sort of word you need to write for each answer.
- Don't worry if you don't hear all the answers the first time you listen.
- When you listen again, write any answers you missed and check that your spelling is correct.

4 2.21 **Listen to an interview with a woman who teaches schoolchildren over the internet. Complete the information.**

ALICE	
Lives in:	*England*
Works as:	1 cloud ....
Teaches:	2 Mondays and ....
Started in:	3
Helps with:	4 English and ....
Photos of:	5

THINK | RESEARCH | CULTURE | LEARN | ME

Write down five questions you would like to ask someone your age who lives in India.

▶ **Workbook Unit 7:** Listening, page 56, exercises 1, 2

GRAMMAR 2 | *will* and *going to*

Grammar in context

Look at these sentences from the audio in the listening lesson. Match the descriptions (a–e) to the sentences (1–5).

1 *What **are** you **going to talk** about?* ____
2 *They**'ll** probably **ask** me lots of questions.* ____
3 *I know! I**'ll talk** about this interview.* ____
4 *I'm not working this afternoon, so I**'m going to have** some free time.*
5 *I**'ll join** you and we can talk to the children together.* ____

a) offering to do something
b) asking about a plan that has already been made
c) saying/predicting what you think will happen
d) deciding to do something
e) saying what you know is going to happen

REMEMBER

- We use *will* when we decide to do something at that moment: *It's cold. I**'ll close** the window.*
- We use *will* when we make offers: *I**'ll go** and buy the bread and milk.*
- We use *will* when we say/predict what we think will happen: *The lesson **will be** interesting. We **won't be** bored.*
- We use *going to* when we already have a plan: *I**'m** not **going to be** at home on Saturday morning. I**'m going to play** tennis with Ali.*
- We use *going to* when it is something we can see or know about: *It says on the radio that there's been an accident. He**'s going to be** late.*

▶ **See Grammar reference, Unit 7,** page 156

1 Choose the correct answer to complete each sentence.

1 **I'll / 'm going to** study English at summer school in July. I've got my plane tickets already.
2 The teacher has just given us lots of homework. I know! **I'll / 'm going to** stay at home tonight and study.
3 I'm new here. **Will you / Are you going to** show me where the library is, please?
4 'Are you going to be away in July?' 'No. We **aren't going to go / won't go** on holiday until August this year.'
5 'Who wants to read the first sentence?' '**I'll / 'm going to** do it.'
6 We've got tickets for the school concert on Friday so we **aren't going to / won't** go to the party.

2 Complete the conversation using *will* or *going to* and the verbs in brackets.

Daniel: So, we need a plan for the end-of-term garden party on Friday.
Casilda: The teacher said we **(1)** ______________ **(make)** the posters in art class tomorrow.
Pete: And everyone knows I **(2)** ______________ **(sell)** the tickets.
Magda: What can I do?
Daniel: Hmm, let me think ... **(3)** __________ you __________ **(choose)** the music, please?
Magda: Yes, of course. I **(4)** ______________ **(buy)** the drinks as well.
Daniel: Good idea. Thanks. What about the food?
Pete: My mum **(5)** ______________ **(prepare)** some pizzas. I asked her yesterday.
Casilda: Great. Everyone is talking about it, so I think lots of people **(6)** ______________ **(come)**.
Pete: Oh, and **(7)** __________ you __________ **(check)** the weather forecast for Friday, Daniel?
Daniel: I checked my phone earlier, Pete. It says it **(8)** ______________ **(be)** sunny.

3 Read the article about how children get to school in a village in China. Complete the text with one word in each gap.

It's Monday morning and 12-year-old Yi Feng Li is **(1)** __________ to go to school. But he isn't **(2)** __________ to walk or take a bus. He and the other children in Atuler **(3)** __________ going to climb 800 metres down the side of a mountain, using a ladder. It takes 90 minutes and it is one of the most dangerous journeys to school in the world.

However, some of the people in the village believe this **(4)** __________ change soon. A Chinese photographer visited the village and took some photos of the journey. 'We want people to see how dangerous it is for the children. And we think they **(5)** __________ help.'

Lots of important people have now seen the photos and have discussed what they can do to help. Next year, they are going **(6)** __________ build some new steps for the children to use. The journey **(7)** __________ still take a long time, but it **(8)** __________ be a lot safer.

▶ **Workbook Unit 7:** Grammar 2, page 55, exercise 1

7 SPEAKING | Interview

Flipped classroom

1 **Watch the *Talk2Me* video and answer the questions.**

1 Why do the twins look sad?
2 How much will they earn a day?
3 When do they start work?

2 **Watch the video again. Underline the phrases in the *Phrase expert* box that you hear on the video.**

PHRASE EXPERT
In (one year's) time / the future
One day, I plan to … | Next week/month/year | tomorrow | tonight | When I (leave school) …

3 **Work in pairs and answer the questions.**

1 What are the best and worst things about going to school?
2 How old are students when they leave school in your country?
3 How will school prepare you for the future?

EXAM SKILL

Talking about the future

- Remember to use *going to* when talking about your plans for the future.
- Use *will* when you decide to do something while you're speaking.
- Use *going to* to make predictions based on something in the present.

4 2.22 **Write the questions in the correct order. Listen and check.**

1 you / to / going / exams / term / Are / take / this / ?
____
2 pass / classmates / Will / the / your / test / ?
____
3 study / will / languages / you / What / year / next / ?
____
4 study / summer holidays / Are / to / in / going / you / the / ?
____

5 2.22 **Listen again and complete the responses.**

1 No, we're not going to take any exams until __________.
2 Yes, they are studying really hard, so I think they __________ pass.
3 I think I'll study French and English __________ .
4 No, when school finishes for the holidays, I __________ work at a summer camp.

OPTIMISE YOUR EXAM

Interview

- Listen carefully to the questions the examiner asks you.
- If you're unsure of your answer about the future, you can say *I think…* or *Perhaps …*
- There are no right or wrong answers in the interview, so you can make up an answer if necessary.

6 **Work in pairs. Take turns asking and answering the questions below. Make notes of your partner's answers.**

1 What are your favourite subjects at school?
____
2 What subjects are you going to study in the future?
____
3 How many hours of homework are you going to do this week?
____
4 What are you going to do when you finish school today?
____
5 What do you think you will do when you leave school?
____

THINK | **RESEARCH** | CULTURE | LEARN | ME

Talk to some students about what they are going to do when they finish school.

 ▶ **Workbook Unit 7:** Speaking, page 56, exercises 1, 2, 3

LANGUAGE IN USE | Multiple-choice cloze

7

1 **Work in pairs. Look at the photo in Exercise 5 and answer the questions.**

1 What do you think is happening?
2 Can you do this in your school?

EXAM SKILL

Learning word phrases

- In this part of the exam, you may be asked to choose a preposition or a verb form.
- It will help if you learn words in phrases not individually (e.g. *a break* ***for*** *lunch, work* ***from*** *nine* ***to*** *five, enjoy* ***singing****, learn* ***to ski****,* etc.).

2 **Choose the correct word to complete each sentence.**

1 I made some new friends **at** / **on** school.
2 Do you usually **have** / **do** lunch at 2pm?
3 The summer holidays last from June **to** / **at** September.
4 Please **do** / **does** exercise 3 for homework.
5 He doesn't want to **make** / **making** a mistake.
6 It's **a** / **one** good idea to take notes in class.

3 **Complete the sentences with the words in the box.**

at	did	had	on	take

1 How often do you do sport ____________ school?
2 I make my own lunch ____________ Saturdays.
3 Everyone ____________ very well in yesterday's test.
4 We ____________ an English class at 9.30 this morning.
5 Lots of students want to ____________ the bus to school.

OPTIMISE YOUR EXAM

Multiple-choice cloze

- Remember that some words go together to make phrases.
- This part of the exam also tests pronouns, prepositions, linking words and words like *this, these* and *them*.
- When you have finished, read the text again with the answers you choose, to check it makes sense.

4 **Work in pairs. Read the text in Exercise 5 quickly and answer the question.**

How long do students play the game for?

a) a term **b)** a month **c)** a year

5 **Read the text. For questions 1–8, choose the best answer (A, B, or C) to fill each gap.**

Playing is learning

Classcraft is a computer game that students can play Example: __*A*__ the classroom. Students work in teams of five or six and can get points **(1)** ____ their team when they do something good, like answering questions in lessons or helping classmates **(2)** ____ their homework. They can also lose points when they do something wrong. When they have a number **(3)** ____ points, they can do special things in the game and also in class. For example, they can ask questions in exams or have more time to do homework. When students do well in class, they can move up a level in the game.

Students play the game for the whole term and stay in **(4)** ____ same teams. This helps **(5)** ____ make friends with other students and work together. Parents can also go online and see how their children are doing in the game and in class. It **(6)** ____ now popular with many teachers and students, and **(7)** ____ of people think it is **(8)** ____ to become very popular all over the world.

Example:

	(A) in	**B** under	**C** next
1	**A** for	**B** on	**C** at
2	**A** with	**B** after	**C** when
3	**A** in	**B** at	**C** of
4	**A** my	**B** the	**C** a
5	**A** him	**B** they	**C** them
6	**A** are	**B** is	**C** was
7	**A** lots	**B** many	**C** much
8	**A** going	**B** will	**C** won't

THINK | RESEARCH | CULTURE | LEARN | ME

Work in groups. Imagine you are going to play *Classcraft* in your class. Think of three good things you can do to get points and two bad things you can do to lose points. Share your ideas with the class.

▶ **Vocabulary reference,** page 166 ▶ **Workbook Unit 7:** Language in Use, page 57, exercises 1, 2, 3

WRITING | Information transfer

1 **In pairs or groups, answer the questions.**

1 How often do you go on trips with your school?
2 What was the last school trip you went on?
3 What was the best school trip you've been on? Why?

2 **Read the notice and the email below about a school trip. Would you like to go on the trip? Why / Why not? Discuss your answers with a partner.**

SCHOOL TRIP
(Meet by the school gates at 7.30 am.)

Tuesday, 5 May SCIENCE MUSEUM

- Would you like to go on the trip? Ask your parents to complete the form.
- Then tell your teacher before the end of school on Friday.
- Bring a bottle of water or juice, a notebook and pen.

From: Phil **To:** Olivia

Hi Olivia,

Do you want to come on the school trip next week? I think it will be really interesting.

You need to tell your teacher before the end of the week.

We are meeting early outside the school on Tuesday, but my dad can take us. Call me after lunch on Saturday.

See you soon,

Phil

EXAM SKILL

Understanding similar information

- In this part of the exam, it is useful to understand different ways of giving the same information.
- Look for words in the texts that have the same or nearly the same meaning.

3 **Match the underlined words and phrases in Olivia's notes (1–5) to words and phrases with a similar meaning (a–e).**

Olivia's notes
School trip to the Science Museum

Where:		*meet by the school gates*
When:	1	7.30 *am*
What to do:	2	give form to *my parents* and
	3	*tell my teacher* this week
What to take:	4	*water* or juice
Phone Phil:	5	*after lunch* on Saturday

a) my mother and father ______

b) in the afternoon ______

c) a drink ______

d) speak to my teacher ______

e) in the morning ______

4 Plan

You are going to complete Alex's notes. Tick the things you need to do before you start writing.

1 Read both texts. ____
2 Look for numbers, days and dates and find out what they mean. ____
3 Make sure I know exactly what information I need to complete the notes. ____

OPTIMISE YOUR EXAM

Information transfer

- Read both texts first, so that you understand the topic.
- Then read the notes and decide what sort of information you need to write, e.g. a word or a number.

Read the information and the email. Fill in the information in Alex's notes.

EXAMS
School exams start next week.
Monday – French
Tuesday – maths
Wednesday – geography
Thursday/Friday – normal lessons

- All exams start at 10 am in the school hall.
- Please bring a pen, pencil, ruler and eraser with you.
- Leave bags and mobile phones in classroom 4A.

From: Rosie **To:** Alex
Hi Alex,
How do you feel about the exams next week? I'm worried.
Do you want to study together this weekend? I'm free after 6 pm on Sunday. Would you like to come for dinner too?
Bye,
Rosie

Alex's notes – Exams

Exams begin on:		*Monday*
What time?	1	in the morning
No exams on:	2	
Take:	3	pen, pencil, ruler and
Don't take:	4	into the exam
Dinner at Rosie's house:	5	After on Sunday evening

5 Write

Write the information to complete Alex's notes in Exercise 4. Check your spelling and use of capital letters.

6 Check

Before you hand in your notes, complete this checklist.

Checklist

- ◯ I've carefully read both texts.
- ◯ I've read everything and decided what type of information I need to write.
- ◯ I've completed all the answers on the form.
- ◯ I've checked my spelling.
- ◯ I've checked my use of capital letters.

Extra writing

7 You're Alex. You're going to write a short reply to Rosie's email in Exercise 4. First answer questions 1–3.

1 Who are you writing to?
____
2 What style should you write in?
____
3 What questions has Rosie asked?
____
____
____

Now write your email in 25–35 words.

8 It's only a game

READING | Right/Wrong/Doesn't say | An online article

1 In pairs or as a group, answer the questions.

1 What's your favourite sport?
2 How often do you practise?
3 Tell your partner about any sports competitions you have entered.
4 Tell your partner about any prizes you have won.

2 In pairs, think of different sports. Write the sports in the correct list below.

Team sports	Sports you play alone
______	______
______	______
______	______
______	______
______	______

EXAM SKILL

Scanning

- Scanning means reading a text quickly to find certain information.
- Look for important dates, numbers or names in the text and underline them.
- Remember that you don't need to understand every word, only the important information.

3 Read the online article on page 81 quickly and answer the questions.

1 What do the best sports people need to do?
2 Where was Garbiñe Muguruza born?
3 What is Garbiñe Muguruza's dream?

4 Read the article again. Match the years (a–e) to the information (1–5).

1 She played her first competition. ____ **a)** 1993
2 She won her first competition. ____ **b)** 1999
3 She was born. ____ **c)** 2012
4 She won a very important competition. ____ **d)** 2014
5 She moved to Spain with her family. ____ **e)** 2016

OPTIMISE YOUR EXAM

Right/Wrong/Doesn't say

- Be careful with the difference between 'Wrong' and 'Doesn't say'.
- 'Wrong' means that the sentence is not true according to the information given in the text.
- Choose 'Doesn't say' when there isn't enough information in the text to choose 'Right' or 'Wrong'.

THE WAY TO WIN

How long do you think it takes a sports person to become one of the best?

1 Can you do any sport really well? Would you like to do it professionally? It may seem easy to you to swim, run or throw a ball for a job. However, to compete at a high level, you must start young and you have to practise for many hours every day for years before you'll be ready to enter important competitions. If you fall over, get tired or injure yourself, you mustn't give up. This might be why only a few people become professional. Garbiñe Muguruza made it. In 2016, when she was 22 years old, she won the French Open, one of the sport's most important competitions.

2 Garbiñe was born in Venezuela in 1993. She could hold a racket when she was three, so she started playing tennis. When her family moved to Spain in 1999, she went to a special tennis school, and in 2012 she entered her first professional competition. Two years later, in 2014, she won a competition for the first time.

3 Garbiñe loves playing tennis, but she thinks that tennis players needn't spend all their time thinking about tennis. 'I like to listen to music, hang out with family and friends, dance, sing.' She is sometimes unhappy that she can't live a normal life. Recently, she couldn't go on holiday with her friends because she needed to play tennis. So why does she do it? Garbiñe says that she is just a normal girl with a dream. And that is to be number one!

5 2.23 **Read the article about a famous tennis player. Are sentences 1–7 'Right' (A) or 'Wrong' (B)? If there is not enough information to answer 'Right' (A) or 'Wrong' (B), choose 'Doesn't say' (C).**

Example: The writer says it takes a long time to become very good at a sport.
(A) Right **B** Wrong **C** Doesn't say

1 Sports people practise alone for many hours a day.
A Right **B** Wrong **C** Doesn't say

2 Garbiñe's family moved to Spain because there are a lot of tennis schools there.
A Right **B** Wrong **C** Doesn't say

3 She learnt to play tennis at school in Spain.
A Right **B** Wrong **C** Doesn't say

4 She won the first competition she entered.
A Right **B** Wrong **C** Doesn't say

5 She likes rock music.
A Right **B** Wrong **C** Doesn't say

6 She thinks it's a good idea for tennis players to spend time with other people.
A Right **B** Wrong **C** Doesn't say

7 She has never been on holiday with her friends.
A Right **B** Wrong **C** Doesn't say

6 **Match the highlighted words in the article to a definition (1–8).**

1 finished first in a competition ____________
2 an object used to hit a ball in tennis, badminton, etc. ____________
3 use your hand to send an object through the air ____________
4 to have something in your hands ____________
5 needing rest or sleep ____________
6 to do an activity very often so you become good at it ____________
7 to move through water by moving your arms and legs ____________
8 feeling sad or upset ____________

THINK | **RESEARCH** | CULTURE | LEARN | ME

Find out about a famous sports person in your country. Make a poster about him or her.

▶ **Workbook Unit 8:** Reading, pages 60–61, exercises 1, 2, 3, 4, 5

GRAMMAR 1 | Modals (1): ability, necessity, obligation, possibility

Grammar in context

Find these sentences in the text on page 81 then choose the correct words to complete sentences a to d.

1 ***Can*** *you do any sport really well?* (paragraph 1)
2 *It* ***may*** *seem easy to you to swim, run or throw a ball for a job.* (paragraph 1)
3 *... to compete at a high level, you* ***must*** *start young...* (paragraph 1)
4 *... you* ***have to*** *practise for many hours every day for years before you'll be ready to enter important competitions.* (paragraph 1)
5 *... tennis players* ***needn't*** *spend all their time thinking about tennis.* (paragraph 3)
6 *Recently, she* ***couldn't*** *go on holiday with her friends because she* ***needed*** *to play tennis.* (paragraph 3)

a) We use *can* to talk about **ability** / **necessity**.
b) We use *have* to talk about **possibility** / **obligation**.
c) We use *may* to talk about **possibility** / **ability**.
d) We use *must* to talk about **possibility** / **obligation**.
e) We use *need(n't)* to talk about **necessity** / **ability**.

REMEMBER

- Modal verbs do not change their form and are followed by the bare infinitive (without *to*) of another verb.
- We use *can/can't (cannot)* to talk about ability in the present and *could/couldn't* to talk about ability in the past.
- We can use *must / have to* for rules made by other people or when the person doing the action believes it is necessary. There is no past form of *must*, we use *had to*. The negative form is *don't have to*.

▶ **See Grammar reference, Unit 8,** page 157

1 Choose the correct words.

1 When my dad was at school, he **can't** / **couldn't** understand maths.
2 All football players **may** / **must** follow the rules of the game.
3 The weather forecast says it's going to snow tomorrow so we **might** / **needn't** go snowboarding.
4 Sports people **could** / **have to** train every day.
5 We **couldn't** / **needn't** go for a run today if we don't want to.
6 You **can't** / **must** tell the sports teacher if you don't feel well.

2 Complete the conversation with the words in the box.

can | can't | don't have
have | might | needn't

Robert: (1) __________ you see who's got the ball?
Anna: No, I (2)__________. I think it's number 10.
Robert: Oh, that's Harry Kane. He's an amazing player. But dad says he (3) __________ move to a different team next year. I hope not.
Anna: Oh, you (4) __________ worry. He loves this team so I don't think he'll want to leave.
Robert: Look! He's scored a goal! That's 1-1.
Anna: That's great! There's only a few more minutes left, so shall we go now?
Robert: No way! We (5) __________ to stay until the end. There's still time for another goal.
Anna: OK, then. We (6) __________ to hurry, anyway. We've got lots of time until the next bus.
Robert: That's good. Now let's enjoy the end of the game!

3 Complete the text with the correct form of the modals *can('t), could(n't), had (to), have (to), may/might, need(n't)*.

Keep on running...!

At 15, Emil Zátopek was a young Czech who worked in a shoe factory. When he was younger he (**1**) __________ do any sports particularly well, so he (**2**) __________ never have become a runner. However, one day, the factory sports coach told him he (**3**) __________ to run in a race. Everyone was surprised when he came second. Zátopek then started to think that he (**4**) __________ work in the factory forever. He thought maybe he could be a runner instead!

Everyone knows that to be the best at any sport you (**5**) __________ to train hard, and he did. Zátopek ran in the 1952 Olympic Games, and he won the 5,000- and 10,000-metre races. He also ran in the marathon, the longest race in the Games. It was his first marathon, but he ran the 42-kilometre race and won! Today most people still (**6**) __________ believe he did this ... but he did! Zátopek showed that if you really want something, you (**7**) __________ worry about what other people (**8**) __________ think. Just believe in yourself.

 ▶ **Workbook Unit 8:** Grammar 1, page 62, exercises 1, 2, 3

Words connected with *sport*

1 2.24 **Write a word from the box to match each definition. There are two extra words you do not need. Listen and check.**

badminton | cricket | kit | pool | skiing | stadium | table tennis | winner

1 You need a small plastic ball to play this game. ___________
2 You can go swimming here. ___________
3 You can do this sport on snow in the mountains. ___________
4 You can watch a football game here. ___________
5 This is the person who is first in a competition or race. ___________
6 You need a racket to play this game. ___________

2 2.25 **Choose the best word to complete each sentence. Listen and check.**

1 The ___________ told us what exercises to do and helped us play better.
A team **B** coach **C** member
2 Can you ___________ a horse?
A play **B** skate **C** ride
3 You need a ___________ to go to the basketball game tonight.
A ticket **B** bat **C** club
4 I can't go swimming because I haven't got my ___________ .
A swimsuit **B** beach **C** pool
5 Ed was the winner of the 800-metre ___________ .
A race **B** bat **C** club
6 They played in a rugby ___________ yesterday, and won 35-3!
A club **B** goal **C** match

Verbs/nouns

3 2.26 **Complete the table. Listen and check.**

verb	noun
win	winner
(1) ___________	surfer
swim	(2) ___________
(3) ___________	runner
play	(4) ___________

4 **Complete the sentences with the correct form of some of the words from Exercise 3.**

1 There are over 50 ___________ in the pool today!
2 Novak Djokovic ___________ the tennis match.
3 The eight best ___________ waited in the stadium to start the 500-metre race.
4 Who do you think is the best football ___________ in the world this year?
5 If you want to learn to ___________ , it's important that you can swim.

Collocations with verbs

5 2.27 **Complete the sentences with the correct form of the verbs in the box. Listen and check.**

climb | enter | go | play | throw | win

1 Greg ___________ the ball into the road.
2 My class ___________ swimming at the city pool every Wednesday.
3 Everyone can ___________ the competition but only one person can win.
4 In the summer, lots of people in England ___________ cricket.
5 Do I need to practise a lot before I ___________ a mountain?
6 Emil Zátopek was very happy when he ___________ the 5,000-metre race at the Olympic Games.

8 LISTENING | Multiple matching

1 **Work in pairs. Look at the poster for a summer camp and answer the questions.**

1 What sports are the young people doing?
2 Would you like to do the sports in the poster? Why / Why not?
3 What other sports would you like to do at a summer camp?

EXAM SKILL

Listening for important information

- You don't need to understand every word to answer the questions.
- The first time you listen, think about the important words.
- When you listen again, think carefully about what the speakers mean.

2 2.28 **Listen to five people talking about sports. Match each speaker to a sport.**

Speaker 1 ____	**a)** running
Speaker 2 ____	**b)** windsurfing
Speaker 3 ____	**c)** badminton
Speaker 4 ____	**d)** cycling
Speaker 5 ____	**e)** table tennis

3 2.28 **Listen again and write the names of the other sports the people talk about in each conversation.**

Conversation 1 _____ *football* _____
Conversation 2 __________
Conversation 3 __________
Conversation 4 __________
Conversation 5 __________

OPTIMISE YOUR EXAM

Multiple matching

- Read the question and all the possible answers carefully.
- Remember that there are three possible answers that you don't need.
- When you listen again, check the three possible answers you didn't choose, to make sure they aren't correct.

4 2.29 **Listen to Bea talking to her dad about her summer camp. What sport did she do on each day? Write a letter A–H next to each day. There are some extra letters you do not need.**

Example:
Monday morning *H*

1 Monday afternoon	____	**A** swimming
2 Tuesday	____	**B** badminton
3 Wednesday	____	**C** volleyball
4 Thursday	____	**D** tennis
5 Friday	____	**E** sailing
		F football
		G cricket
		~~**H** running~~

THINK | RESEARCH | **CULTURE** | LEARN | ME

Work in pairs and answer the questions.

- How popular are summer camps in your country?
- What sports and other activities can you do there?

▶ **Workbook Unit 8:** Listening, page 64, exercises 1, 2, 3

GRAMMAR 2 | Modals (2): advice, permission, polite requests, prohibition

Grammar in context

Look at these sentences from the audio in the listening lesson then match them to the descriptions (a–e).

1 *You **should** start playing again, Dad – it's good exercise ...*

2 *Camp rules say we **mustn't** swim if there's a strong wind ...*

3 *... **could** you take some photos of the boats, please?*

4 *You **shouldn't** be out all day in the sun if it's very hot.*

5 *The camp leader says we **can** go to the pool today instead.*

a) something is not allowed ____

b) we have permission ____

c) someone is making a request ____

d) something is a good idea ____

e) something isn't a good idea ____

REMEMBER

- We use modals to:
  - ask for / give advice: *should/shouldn't*
  - ask for / give permission: *can/could*
  - refuse permission: *can't/couldn't*
  - make a polite request: *could*
  - say something is prohibited: *mustn't*
- To make the negative form, you add 'not' after the modal verb and this is usually contracted, e.g. *need not = needn't*.
- Sometimes the negative form changes the modal's meaning: *In the UK, you **must** drive on the left.* (obligation) *In the UK, you **mustn't** drive on the right.* (prohibition)
- To make a question, the subject and modal swap position: ***Could you** pass me my racket, please?*

▶ **See Grammar reference, Unit 8,** page 158

1 Choose the correct words.

1 We're very happy because the teacher says we **shouldn't** / **can** all watch a video for the last half hour this afternoon.

2 'Amber, come back and get your helmet! You **could** / **mustn't** ever go out on your bike without it.'

3 Ed, **should** / **could** you help me with my school project, please?

4 Please turn the computer off. You **shouldn't** / **can** play video games all evening. It's not a good thing to do!

5 You look very tired. You **mustn't** / **should** go to bed earlier.

2 Choose the correct words (a, b or c) to complete each sentence.

1 I'm not sure how to do this. ____ you help me, please?
a) Could **b)** Should **c)** Shouldn't

2 You ____ eat for 30 minutes before you go swimming.
a) could **b)** can **c)** shouldn't

3 I think you ____ try learning a new sport. It's fun!
a) mustn't **b)** couldn't **c)** should

4 The teacher says we ____ use her tennis rackets. That's kind of her.
a) can **b)** shouldn't **c)** couldn't

5 The boys ____ go to the match last night because their dad said no.
a) shouldn't **b)** couldn't **c)** mustn't

6 The rule here is that you ____ do any water sports if you ____ swim 500 metres.
a) should, can **b)** mustn't, can't **c)** could, mustn't

3 Complete the text about a summer camp with the phrases from the word box.

can use | can't do | could you ask
could you bring | mustn't leave
should bring (×2) | should have
shouldn't arrive

A WELCOME
from our Camp Manager

We're really excited about meeting everyone at Super Sports Summer Camp next month. Before you come, I want to give you some important information.

- **What to bring** First of all, everyone (**1**) ______________ these things to camp: a pair of trainers, shorts or leggings and a T-shirt. You (**2**) ______________ sports without them. Secondly, don't bring your best clothes, because we don't want them to get dirty. So (**3**) ______________ some old clothes for art activities, please? People often ask us if they (**4**) ______________ their own rackets, bats or balls. The answer is no. We have all the equipment here and you (**5**) ______________ it whenever you want.
- **When to arrive** The camp starts at 11:30 am on Saturday 7th July. You (**6**) ______________ too early, as the leaders won't all be here until 10, so please try and arrive at about 10:30 if possible.
- **And finally ...** When you arrive, (**7**) ______________ your parents to park in the Rees Lane car park. There's plenty of room there for everyone. And, one last thing ... always remember the camp rule while you're here – you (**8**) ______________ the camp at any time without permission. See you on Saturday!

8 SPEAKING | Collaborative task

Flipped classroom

1 **Watch the *Talk2Me* video and answer the questions.**

1 What can the twins' new phones do?
2 What question does Jojo ask her phone?
3 What surprising thing do the phones do at the end?

2 **Watch the video again. Underline the phrases in the *Phrase expert* box that you hear on the video.**

PHRASE EXPERT

Can I buy ...? | Do I need ...? | How much is/are ...? | What's the ...? | What time ...? | Where is the ...?

EXAM SKILL

Asking questions

- In this part of the test, you ask and answer questions to exchange information.
- Remember that the order of the words is different in questions from the order in positive sentences.

3 **Work in pairs and answer the questions.**

1 Are there any sports shops where you live?
2 How often do you go to them?
3 What have you bought from them?

4 **Write the questions in the correct order.**

1 does / start / it / what time / ?

______

2 a ticket / can / buy / online / I / ?

______

3 a website / they / have / got / ?

______

4 it / how much / cost / does / ?

______

5 open / school / is / after / it / ?

______

6 have to / a racket / I / take / do / ?

______

5 2.30 **Match each question from Exercise 4 to the answers below. Listen and check.**

a) ___ Yes, you can.
b) ___ It's £8 for teenagers.
c) ___ No, it isn't.
d) ___ At 5:30pm.
e) ___ No, you don't.
f) ___ Yes, they have.

OPTIMISE YOUR EXAM

Collaborative task

- Listen carefully to your partner's questions, so you know exactly what information you are being asked for.
- All the answers can be found in the information given to you.

6 **In pairs (Student A and Student B), do the exam task.**

Student A: turn to page 137 and look at the information about a new sports shop. Answer Student B's questions about it.
Student B: look at the question prompts on page 140. Ask Student A your questions.

Student B: turn to page 140 and look at the information about cricket lessons. Answer Student A's questions about them.
Student A: look at the question prompts on page 137. Ask Student B your questions.

SAY IT RIGHT

Resource centre: Unit 8
Intonation in questions

THINK | RESEARCH | CULTURE | LEARN | ME

Do you like learning new sports? Are there any sports you would like to learn? Which ones?

▶ **Workbook Unit 8:** Speaking, page 64, exercises 1, 2, 3

LANGUAGE IN USE | Multiple-choice cloze

1 In pairs or as a group, answer the questions below.

1 What different places can you do sports in?
2 Do you prefer to do sports inside or outside?

EXAM SKILL

Modal verbs

- Modal verbs add meaning to the main verb to express ability, possibility, permission or obligation.
- They usually change to express the present, past or future tense and are mostly followed by the infinitive without 'to'.
- You need to understand the meaning and time period (present, past, etc.) of the text in order to select the correct modal verb.

2 Complete the sentences with a modal verb from the box.

can	could	may	must	shouldn't

1 You ___________ do sport after eating a big meal.
2 Running is popular because you ___________ do it everywhere.
3 We ___________ go swimming later today if we have time.
4 The whole class ___________ run round the field twice for being late.
5 ___________ you pass me the ball, please?

OPTIMISE YOUR EXAM

Multiple-choice cloze

- Read the text carefully so you understand what it is about.
- Try to think of possible answers for each gap before you look at the answer options.
- Read each sentence again to check that your answers fit the grammar and meaning.

3 In pairs, read the text in Exercise 4 quickly and answer the questions.

1 What does *StreetGames* do?
   A It organises football competitions.
   B It gives money to young people.
   C It helps poor young people do sport.
2 Where do most games happen?
   A inside
   B outside
   C inside and outside

4 Choose the correct word to fill each gap.

Changing lives with sport

StreetGames is an organisation Example: _B_ the UK which wants more children and young people to get fit and do sport. The idea began in 2005, **(1)** ____ a number of local sports organisations met at a football competition. Two years later, *StreetGames* started **(2)** ____ it has now helped more than 50,000 young people take part in sport. *StreetGames* organises sports events in areas where people **(3)** ____ go to a sports centre or join a club because of money. These events are called 'Doorstep sports' **(4)** ____ they often happen in the streets where the young people live. So young people **(5)** ____ can't usually play sports get the chance to play them. Sports like basketball, football, tennis and cricket have **(6)** ____ become popular with lots of the young people..

StreetGames believes that all young people **(7)** ____ be able to play sports, because children who do sport are healthier, happier and **(8)** ____ live longer than children who don't.

Example:

	A	B	C
	A of	**(B)** in	**C** to
1	**A** after	**B** while	**C** until
2	**A** but	**B** and	**C** until
3	**A** would	**B** mustn't	**C** can't
4	**A** because	**B** after	**C** before
5	**A** what	**B** where	**C** who
6	**A** quick	**B** quickly	**C** quickest
7	**A** should	**B** can	**C** need
8	**A** mustn't	**B** couldn't	**C** can

THINK | **RESEARCH** | CULTURE | LEARN | ME

Find out about the sports that young people played in the streets in your country in the past. Are they similar to the sports of today?

▶ **Vocabulary reference,** page 166 ▶ **Workbook Unit 8:** Language in Use, page 65, exercises 1, 2

WRITING | An email

1 In pairs, answer the questions.

1 What sports do you do at your school:
- in the winter?
- in the summer?

2 Do boys and girls do sports together or separately?

3 How many hours a week do you do sport?

EXAM SKILL

Writing in an informal style

- When you write an email to a friend, use informal language, e.g. *Hi, See you soon, Write soon, Bye.*
- Use contractions, e.g. *I'm, he can't, we've got.*
- We often use phrasal verbs in informal writing, e.g. *go out, put on.*
- We use more exclamation marks than we do in formal writing.

2 Write the contractions of the words in bold in each sentence.

1 **I would** like to learn how to play golf next year. *I'd*

2 **Sally has** got a new pair of trainers. ______

3 **They will** start playing baseball in May. ______

4 Those two teams **were not** good enough to win the competition. ______

5 He **did not** score any goals in the match. ______

6 **Who is** the new player in the cricket team? ______

7 **I am** excited because my team is winning! ______

8 **We have** trained really hard this winter. ______

3 Write the words/phrases in the correct column to complete the table.

Hi! | How about …
I am looking forward to …
Love, | Thanks a lot for …

formal	informal
Dear …	
I suggest we …	
	Can't wait to …
I would like to thank you for …	
Yours sincerely,	

4 Read the email. Then tick the three questions that the email answers.

From: Chris **To:** Sam

Hi Sam,

We play football, cricket, hockey and basketball and do athletics at school. Yes, everyone's got to do one sport! We have to go to the park to do sports.

Write soon,

Chris

1 What sports do you do at school? ☐
2 Do all the students have to do sport? ☐
3 How many students play cricket? ☐
4 When do you do sport at school? ☐
5 Where do you do sport? ☐

5 Find examples of informal style in the email in Exercise 4. Write them in the correct place below.

1 informal words or phrases
______ , ______

2 a contraction ______

OPTIMISE YOUR EXAM

An email

- The exam task may ask you to write an email to a friend.
- Read their email carefully so you know what you need to write.
- Make sure you answer the three questions in your friend's email.

6 **Look at this writing task. What information do you need to give Lee? Choose the correct answers.**

1 **the amount of time / the places where** they practise
2 **the person who teaches / the students who play** tennis
3 **the training you need to do / the clothes you need to wear**

Read the email from your English friend, Lee.

From: Lee

I'm happy that we'll be at the same tennis club this summer.
I'd like some information. How many hours a day do we practise?
Who's the coach? What special kit do you have to have?

Write an email to Lee and answer his questions.
Write **25–35** words.

7 Plan

Plan your email. Use the chart to help you.

	Purpose	Useful language	My notes
First line	use informal language to greet the person you are writing to	*Hello …,* *Hi …,* *Dear …,*	
Question 1	answer the first question: How many hours a day do we practise?	*We practise …* *once a month / once a week / two or three times a week / every day*	
Question 2	answer the second question: Who's the coach?	*The coach is called …* *The coach's name is …*	
Question 3	answer the third question: What special kit do you have to have?	*You have to / don't have to have …* *shorts / a T-shirt / trainers / a racket*	
Last line	use informal language to say goodbye	*See you soon,* *Write soon,* *Love,* *Bye,*	

8 Write

Write your email to Lee in an appropriate style. Write 25–35 words.

9 Check

Before you hand in your email, complete this checklist.

Checklist

- ◯ I've followed my writing plan.
- ◯ I've started and ended my email in the right way.
- ◯ I've answered the three questions.
- ◯ I've used a good range of vocabulary.
- ◯ I've used an informal style.
- ◯ I've written about 25–35 words.
- ◯ I've checked my spelling and grammar.

▶ **Writing reference,** page 169 ▶ **Workbook Unit 8:** Writing, page 66, exercises 1, 2, 3, 4 and Progress check 8, page 67

PROGRESS CHECK UNITS 7–8

GRAMMAR AND VOCABULARY

1 Complete the conversation using the correct form of *will* or *going to*.

Simona: What **(1)** ___________ you ______________ do in the summer holidays?

Martin: I **(2)** ______________ stay with my cousins in France for two weeks. After that, I **(3)** ______________ visit my grandparents. **(4)** ___________ you ______________ go on holiday?

Simona: No, I'm not. I **(5)** ______________ study English at a summer school in London. But I need to pass an exam first.

Martin: You're one of the best students in the class. I'm sure you **(6)** ______________ pass.

Simona: I hope so. I have to go now. I **(7)** ______________ do my history homework in the library.

Martin: I'm really bad at history. **(8)** ______________ you help me?

Simona: OK. I **(9)** ______________ help you find the information you need, but I **(10)** ______________ tell you the answers.

Martin: That's great. Thanks a lot.

__/10

2 Choose the correct answers (A, B or C).

1 What do I need to play tennis?
A It's a good idea.
B A racket and some trainers.
C Don't forget your bat and ball.

2 I want to take an English course in September.
A You should speak to my teacher. He's great.
B I don't think so.
C Can you help me?

3 Have you seen my dictionary?
A I have to go.
B It's on the bookshelf.
C It's after lunch.

4 Who won the race?
A Not at the moment.
B It doesn't take long.
C I don't know. They're still running.

5 I'm going to enter this competition.
A I hope you win.
B You don't have to run.
C Wait until it finishes.

__/5

3 Choose the correct modal verb to complete each sentence.

1 My sister **could** / **may** / **should** play tennis when she was five.
2 My cousin **can't** / **couldn't** / **shouldn't** read or write until he was eight.
3 I **can** / **have to** / **may** need your help with my homework, but I'm not sure yet.
4 You **can't** / **needn't** / **couldn't** use your mobile phone during the exam. Leave it in your bag.
5 You **don't have to** / **should** / **may** wear a coat to school because it might be cold later on.
6 In football, only the goalkeeper **doesn't have to** / **has to** / **can** touch the ball with his hands.
7 You **have to** / **shouldn't** / **couldn't** eat too much before you do sport.
8 The runners **don't have to** / **can** / **shouldn't** stop for water, but it is a good idea.
9 You **can** / **needn't** / **have to** use a dictionary during French lessons if you want to find a word.
10 Everyone **could** / **may** / **has to** wear a swimsuit in the pool.
11 You **can** / **may** / **don't have to** go to school in the holidays.
12 I **may** / **couldn't** / **can't** come to the match on Saturday, but at the moment I don't know. I'll tell you tomorrow.

__/12

4 Complete the blog post by a Spanish teenager with one word in each gap.

I'm Paz Nevado, I'm 14 years old, I'm from Spain (**1**) ____________ I love sport. I (**2**) ____________ tennis three times a week and I'm also in the school team. Every year, we enter a big competition (**3**) ____________ May. This year, it's (**4**) ____________ to be in Madrid. We have (**5**) ____________ practise a lot (**6**) ____________ we go to the competition. We've never won it, (**7**) ____________ last year we came second. It's great fun and I always (**8**) ____________ lots of new friends there. I also love swimming. I can't swim very often (**9**) ____________ there isn't a pool in my town. Every summer, we (**10**) ________ to the beach and I swim in the sea. I love it!

__/10

5 Complete the sentences with the verbs in the box.

climb	do	go	make	ride	take	throw	win

1 When you're at school, you need to ____________ homework every night.
2 It's really useful to ____________ notes when the teacher is talking.
3 Cora wants to ____________ a really high mountain when she is older.
4 Who do you think will ____________ the 10,000-metre race at the Olympics?
5 Lots of young people ____________ to university when they're 18.
6 Don't ____________ the ball into the road. It's dangerous.
7 It's OK to ____________ mistakes when you're learning something new.
8 I'd really like to learn how to ____________ a horse next year.

__/8

6 Read the descriptions about sports. What is the word for each one? The first letter is already there.

1 Two or four people play this game with a ball and rackets. t_ _ _ _ _
2 You hit a ball with a bat in this English summer game. c_ _ _ _ _ _
3 Moving through water. s_ _ _ _ _ _ _
4 You hit a ball with your hands in this team game. v_ _ _ _ _ _ _ _ _
5 Riding a board on the sea. s_ _ _ _ _ _

__/5

Total score __/50

EXAM SKILLS

Tick the statements that are true for you. Review the skills in the unit if you need more help.

I can …	Unit/page
☐ understand *this, that, these, it* and *them* in a text.	Unit 7 p70
☐ think about the missing information I need to listen for.	Unit 7 p74
☐ talk about the future and make predictions.	Unit 7 p76
☐ make collocations with *make, do, have* and *take*.	Unit 7 p77
☐ understand similar information.	Unit 7 p78
☐ scan a text to find certain information.	Unit 8 p80
☐ listen for important information.	Unit 8 p84
☐ ask and answer questions.	Unit 8 p86
☐ use modal verbs.	Unit 8 p87
☐ write emails using an informal style.	Unit 8 p88

9 Whatever the weather

READING | Multiple-choice cloze | A magazine article

1 In pairs or as a group, answer the questions.

1 What is the weather like today?
2 What is the weather like in January, April, July and October in your country?
3 What is your favourite time of the year? Why?

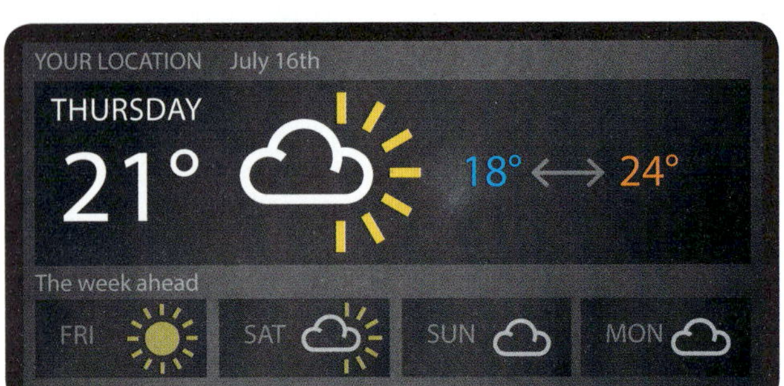

EXAM SKILL

Skimming

- Skimming means reading a text very quickly to understand the general idea.
- You don't read every word when you skim a text.
- Skimming can help you understand where the text is from and who it is for.

2 Read the magazine article on page 93 quickly and choose the correct answers (A, B or C).

1 What is it about?
   A the weather this week
   B unusual weather
   C the weather in one year
2 How many different places does the text talk about?
   A three
   B four
   C five
3 Who is the text for?
   A scientists
   B children
   C adults and teenagers

3 Read the article quickly again and tick the stories that it talks about.

1 a very hot day in a cold country ☐
2 coloured rain ☐
3 a very bad snowstorm ☐
4 an amazing lightning storm ☐
5 raining fish ☐
6 moving ice ☐

THE WORLD'S Strangest WEATHER

1

If it rains a lot in England, some people **Example:** *A* it is raining cats and dogs. Of course, it doesn't really mean that pets are falling **(1)** ____ the sky. However, one day **(2)** ____ did actually happen in Sri Lanka, when a different type of animal fell like rain.

2

In May 2014, people in a village in Sri Lanka were surprised when it started raining fish. Over 50 kg of fish fell on the roads, gardens and roofs, and in a local forest. Fortunately, the local people liked fish very much and **(3)** ____ many of them. But **(4)** ____ often do strange things like this happen? Scientists think that if strong winds move over water, such as large rivers or the sea, they can take small animals like fish up into the clouds. Then if it rains, the fish fall on the ground.

3

Sometimes the colour of the rain **(5)** ____ also surprise people. In southern India, in the summer of 2001, red rain fell from the sky. It turned houses, animals and people's clothes pink and **(6)** ____ a long time no-one knew what it was. Scientists found that there were very small parts of a red plant in the rain. So if red rain falls from the sky again in India, people will know what it is.

4

Fish rain and red rain aren't dangerous. But if ice starts moving towards your house, it probably will be. This is what happened **(7)** ____ the winter of 2014 in Lake Winnebago, USA. Strong winds pushed the ice that was on top of the lake onto the beaches and slowly towards the local town. Nothing **(8)** ____ stop it. The ice went into people's houses, covered the roads and moved their cars. People were afraid, but luckily nobody was badly hurt.

OPTIMISE YOUR EXAM

Multiple-choice cloze

- If you aren't sure of the answer, cross out the possible answers that you **know** are wrong.
- Then choose the word that sounds right from the other possible answers.

4 3.01 **Read the magazine article about unusual weather. For questions 1–8, choose the best answer (A, B or C) to fill each gap.**

Example:

	A	B	C
	(A) say	B says	C saying
1	A to	B on	C from
2	A they	B these	C this
3	A ate	B eat	C eaten
4	A when	B how	C what
5	A must	B need	C can
6	A since	B for	C during
7	A at	B on	C in
8	A could	B should	C have to

5 Match the definitions (a–h) to the highlighted words in the article (1–8).

1 village ____
2 surprised ____
3 roofs ____
4 clouds ____
5 pink ____
6 dangerous ____
7 ice ____
8 lake ____

a water that is below 0 °C
b the things that cover the tops of buildings
c a very small town in the countryside
d white or grey things in the sky which are made of water
e how you feel when something unusual happens
f the opposite of safe
g a large area of water
h the name for the colour that is pale red

THINK | **RESEARCH** | CULTURE | LEARN | ME

Find out about some unusual weather that has happened in your country. Make a poster about it.

▶ **Workbook Unit 9:** Reading, pages 68–69, exercises 1, 2, 3, 4

Grammar in context

Find the sentences in the text on page 93 then answer the questions

1 *If it **rains** a lot in England, some people **say** it is raining cats and dogs.* (paragraph 1)

2 *So if red rain **falls** from the sky again in India, people **will know** what it is.* (paragraph 3)

Which sentence talks about:

a) something that is a fact or is always true? ____

b) something that is possible in the future? ____

REMEMBER

Zero conditional

- We use present tenses in both parts of the sentence: *If the weather **is** bad, he **stays** at home.*
- We use the zero conditional to talk about things that are true and scientific facts: *If you **heat** water to 100° Celsius, it **boils**.*

First conditional

- We use ***If*** + the present simple in one part of the sentence and ***will*** in the other: ***If** the weather **is** good tomorrow, we**'ll have** a barbecue.*
- We use the first conditional to talk about real, likely or possible situations in the future: ***If** the weather **is** bad **tomorrow**, he**'ll stay** at home.*

Note: in zero conditional sentences, *If* can be changed to *When* with no change in meaning.

▶ **See Grammar reference, Unit 9,** page 158

1 Choose the correct words to complete the zero conditional sentences.

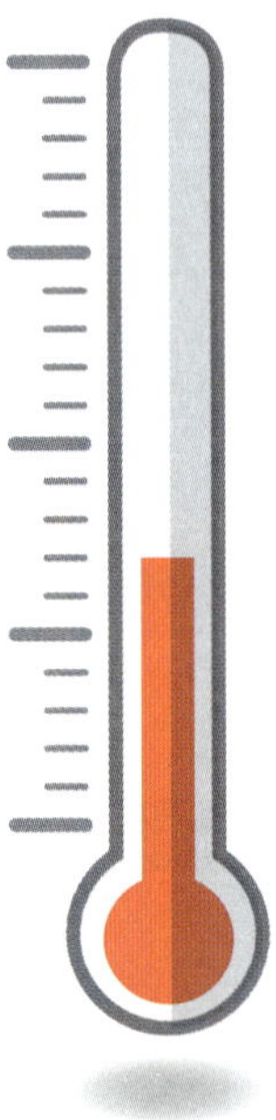

1 If the temperature **is** / **will be** below 0 °C, water **changes** / **will change** to ice.

2 When **it is** / **will be** very windy, trees sometimes **will fall** / **fall** down.

3 I always **will feel** / **feel** better when the sun **shines** / **will shine**.

4 If plants **don't** / **won't** have enough air and water, they **don't** / **won't** grow.

5 **Do** / **Will** you usually go out for long walks in the forest when it **will snow** / **snows**?

6 When I **will have** / **have** a bad cold, I **won't** / **don't** go to school.

2 Choose the correct words to complete the first conditional sentences.

1 If it **rains** / **will rain** this afternoon, I **don't** / **won't** go and play football in the park.

2 If the weather **gets** / **will get** very cold tonight, some of the flowers in our garden **will die** / **die**.

3 There **isn't** / **won't be** any cars on the road if it **snows** / **will snow** a lot later.

4 **Will** / **Do** you come with me if I **will go** / **go** out to make a snowman?

5 If you **go** / **will go** out in this cold weather, you **need** / **will need** a warm jacket.

6 We **are not** / **won't** go out if there **is** / **will be** a storm tonight.

3 Complete the article using the correct form (present simple or *will*) of the verbs in brackets.

Using plants in science

When you **(1)** ___________ **(go)** to bed tonight, will you take your mobile phone with you? And if you **(2)** ___________ **(keep)** it with you, will it be near your bed? If your phone **(3)** ___________ **(be)** usually near your head during the night, how do you feel in the morning? If you **(4)** ___________ **(feel)** tired and don't do well at school, this **(5)** ___________ **(not be)** unusual.

Five teenagers from Denmark found that on nights when they **(6)** ___________ **(sleep)** with their phones near their heads, they can't **(7)** ___________ **(think)** very well at school the next day. They wanted to know why, so they did an experiment with plants. They grew plants in two rooms. In one room there was a wi-fi router and in the other room there wasn't. Before they started, the girls thought, 'If wi-fi and mobile phones **(8)** ___________ **(be)** totally safe, then the plants **(9)** ___________ **(grow)** normally.'

After 12 days, they were surprised. The plants near the router didn't grow, and many of them died. But the plants in the other room were healthy and grew well. So, if wi-fi **(10)** ___________ (stop) plants from growing, what does it do to us? Because of what these girls did at school, scientists now want to find out.

THINK | RESEARCH | CULTURE | LEARN | **ME**

Work in pairs and discuss the questions.

What will you do if …

- it rains all weekend?
- it is sunny tomorrow?
- it snows on a Sunday?

▶ **Workbook Unit 9:** Grammar 1, page 70, exercises 1, 2, 3

Words connected with *weather and nature*

1 3.02 **Look at the weather map of Europe and choose the correct word to complete each sentence. Listen and check.**

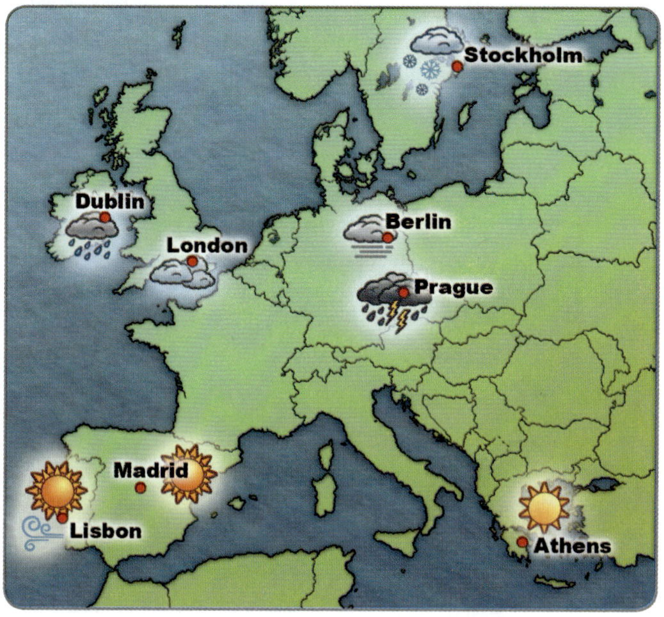

1 It is warm and **foggy** / **sunny** in Madrid.
2 There is **snow** / **sun** in Stockholm.
3 It is **rainy** / **sunny** in Dublin.
4 It is **rainy and windy** / **sunny and windy** in Lisbon.
5 There is **ice** / **fog** in Berlin.
6 There **is ice** / **are thunderstorms** in Prague.
7 It's **foggy** / **cloudy** in London.

2 3.03 **Complete the descriptions with the words in the box. Listen and check.**

beach | forest | hill | mountain | river | sky

1 A large area of trees and other plants.
____
2 It is very tall and sometimes there is snow on the top.
____
3 It takes water from the mountains to the sea.
____
4 It's by the sea and people go there in the summer.
____
5 The space above you that you see when you look up into the air.
____
6 It is smaller than a mountain.
____

Words + prepositions

3 3.04 **Match to make sentences. Listen and check.**

1 The students did experiments ____
2 It is important ____
3 The students were good at ____
4 Scientists want to ____
5 Summer is the best time ____
6 They learnt about animals by ____

a) to visit the beach, because it's sunny.
b) to protect our forests and rivers.
c) to see if wi-fi was dangerous.
d) visiting the zoo.
e) thinking of new science experiments.
f) find out why things happen.

Nouns/adjectives

4 3.05 **Complete the table with a noun or adjective. Listen and check.**

noun	adjective
cloud	*cloudy*
fog	(1) ________
(2) ________	icy
rain	(3) ________
(4) ________	snowy
sun	(5) ________

5 **Complete the sentences using the correct form of some of the words from Exercise 4.**

1 There are lots of ________ in the sky. I think it's going to rain.
2 It was very cold and wet and the path was very ________ . Lots of people fell down.
3 If it's ________ tomorrow, we will go to the beach.
4 When there is lots of ________ , you can't see very far.
5 A lot of ________ fell in the night and now everything outside is white.
6 It was a ________ day and everyone at the volleyball game got wet.

SAY IT RIGHT

Resource centre: Unit 9
/əʊ/ and /aʊ/

9 LISTENING | Picture multiple choice

1 Work in pairs and answer the questions.

1 What do you like doing in your free time in the summer?

2 What are you going to do in the next summer holiday?

EXAM SKILL

Understanding the speakers' questions

- It is important to understand exactly what the speakers mean when they answer a question.
- When the speakers agree or disagree with someone, they don't always say *yes* or *no*.
- Listen carefully to the words the speakers use and try to decide exactly what they mean.

2 3.06 Listen to five short conversations. Are the answers *yes*, *no* or *don't know*? Tick the correct box for each conversation (1–5).

	yes	no	don't know
1			
2			
3			
4			
5			

3 Complete the conversations with the words in the box.

idea | maybe | really | sure

1 **A:** Do you want to go skiing next winter?
B: Good ___________ ! I love skiing.

2 **A:** I'm going to the lake on Sunday. Can you come?
B: I'm not ___________ . I think my cousins are coming to visit me.

3 **A:** Do you want to go horse-riding in the forest?
B: Not ___________ . It's too cold today.

4 **A:** Would you like to go to the countryside on Saturday?
B: ___________ . But I need to ask my mum first.

OPTIMISE YOUR EXAM

Picture multiple choice

- When you choose the correct picture, you may need to listen for numbers, descriptions or the correct word for something.
- Be careful. Sometimes you will hear more than one possible answer.
- When you listen again, check that the picture you chose is correct.

4 3.07 You will hear people talking in five different situations. For each question, choose the best answer (A, B or C).

Example: Where will both boys be later?

A ☐

B ☑

C ☐

1 Where does Sophie want to go at the weekend if the weather is good?

A ☐

B ☐

C ☐

2 What's the weather like today?

A ☐

B ☐

C ☐

3 Which place is the boy NOT going to visit this summer?

A ☐

B ☐

C ☐

4 What's the weather going to be like here tomorrow afternoon?

A ☐

B ☐

C ☐

5 Which season does the girl like the best?

A ☐

B ☐

C ☐

THINK | RESEARCH | **CULTURE** | LEARN | ME

What are the most popular free-time activities for young people in the winter in your country?

▶ **Workbook Unit 9:** Listening, page 72, exercises 1, 2, 3

GRAMMAR 2 | Second conditional

9

Grammar in context

Look at these sentences from the audio in the listening lesson and answer the questions.

1 If it was sunny, I would go to the beach today.
  a) Is it sunny? ______
  b) Is the speaker going to the beach today? ______
2 We'd go to the beach in Spain if we had more money.
  a) Is the speaker going to the beach in Spain? ______
  b) Does the speaker have a lot of money? ______
3 If I didn't have a guitar lesson at 1 o'clock, I'd come with you.
  a) Does the speaker have a guitar lesson at 1 o'clock? ______
  b) Can the speaker go with his friends at 1 o'clock? ______

REMEMBER

- We use ***If*** + past simple in one part of the second conditional, and ***would*** in the other part: ***If*** *my brother* ***were*** *here right now, he* ***would*** *know what to do.*
- We use the second conditional to talk about unlikely or impossible situations now, generally or in the future: *If I* ***lived*** *in England, I'****d eat*** *fish and chips every day.*

Note: we use *were* for the first and third person singular in second conditional sentences using the verb *to be*: *If I* ***were*** *you, I'd stay at home until the rain stops.*

▶ **See Grammar reference, Unit 9,** page 159

1 **Choose the correct word to complete the sentences.**

1 If there **is** / **was** lots of snow outside, we would go skiing in the mountains.
2 If there were no rivers, we **won't** / **wouldn't** have fresh water to drink.
3 If the grass **won't** / **didn't** grow in spring, the cows in the field wouldn't have any food.
4 If it wasn't warm and sunny in the summer, **will** / **would** the fruit grow on the trees?
5 If there **are** / **were** no people, what would the world be like?

2 **Complete the second conditional sentences using the correct form of the verbs in brackets.**

1 If he ______ (**can**) travel into space, he ______ (**visit**) the moon.
2 If Harry ______ (**not own**) a bike, he ______ (**not cycle**) to school and back every day.
3 Would you ______ (**go**) swimming every day if you ______ (**live**) by the beach?
4 If they ______ (**have**) a lot of money, they ______ (**buy**) a big house.
5 If everyone ______ (**stop**) driving cars, the air ______ (**be**) cleaner.

3 **Work in pairs. Complete the second conditional sentences using your own ideas.**

1 If I owned a plane, I ______ .
2 If I were famous, I ______ .
3 If I lived in a forest, I ______ .
4 If I were good at singing, I ______ .
5 If I could live anywhere, I ______ .

4 **Complete the text by making second conditional sentences using the correct form of the verbs in the box.**

be	be able to	can	do	not have	wash

Living With Nature

When you wake up in the morning, what do you usually do? Perhaps you turn on the light and have a warm shower. But what do you think you would (**1**) ______ if you didn't have electricity? How would you (**2**) ______ if you (**3**) ______ hot water to use? Well, if you wanted to know, you (**4**) ______ always ask 16-year-old Zeki Basan. Zeki lives by himself in a forest on the island of Skye, near Scotland.

Zeki is a student at the School of Adventure Studies on Skye and he decided to live in a tent in the forest to learn more about life in the countryside. He gets up at six every morning and lights the fire. If he didn't have a fire, he wouldn't (**5**) ______ cook food or keep warm. He washes his clothes in the river. He doesn't use the internet and can't watch TV.

If he lived in a normal house, his life (**6**) ______ a lot easier. But out here in the forest, Zeki loves the fresh air, the highland cows and living close to nature.

THINK | RESEARCH | CULTURE | LEARN | ME

If you lived in a forest by yourself, what would you eat and drink? Do you think you would be happy?

9 SPEAKING | Interview

Talk2Me — *It's a fun place to live.*

Flipped classroom

1 **Watch the *Talk2Me* video and answer the questions.**

1 Who has a French exchange partner?
2 Where does Anouk live?
3 Why are the twins excited at the end?

2 **Watch the video again. Underline the phrases in the *Phrase expert* box that you hear on the video.**

> **PHRASE EXPERT**
> I live in a village/town/city. | In my … there is/are … | It's a (beautiful/fun/quiet) place to live.
> The thing I like the most/least about … is …

3 **Work in pairs and answer the questions.**

1 What's your favourite time of year for the weather? Why?
2 Do you travel more in the summer or the winter? Why?
3 What do you enjoy eating on a hot day? Why?

> **EXAM SKILL**
> ### Talking about a topic
> - During the Speaking test, the examiner will ask personal questions and then ask about a topic.
> - The examiner often does this by saying *Tell me something about …*
> - Be ready to give examples about the main topics of the exam, e.g. daily life, interests, likes.
> - To give examples, you can use words and phrases like *For example, Let me give an example, One example is …*

4 3.08 **Listen to four students and match each one to a topic. There is one extra topic you do not need.**

> city where you live | family and friends
> hobbies | places you go on holiday | technology

5 3.08 **Listen again and write down the examples each student gives.**

Student 1 ______________________________
Student 2 ______________________________
Student 3 ______________________________
Student 4 ______________________________

6 3.09 **Listen to another student. Write down the topic, the examples given and the phrase used to correct a mistake.**

Topic: ______________________________
Examples: ______________________________
Correction phrase: ______________________________

> **OPTIMISE YOUR EXAM**
> ### Interview
> - Sometimes you might make a mistake when you are speaking.
> - Use phrases like *Sorry, I mean …, Sorry, I'll do that again.*, or *No, that's wrong. I mean …* to show that you know you made a mistake and want to correct it.
> - These phrases show the examiner your understanding of language and give you another chance to get it right.

7 **Spend one minute planning your answers for the topics (1–3) below. Then, in pairs, take turns to talk about the topics.**

1 Tell me something about the place where you live.
____
2 Tell me something about your friends.
____
3 Tell me something about your family.
____

> THINK | **RESEARCH** | CULTURE | LEARN | ME
>
> Find out what the weather is like today in the following cities:
> Bangkok, Buenos Aires, London, Melbourne, Oslo and Tokyo.

▶ **Workbook Unit 9:** Speaking, pages 72–73, exercises 1, 2, 3, 4

1 Work in pairs and answer the questions.

1 Would you like to live in the mountains? Why / Why not?
2 Do you like going to the countryside? Why / Why not?

EXAM SKILL

Identifying key words

- Look for key words in the sentence that help you choose the correct answer.
- Key words include functional phrases (a greeting, an apology, a request, an opinion, etc.), question words (*Who*, *How long*, *Where*, etc.) or a subject/object and pronoun.

2 Match the two sentences. The important key words are underlined.

1 Are the students in class now? ____
2 I'm sorry. There isn't enough snow to go skiing. ____
3 Jo lives near me. ____
4 Can I borrow a pen? ____
5 How long have you been in the sun? ____

a) Her house is over there.
b) Yes, of course.
c) For half an hour.
d) No, they are outside.
e) What a shame!

3 Underline the key phrases in the conversations.

1 **A:** Have you seen Peter today?
B: Yes, he's here.
2 **A:** See you at the weekend.
B: I'll be a bit late.
3 **A:** Can you see that bird?
B: Do you mean the one in the tree?
4 **A:** I don't like the snow.
B: Stay inside then.

4 Work in pairs and compare your answers. Are the key phrases you underlined the same? Explain how the answer matches the first line in each conversation.

OPTIMISE YOUR EXAM

Multiple-choice dialogue

- Remember, in this part of the exam you will read five short, everyday conversations.
- There is no connection between the conversations, so answer the easy questions first.
- Always write down an answer for each conversation.

5 Work in pairs. Read the example conversation in Exercise 6. Why is the answer B?

6 Complete the five conversations. For questions 1–5, choose the best answer (A, B or C).

Example:

Is it raining at the moment?

A Yes, it's late.
(B) No, it's sunny.
C We can go skiing.

1 Have you been to this beach before?
A No, thanks.
B Yes, it's here.
C Yes, it's really beautiful.

2 There was a thunderstorm last night.
A I didn't hear it.
B I'm very busy.
C I hope so.

3 What are you going to do tomorrow?
A I don't like this weather.
B I'm going now.
C I'm going to the beach.

4 There's a lot of snow in the mountains.
A Let's go skiing.
B We're very early.
C It's over there.

5 Look out! It's going to fall.
A It's by the lake.
B That was close!
C Great idea.

THINK | RESEARCH | CULTURE | LEARN | ME

What is the worst weather you have ever been in? Write a few sentences then tell your partner.

WRITING | A note

1 In pairs or as a group, answer the questions.

1 Have you been on a holiday or trip with your friends? Did you enjoy it? Why / Why not?

2 Would you prefer a holiday in a city, in the mountains or near the beach? Why?

EXAM SKILL

Giving advice and instructions

- We often use the first conditional to explain what you'll need in certain conditions, e.g. *If it's sunny, you'll need a hat.* and the second conditional or *should* to give advice, e.g. *If I were you, I'd …, You should …*
- Remember, when we want to give short, clear instructions, we can use the imperative, e.g. *Meet me in the café.* or *Don't be late!*

2 Complete the sentences with the correct form of the verbs in the box.

be | bring | need | not go
not stay | wait

1 ____________ a coat. It's going to be cold tonight.

2 If I were you, I ____________ in the mountains in this weather.

3 ____________ into the forest. It's dangerous.

4 If I were you, I ____________ until it stops raining.

5 ____________ careful. The river is very deep.

6 You ____________ sun cream if it's very sunny.

3 Read the note. What three things does Amelia want Rosie to bring?

Hi Rosie,

Are you ready for our summer camp?

If it's wet, we'll need raincoats. Have you got one?

Don't forget a hat! And if I were you, I'd bring some food.

What time shall we meet?

See you soon,

Amelia

1 ____________

2 ____________

3 ____________

4 Read the email in Exercise 3 again and find examples of:

1 giving an instruction.

____

2 giving advice.

____

OPTIMISE YOUR EXAM

A note

- Remember to use informal language when you write a note.
- Check your answer for correct spelling and grammar.
- Make sure your note answers all three questions.

5 **Look at the writing task below. Tick the three things that Tom asks about.**

Read the note from your English friend, Tom.

> *Hi Jessica,*
> *I'm excited about summer camp! Do you think it will be cold at night? What should I bring to eat? I've forgotten where we're meeting. Can you tell me?*
> *See you on Saturday,*
> *Tom*

Write a note to Tom and answer the questions.
Write **25–35** words.

- the place to meet ___
- the time to meet ___
- the weather ___
- what they'll do ___
- what to take ___
- where they'll stay ___

6 **Plan** **Plan your note. Use the chart to help you.**

	Detail	Useful language	My notes
First line		*Hello …,* *Hi …,*	
Question 1		*I think …* *I don't think …* *I'm not sure …*	
Question 2		*If I were you, I'd …* *You should …*	
Question 3		*Meet me at …* *Let's meet at …*	
Last line		*See you soon,* *Love,*	

7 **Write** **Write your note to Tom in an appropriate style. Write 25–35 words.**

8 **Check** **Before you hand in your note, complete this checklist.**

Checklist

- ◯ I've followed my writing plan.
- ◯ I've started and ended my note in the right way.
- ◯ I've answered the three questions.
- ◯ I've used phrases for giving advice and instructions.
- ◯ I've used a good range of vocabulary.
- ◯ I've used informal language.
- ◯ I've written 25–35 words.
- ◯ I've checked my spelling and grammar.

▶ **Writing reference,** page 169 ▶ **Workbook Unit 9:** Writing, page 74, exercises 1, 2, 3, 4 and Progress check 9, page 75

10 Looking after yourself

READING | Matching | Signs and notices

1 In pairs or as a group, answer the questions.

1 When was the last time you felt ill?
2 What did you do?
3 Do you usually take medicine when you're ill? Do you do anything else?

2 3.10 **Read the online article on page 103 and answer the questions T (True) or F (False).**

1 The writer started working as a doctor 10 years ago. **T / F**
2 Many ill people don't live near a hospital. **T / F**
3 Abbey was 15 last month. **T / F**
4 Abbey didn't get a birthday cake on her birthday. **T / F**

EXAM SKILL

Guessing the meaning of new words

- If you don't understand a new word, read the whole sentence and try to guess what it means.
- Remember to think about where the signs and notices are from, and who they are for and what their function is. This will help you understand the meaning of new words.

3 Match the highlighted words in the article to a definition (1–8).

1 arrangements to meet people like doctors or dentists at agreed times ______________
2 an aeroplane that takes people to hospital ______________
3 people trained to care for sick and injured people ______________
4 facts and information ______________
5 a journey by plane ______________
6 to examine someone or something to make sure everything is as it should be ______________
7 very sad or worried about something ______________
8 areas of land used for growing plants or keeping animals ______________

OPTIMISE YOUR EXAM

Matching

- Remember to underline the important words in the questions first, then to look for words that mean the same in the signs and notices.
- Decide if each sign is positive (telling you to do something) or negative (telling you not to do something).

Doctors in the air

1 I have been a doctor for 10 years, but I don't work in a normal hospital. I work for the Royal Flying Doctor Service of Australia. Australia is a very big country and some people live thousands of kilometres from the nearest city. When they get ill or have an accident, they can't get to a hospital easily because they're so far away, so they call us. We can get to them fast.

2 Flying doctors have worked in Australia since 1928. It has become a really important service for people who live in the Australian countryside.

3 When someone calls us, our staff need to find out about the person and the details of their illness or the accident that has just happened. If it's very serious, we might send an air ambulance to take them to hospital.

4 Doctors and nurses also fly to different villages and farms in the outback, which is what we call the countryside in Australia. We see people who have already made appointments and we also visit people we haven't met yet, to check on their health. I love meeting different people every day.

5 Last month I flew out to Abbey, after she fell and broke her arm while she was playing with her sister. To make things worse, it was Abbey's 14th birthday, so she missed her own birthday party. Abbey was in pain, but she looked happy as we flew to the hospital. It was her first ever flight and she said that she loved being high in the sky looking down at the little houses and trees below. When we arrived, the nurses gave Abbey a birthday cake and sang 'Happy birthday' to her. Abbey was upset about her arm, but she told us, 'The flying doctor service made my birthday special.'

4 Read the signs and notices (A–H) in Exercise 5 and choose the correct meaning for each word.

1 enter – **go out of** / **go into**
2 emergency – a **serious** / **normal** situation
3 parking – **stopping and leaving** / **driving** a car
4 hours – **start and end time of working** / **appointments**
5 patient – a person **being cared for** / **working** in a hospital

5 Which sign or notice (A–H) says this (1–5)? There are some extra letters you do not need.

Example:
You cannot see people here for two hours at lunchtime. _H_

1 You can't leave your car here. ____
2 This is not for normal calls. ____
3 You can't see this person in the evening. ____
4 You can't eat your sandwiches here. ____
5 Speak to someone before you go. ____

A WASH YOUR HANDS BEFORE YOU ENTER THE HOSPITAL.

B No food allowed in the waiting room.

C See your doctor before leaving the hospital.

D USE THIS PHONE ONLY IN AN EMERGENCY.

E NO PARKING. AMBULANCES ONLY.

F The nurse's hours are 9:00 and 17:00 every day.

G DANGEROUS: Do not enter this room when the red light is on.

H No visiting patients between 12:00 and 14:00.

▶ **Workbook Unit 10:** Reading, pages 76–77, exercises 1, 2, 3, 4

Grammar in context

Find the sentences in the text on page 103 then answer the questions.

1 *I **have been** a doctor for 10 years, …* (paragraph 1)
2 *Flying doctors **have worked** in Australia since 1928.* (paragraph 2)
3 *… the details of their illness or the accident that **has just happened**.* (paragraph 3)
4 *We see people who **have already made** appointments …* (paragraph 4)
5 *… we also visit people we **haven't met** yet, …* (paragraph 4)

Which sentence (1–5) talks about

a) when something started? ____
b) a length of time? ____
c) something arranged earlier? ____
d) something that has not happened up to now? ____
e) something that happened a short time before? ____

REMEMBER

- We use *for* to talk about a period of time.
- We use *since* to talk about when something started in the past.
- We use *already* to talk about something that has happened earlier. *Already* can go between *have/has* and the main verb, or at the end of the sentence.
- We use *just* to talk about something that happened a short time ago. *Just* goes between *have/has* and the main verb.
- We use *yet* with negative sentences and questions, to talk/ask about 'any time up to now'. *Yet* usually goes at the end of the sentence.

▶ **See Grammar reference, Unit 10,** page 159

1 Complete the sentences with the words in the box.

already	for	just	since	yet (× 2)

1 Can you help me, please? I've ____________ hurt my hand.
2 Have you seen the doctor ____________ ?
3 Sara's had a headache ____________ last night.
4 I've ____________ taken some medicine today so I don't need any more until tomorrow.
5 Max hasn't been to the doctor ____________ over a year.
6 Where's the ambulance? It hasn't arrived ____________ .

2 Complete the sentences using the present perfect simple form of the verbs in brackets and choose the correct word.

1 I ______________ (**not / see**) the doctor about the pain in my legs **since / yet**.
2 How long ____________ you ____________ (**have**) toothache **for / since**?
3 Dad ____________ **just / yet** ______________ (**hurt**) his back.
4 The children ______________ (**not eat**) anything **for / since** 7 o'clock this morning.
5 The nurse ____________ **already / yet** ____________ (**check**) my temperature.

3 Complete the article with the correct present perfect form of the verbs in brackets. If there is no verb, use *already, for, just, since* or *yet*.

Lessons for life

Imagine this – you've been on a bike ride with your friends, but one of them (1) ____________ (**fall**) and hit their head. You (2) ____________ (**phone**) for an ambulance (3) ____________ , but it (4) ____________ (**not arrive**) (5) ____________ . Would you know what to do next?

Something like this happened to Lily Kent a few weeks ago when she was out cycling. Her friend, Annie, fell and hurt her leg, but Lily (6) ____________ (**be**) on a first aid course, so she knew exactly what to do. She phoned the ambulance then sat with Annie and held her hand while they waited for help to arrive. Annie felt safe knowing Lily was there.

Annie is fine now, but the accident (7) ____________ (**change**) her views about first aid. 'I've wanted to learn about first aid (8) ____________ a long time, but (9) ____________ the accident, I've been even more interested.' said Annie. 'So I've (10) ____________ started a first aid course – and it's really interesting!'

THINK | RESEARCH | CULTURE | LEARN | **ME**

Write a sentence about a time when you've hurt yourself and needed help.

Words connected with *health*

1 3.11 **Write the names for the different parts of the body. Use the words in the box. Listen and check.**

ankle | arm | back | ear | eye | face finger | foot | hand | knee | leg neck | nose | stomach | throat

2 **Choose the correct word or phrase to complete each sentence.**

1 If I eat too quickly, I usually get **neck** / **stomach** ache.
2 Sarah has hurt her **ankle** / **eye** and now she can't walk.
3 I hurt my **face** / **foot** when I kicked the ball during the football match.
4 Alex can't talk because he has a problem with his **finger** / **throat**.
5 My mum has hurt her **neck** / **nose** and she can't move her head very well.
6 If you can't read the board, maybe you should get your **ears** / **eyes** checked.
7 I've run 10 kilometres and now my **fingers** / **knees** hurt.
8 Arthur threw the ball so fast that it hurt Dan's **foot** / **hand** when he caught it.

Words + prepositions

3 3.12 **Complete the sentences. Choose the best word (A, B or C) for each gap. Listen and check.**

1 I had a bad pain ____ my foot this morning.
A with **B** for **C** in
2 Ashley has a problem ____ his stomach so he can't eat bread.
A for **B** with **C** to
3 This is a hospital ____ children and babies.
A with **B** for **C** to
4 Sitting down all day can be a danger ____ your health.
A to **B** in **C** with
5 I'd like an appointment ____ the doctor, please.
A for **B** with **C** to
6 Have you got any medicine ____ a bad cold?
A with **B** in **C** for
7 What's the matter ____ you?
A with **B** in **C** for
8 I hope to do a course ____ nursing.
A of **B** in **C** at

Collocations with verbs

4 3.13 **Match the nouns (a–f) to the verbs (1–6) to make expressions about health. Listen and check.**

1 take ____ **a)** your leg
2 make ____ **b)** ill/better
3 break ____ **c)** a cold
4 brush ____ **d)** an appointment
5 catch ____ **e)** your temperature
6 feel ____ **f)** your teeth

5 **Complete the sentences using the correct form of the expressions from Exercise 4.**

1 I ______________ from one of my friends at school and had to stay in bed for two days.
2 Jack couldn't walk for eight weeks after he ______________ during a skiing holiday last year.
3 Have you ______________ to see the doctor yet?
4 Your head feels very warm. I think I need to ______________ to see if you are ill.
5 It's important to ______________ every morning and evening so they are clean and healthy.
6 If you ______________ at school, you should tell the school nurse.

▶ Vocabulary reference, page 167 ▶ Workbook Unit 10: Vocabulary, pages 78–79, exercises 1, 2, 3

10 LISTENING | Multiple matching

1 **Work in pairs and do the following:**

1 Make a list of all the health problems you can think of.

2 Look at the list together and decide which health problems you should go to hospital with.

EXAM SKILL

Understanding when something happened

- Listen carefully to the tenses the speakers use.
- Speakers may use the present simple with adverbs like *usually* and *often* to talk about things generally or routine events.
- Speakers use the past simple to talk about actions that happened at a known time in the past and are finished. They use the present perfect when the exact time of the action is not important or not known, or for unfinished actions that started in the past but are connected to the present.

2 **Complete the sentences using the present simple, present perfect or past simple of the verbs in brackets.**

1 Mike ______________ (**just / break**) his arm and needs to go to hospital.

2 The doctor ______________ (**check**) her temperature two hours ago and it was normal.

3 We usually ______________ (**see**) more people on Monday morning.

4 Mrs Richards ______________ (**have**) a bad stomach ache on Wednesday afternoon.

5 I ______________ (**have**) this earache for four days already.

3 3.14 **Listen to six speakers talking about events. When do/did the events happen? Tick the correct box.**

	a routine event or habit (present simple)	a time in the past (past simple)	an unknown time in the past (present perfect)
1			
2			
3			
4			
5			
6			

OPTIMISE YOUR EXAM

Multiple matching

- Try to understand exactly what the speakers are saying if they talk about any of the possible answers.
- Be careful. Sometimes speakers will say something negative about one of the answers or use a different tense to talk about it, so it might not be a correct answer.

4 3.15 **Listen to two school nurses talking about who they have seen this week. For each person (1–5), choose a problem (A–H). There are some extra letters you do not need.**

Wesley	*D*		
1 Evan	____	**A**	a broken arm
2 Rosie	____	**B**	a high temperature
3 Amber Mistry	____	**C**	a stomach ache
4 Ben Sharp	____	**D**	~~backache~~
5 Oliver	____	**E**	a cold
		F	had a fall
		G	a broken leg
		H	an ear problem

THINK | RESEARCH | CULTURE | **LEARN** | ME

Cover Exercise 4. Complete the words to make health problems from the audio.

1 a h_ _h t_ _ _ _ _ _ _ _ _ _ _

2 b_ _ _ _ _ _ _ _

3 a s_ _ _ _ _ _ _ a_ _ _

4 a b_ _ _ _ _ _ l_ _

▶ **Workbook Unit 10:** Listening, page 80, exercises 1, 2, 3

Grammar in context

Look at these sentences from the audio in the listening lesson and answer the questions.

1 *I **offered to give** him some medicine, …*
2 *… he **hates taking** it.*
3 *She **decided to climb** a tree, but she fell.*
4 *… I **told** him **to drink** lots of water …*
5 *… he **keeps coming** to see me.*

a) Which verbs are followed by the infinitive?
__________ , __________ , __________

b) Which verbs are followed by the -*ing* form?
__________ , __________

REMEMBER

- When we use two verbs in a sentence, there isn't a rule about whether the second verb is in the infinitive or ends in -*ing*. You have to learn the verb patterns.
- Common verbs followed by the infinitive are: *agree, choose, decide, help, hope, try* and *want*.
- Common verbs followed by the -*ing* form are: *don't mind, enjoy, keep, spend time* and *stop*.

▶ **See Grammar reference, Unit 10,** page 159

1 Choose the correct verb to complete each sentence.

1 My dad **decided** / **enjoyed** to do more exercise.
2 The nurses wanted **helping** / **to help** my grandmother when she was in hospital.
3 My brother **didn't mind** / **agreed** taking the medicine.
4 Paul **hoped** / **kept** to visit his best friend in hospital.
5 Pippa **chose** / **stopped** eating unhealthy food when she felt ill.
6 Yasmin **wanted** / **kept** getting stomach aches when she ate bread.

2 Complete the sentences using the correct form of the verbs in brackets.

1 Leo decided ______________ (**make**) an appointment to see the doctor.
2 Laura stopped ______________ (**take**) the medicine after she felt better.
3 The students enjoyed ______________ (**hear**) about what the nurses did at work.
4 They wanted ______________ (**eat**) healthier food and do more exercise.
5 My grandfather didn't mind ______________ (**take**) the medicine for his stomach problem.
6 The nurse spent time ______________ (**put on**) a new bandage for me.

3 Complete the article using the infinitive or -*ing* form of the verbs in brackets.

Everyday solutions for everyday problems

When we feel ill or have a health problem most of us decide (**1**) ______________ (**visit**) a chemist or doctor. But sometimes the things we have at home can help us too.

Do you get sick when you travel by car or bus? It happens to a lot of people. Many hope (**2**) ______________ (**feel**) better after taking expensive medicines, while other people just stop (**3**) ______________ (**travel**) in cars and buses. Before you do that, you might want (**4**) ______________ (**try**) this. Scientists have found that the smell of fresh lemon can stop you feeling sick. So the next time you travel by car, just cut a lemon in half and put it under your nose. It will help you (**5**) ______________ (**enjoy**) the journey.

We all know that it's important to exercise regularly. A lot of people try (**6**) ______________ (**get**) fit by running or going to the gym once or twice a week. This is usually a good thing. However, it can sometimes be a problem. One surprising thing happens to a few people when they stop (**7**) ______________ (**run**) and take off their shoes. Smelly feet! If this happens to you, the solution is to put your feet in a bowl of warm black tea. There is something in the tea that stops the smell. If you keep (**8**) ______________ (**do**) this every day for a few weeks, your feet will smell much nicer!

SAY IT RIGHT

Resource centre: Unit 10
/ɪ/ and /iː/

THINK | RESEARCH | CULTURE | LEARN | **ME**

Write sentences about things …

- you enjoy doing now to get fit.
- you would like to do to be healthier.

▶ **Workbook Unit 10:** Grammar 2, page 79, exercises 1, 2

Flipped classroom

1 **Watch the *Talk2Me* video and answer the questions.**

1 How much are the tickets for students?
2 What time is it when their call is answered?
3 How many tickets do they buy?

2 **Watch the video again. Underline the words and phrases in the *Phrase expert* box that you hear on the video.**

> **PHRASE EXPERT**
> Just a minute, please. | Let's have a look at … | Let me think … | Let's see … | Looking at the information, it says … | OK. | Well …

3 **Work in pairs and answer the questions.**

1 What do you do to stay healthy?
2 What do you do when you feel ill?

4 3.16 **Write full questions from these prompts. Listen and check.**

1 open / evenings ?
____
2 big / small ?
____
3 swimming pool ?
____
4 telephone number ?
____
5 address ?
____

5 3.17 **Now listen to the answers and complete the advert.**

> **JUMP! Sports Club**
>
> **NEW! Come and try for free!**
>
> Open daily 6am – 10am
>
> (**1**) __________ but there's something for everyone
>
> gym, sports hall (**2**) __________
>
> Tel: (**3**) __________
>
> (**4**) __________ George (**5**) __________

EXAM SKILL

Giving yourself time to think

- In the collaborative task, you may need a little time to find the information you are looking for.
- Learn useful phrases such as: *just a minute, please* or *let me think* to give you time to find the answer.

6 3.17 **Listen again and note down the phrases you hear that give the speaker time to think.**

1 ______________________
2 ______________________
3 ______________________

OPTIMISE YOUR EXAM

Collaborative task

- This task is about working with your partner.
- Give them time to think and say their answers. Listen carefully and respond with phrases like *'That's interesting.'* or simply *'Thank you.'*
- If there is a long pause before a question, you could ask *'Do you have another question?'.*

7 **In pairs (Student A and Student B), do the exam task.**

> **Student A:** turn to page 138 and look at the information about some *Health and wellbeing lessons*. Answer Student B's questions about it.
>
> **Student B:** look at the question prompts on page 141. Ask Student A your questions.
>
> **Student B:** turn to page 141 and look at the information about the *Health Food Shop*. Answer Student A's questions about it.
>
> **Student A:** look at the question prompts on page 138. Ask Student B your questions.

THINK | RESEARCH | CULTURE | LEARN | ME

Keep a diary in English for a day. Note down everything you eat and the physical activities you take part during that day.

 ▶ **Workbook Unit 10:** Speaking, pages 80–81, exercises 1, 2, 3, 4

1 Work in pairs. Look at the photos and answer the questions.

1 What do you think about the food in these two photos?
2 Which food would you rather eat? Why?
3 Do you usually eat a healthy diet?
4 Have you ever had stomach ache?

A

B

EXAM SKILL

Giving short answers

- When someone answers a question, they often give a short answer.
- The verb in the short answer matches the verb at the beginning of the question, e.g. ***Do** you like it? Yes, I **do**. / No, I **don't**.*
- The pronoun in the short answer often matches the pronoun in the question, e.g. *Is **he** here? Yes, **he** is.* If the question includes 'you', the pronoun may change, e.g. *'Do **you** like it?' 'Yes **I/we** do.'*

2 Match the short answers (a–f) to the questions (1–6).

1 Do you think this will help? ____
2 Has Matthew got a headache? ____
3 Would you like to have a rest? ____
4 Are there many nurses in the hospital? ____
5 Should I take this medicine? ____
6 Will the children get to school on time? ____

a) Yes, he has.
b) Yes, we would.
c) No, they won't.
d) No, you shouldn't.
e) No, I don't.
f) Yes, there are.

3 Complete the questions and short answers.

1 Did you call an ambulance? __________ , I did.
2 Have you got a stomach ache? No, I __________ .
3 __________ he going to see a doctor? No, he isn't.
4 Does this medicine work? No, __________ .
5 __________ you had back pain? Yes, I have.
6 Would they like to come in? __________ , __________ wouldn't.

OPTIMISE YOUR EXAM

Multiple-matching dialogue

- When you choose an answer, put a line through it.
- Read the complete dialogue with the answers you chose, to check it makes sense.
- Look at the three answers you didn't choose. Make sure they don't fit in any of the gaps.

4 Complete the conversation at the doctor's with sentences A–H. There are some extra letters which you do not need.

Doctor: What's the problem?
Sarah: Example: D
Doctor: Yes, there is. How often are you having them?
Sarah: (1) ____
Doctor: That's interesting. What do you usually eat?
Sarah: (2) ____
Doctor: OK. How long does the pain last for?
Sarah: (3) ____
Doctor: I think you should stop eating fried food. Can you do that?
Sarah: (4) ____
Doctor: Yes, I'd like you to eat at least five types of fruit and vegetables every day.
Sarah: (5) ____
Doctor: OK, goodbye Sarah.

A Fried chicken and chips or pasta with cheese sauce.
B Yes, I can. Is there anything else I should do?
C OK, I'll do that, too. Thank you, doctor.
~~**D** I get a lot of bad stomach aches. Is there anything you can do?~~
E About six months ago.
F Two or three hours.
G About three times a week. They usually start after I've eaten dinner.
H Yes, I do. But it isn't a problem.

THINK | RESEARCH | CULTURE | LEARN | ME

Find out about which types of food are the best and worst for your:
a) stomach, **b)** throat, **c)** eyes.

1 **In pairs or groups, answer the questions.**

1 What do you think has happened to the young person in the picture?
2 Do you ever use the internet to get health advice? Why / Why not?

EXAM SKILL

Giving advice

- We use *should* to give advice or say something is a good idea, e.g. *You should drink more water.*
- We use *must* to give strong advice or to say something is necessary, e.g. *You must see a doctor.*
- We use *mustn't* to say something is not allowed, usually because someone else has said so, e.g. *You mustn't eat too much fried food.*
- We use *don't have to* to say something isn't necessary, e.g. *You don't have to go to hospital.*

2 **Choose the correct word or phrase to complete each sentence.**

1 You **should** / **mustn't** drink milk after taking this medicine because it stops the medicine working properly.
2 You **mustn't** / **don't have to** take this medicine in the morning. You can take it at whatever time you prefer.
3 I **shouldn't** / **don't have to** eat unhealthy food. It isn't good for me and it makes me feel ill.
4 We **mustn't** / **should** drink lots of water today because it's a very hot day.
5 If you have a bad pain in your chest, you **must** / **don't have to** see a doctor as soon as you can.

3 **Read the internet forum posts. Then tick the problem below that each one answers.**

LET'S GET HEALTHY
The best forum for healthy bodies

Maxy2020 18:34, Thursday, 10 May

Don't worry. I often get a pain there too. You should have an ice bath after you run. That helps my legs feel better. And you must have a rest after a big race. Good luck!

1 I have back pain when I do exercise. ☐
2 My legs hurt after I do exercise. ☐
3 I'd like to do more exercise. ☐

LET'S GET HEALTHY
The best forum for healthy bodies

Maxy2020 15:28, Sunday, 1 June

I sometimes eat the wrong food, too, JoJO33. You must try to plan what you're going to eat each day. Then, when you're hungry, you should eat a healthy snack. You mustn't eat burgers every day!

1 I'd like to learn to cook. ☐
2 I get stomach ache if I exercise. ☐
3 I want to stop eating unhealthy food. ☐

OPTIMISE YOUR EXAM

An online post

- Read the internet forum post carefully.
- Underline the three questions or problems.
- Plan your answer before you start writing. Make sure you include all the information in the exam task.

4 Look at this writing task and answer the questions.

Read the blog post from Arno95.

LET'S GET HEALTHY
The best blog for healthy bodies

Arno95 15:28, Sunday, 1 June

Hi. I get headaches and I can't sleep after I play video games. Is this bad? I play for three hours every night. Should I stop playing? It's my favourite hobby. What else can I do?

Write a reply to Arno95 and answer the questions.
Write **25–35** words.

1 What is Arno95's problem?

___

2 What three questions does he ask?

___

___

___

5 Plan Plan your reply. Use the chart to help you.

	Detail	Useful language	My notes
First line		*Hello …,* *Hi …,*	
Question 1		*I think …* *I don't think …* *I'm not sure …*	
Question 2		*I think you should …* *You shouldn't/mustn't / don't have to …*	
Question 3		*You should/must …* *What about …*	
Last line		*Good luck!* *Bye!*	

6 Write Write your reply to Arno95 in an appropriate style. Write 25–35 words.

7 Check Before you hand in your internet forum post, complete this checklist.

Checklist

- ◯ I've followed my writing plan.
- ◯ I've started and ended my post in the right way.
- ◯ I've answered the three questions.
- ◯ I've used phrases for giving advice.
- ◯ I've written 25–35 words.
- ◯ I've checked my spelling and grammar.

PROGRESS CHECK UNITS 9–10

GRAMMAR AND VOCABULARY

1 Complete the zero, first and second conditional sentences using the correct form of the verbs in brackets.

1 If we _______________ **(live)** in a warmer country, we could go to the beach every day.
2 When I have a headache, I _______________ **(lie)** on my bed and rest.
3 My mum always _______________ **(give)** me lots to drink if I have a temperature.
4 If my legs were longer, I _______________ **(be)** really good at volleyball.
5 If they get up early tomorrow, they _______________ **(go)** to the mountains.
6 How would you feel if you _______________ **(win)** a race at the Olympics?
7 If I _______________ **(pass)** all my exams, I'll become a dentist.
8 They _______________ **(enjoy)** their holiday in India more if they learn about the culture.
9 She _______________ **(feel)** a lot better if she stopped watching so much TV.
10 If you brush your teeth twice a day, you _______________ **(not need)** to see the dentist so much.

__/10

2 Choose the correct word to complete each sentence.

1 Afonso Mendes works in a hospital **for** / **of** / **to** children in Liverpool.
2 This morning, he is **giving** / **having** / **taking** the temperature of Eddie, a 10-year-old boy.
3 Eddie has a problem **on** / **with** / **for** his ears.
4 He **feels** / **catches** / **takes** pain when he opens his mouth.
5 Afonso spends a long time **tries** / **try** / **trying** to help Eddie feel better.

__/5

3 Read the descriptions. What is the word for each one? The first letter is given.

1 It is between the eyes and the mouth. n__ __ __
2 You listen with these. e__ __ __
3 Food goes here. s__ __ __ __ __ __
4 You walk on these. f__ __ __
5 This joins your head to your body. n__ __ __
6 You hold your pen with this. h__ __ __
7 You move these fast when you run. l__ __ __
8 The person who checks your teeth. d__ __ __ __ __ __
9 It's behind you. b__ __ __
10 You can put this round your knee if you hurt it. b__ __ __ __ __ __

__/10

4 Choose the correct word or phrase to complete each sentence.

1 Mark has been a doctor **since** / **for** ten years.
2 Charlotte hopes **to work** / **working** in a children's hospital when she finishes university.
3 Jack wants to be a nurse, but he hasn't left school **yet** / **already**.
4 It's **just** / **since** stopped raining, so we can go outside now.
5 Mrs Oliver keeps **to go** / **going** to see the doctor with her back pain.
6 I've **already** / **just** been swimming and done my homework this morning.
7 My dad has just stopped **to eat** / **eating** unhealthy food. I'm really happy about it.
8 Tim didn't enjoy **to take** / **taking** the medicine, but he knew it would make him feel better.
9 I haven't been to the doctor **since** / **for** last January.
10 My sister has always been interested in **to learn** / **learning** about animals and birds.

__/10

5 Complete the dialogue between two friends. Choose from the list (A–H) what Fiona says to Jake. Use the letters only once. There are three extra letters you do not need.

Jake: I've just heard some news about Sophie.
Fiona: (1) ____
Jake: She's got a problem with her leg. She's in hospital now.
Fiona: (2) ____
Jake: If it is, I don't think she'll be able to go anywhere.
Fiona: (3) ____
Jake: I don't know what they said. I haven't spoken to her yet.
Fiona: (4) ____
Jake: She fell off her bike.
Fiona: (5) ____
Jake: Good idea. Me too.

A I think I'll go and see her tonight.
B Where did she go?
C I think she'll be fine. It's nothing serious.
D What have the doctors said?
E How did it happen?
F She's going skiing on Saturday. I hope it isn't broken.
G What is it?
H Can I borrow your phone?

__/5

6 Complete the sentences with the words in the box.

clouds	foggy	forest	hill	ice	river	snow	sunny	thunderstorm	wet

1 I prefer to go to the beach when it's warm and ____________ .
2 The Thames is a ____________ that takes water through London to the sea.
3 There is lots of ____________ on the mountains. We can go skiing.
4 Did you hear the ____________ last night? It woke me up.
5 There are lots of ____________ in the sky. I think it's going to rain.
6 You shouldn't drive when there is ____________ on the road. It's dangerous.
7 It is so ____________ today I can't see anything outside.
8 If you walk to the top of that ____________ you can see the whole of the city.
9 You'll need an umbrella because it's very ____________ today.
10 Take your jacket when you go for a walk in the ____________ . It can be cold under the trees.

__/10

Total score __/50

EXAM SKILLS

Tick the statements that are true for you. Review the skills in the unit if you need more help.

I can …	**Unit/page**
☐ skim a text to understand the general idea.	Unit 9 p92
☐ understand a speaker's questions.	Unit 9 p96
☐ talk about the weather.	Unit 9 p98
☐ identify key words.	Unit 9 p99
☐ give advice and instructions.	Unit 9 p100
☐ guess the meaning of new words.	Unit 10 p102
☐ understand when something happened.	Unit 10 p106
☐ talk about health problems.	Unit 10 p108
☐ give short answers to questions.	Unit 10 p109
☐ give advice using *should, must, mustn't* and *don't have to*.	Unit 10 p110

11 The world of work

READING | Right/Wrong/Doesn't say | A magazine article

1 In pairs or as a group, answer the questions.

1 What job did you want to do when you were six years old?

2 What do you want to do now? Why?

EXAM SKILL

Understanding the reason for / purpose of a text

- It is important to understand the reason for / purpose of a text.
- Texts can give descriptions and opinions, or advice and instructions.
- Look carefully at the writer's language to work out what kind of text it is.

2 Read the sentences (1–5). Then match the purposes (a–e) to the sentences.

a) to describe
b) to give a personal message
c) to give advice
d) to give an instruction
e) to give an opinion

1 The museums are open until 5pm, but go early. _____

2 Do not use the machine before cleaning it. _____

3 Good luck in your new job! _____

4 Mr Lee was tall with dark hair and a beard. _____

5 They're the funniest animals I've ever seen. _____

3 Read the sentences in Exercise 2 again and match them to the text types a–e.

a) a story ____ **b)** a tourist guide ____
c) a magazine article ____ **d)** a card ____
e) some instructions ____

4 Read the magazine article on page 115 quickly. Which purpose from the list in Exercise 2 best explains why the article was written?

OPTIMISE YOUR EXAM

Right/Wrong/Doesn't say

- Remember to read the text quickly to understand what it is about.
- Underline the important information in the sentences.
- If you choose 'Doesn't say', make sure there isn't any information in the text.

ALL ABOARD THE CHILDREN'S RAILWAY

1 Are you interested in trains? Have you ever thought about all the jobs people do on a railway? It isn't easy. All the trains have to be clean, the engineers need to check everything is working, someone needs to sell the tickets and take the money, and the trains mustn't be late. The trains must leave and arrive on time and this must match the timetable. And, very importantly – the trains must be safe. Almost everywhere in the world, railway staff are adults. But in Budapest, there is a special railway and nearly everyone who works there is a child.

2 The Gyermekvasút, or Children's Railway, in Hungary, first opened to customers in 1948. And it is still taking passengers on journeys from a few hundred metres to 11 kilometres, through the hills in the west of the city. The train drivers and engineers are adults, but all the other staff, from the ticket sellers to the station managers, are between 10 and 14 years old. All the workers have to wear a smart uniform, and they are all volunteers, which means they don't get paid. Every year, lots of children want to work on the railway, but they don't give jobs to everyone. Anyone who doesn't get good marks at school won't get a job. The children who get jobs have two days off school every month to work on the railway.

3 The Children's Railway isn't a toy or a model railway. It is part of the national railway system of Hungary and an important part of Budapest's transport system. Each year over 300,000 customers use the Railway to get to work, visit friends or just to see how well the children do their jobs!

5 3.18 **Read the magazine article about a children's railway. Are sentences 1–7 'Right' (A) or 'Wrong' (B)? If there is not enough information to answer 'Right' (A) or 'Wrong' (B), choose 'Doesn't say' (C).**

Example: The trains are never late.
A Right **B** Wrong (**C**) Doesn't say

1 Everyone who works at the special railway in Budapest is a child.
A Right **B** Wrong **C** Doesn't say

2 The longest journey you can take on the Children's Railway is 11 kilometres.
A Right **B** Wrong **C** Doesn't say

3 Children sometimes drive the trains.
A Right **B** Wrong **C** Doesn't say

4 Staff can wear their own clothes when they work on the railway.
A Right **B** Wrong **C** Doesn't say

5 The children get a little bit of money each month for working there.
A Right **B** Wrong **C** Doesn't say

6 More than 300,000 people use the Children's Railway each year.
A Right **B** Wrong **C** Doesn't say

7 Some people use the railway to go on holiday.
A Right **B** Wrong **C** Doesn't say

6 Match the highlighted words in the article to a definition (1–8).

1 clothes that all people who work or study at the same organisation wear ____________
2 the opposite of 'dirty' ____________
3 the ways of moving people or things from one place to another ____________
4 a piece of paper or online text that allows you to enter a place, travel on a bus or train, etc. ____________
5 the opposite of 'early' ____________
6 the people who work somewhere ____________
7 a list of times that says when all buses, trains, etc. arrive or leave ____________
8 the opposite of 'dangerous' ____________

THINK | RESEARCH | CULTURE | LEARN | ME

Why do you think young people want to work on the Children's Railway?
Would you like to work there? Why / Why not?

▶ **Workbook Unit 11:** Reading, pages 84–85, exercises 1, 2, 3, 4

11 GRAMMAR 1 | Indefinite pronouns

Grammar in context

Find the sentences in the text on page 115 then do the task below.

1 *… the engineers need to check* ***everything*** *is working, …* (paragraph 1)
2 *…* ***someone*** *needs to sell the tickets and take the money, …* (paragraph 1)
3 *Almost* ***everywhere*** *in the world, railway staff are adults.* (paragraph 1)
4 *… but they don't give jobs to* ***everyone.*** (paragraph 2)
5 ***Anyone*** *who doesn't get good marks at school won't get a job.* (paragraph 2)

Complete the sentences with *-one*, *-thing* or *-where*.

a) We use ___________ to talk about objects and actions.
b) We use ___________ to talk about people.
c) We use ___________ to talk about places.

REMEMBER

- We use indefinite pronouns to talk about people or things without saying exactly who or what they are.
- We use *every-* to talk about all of the things, places or people: ***Everyone*** *in my family likes trains.*
- We use *some-* in positive sentences: *I want* ***something*** *to eat, but I'm not sure what.*
- We use *any-* in negative sentences and questions: *Does* ***anyone*** *in your family like trains? / I don't want* ***anything*** *to eat.*

▶ **See Grammar reference, Unit 11,** page 160

1 Choose the correct word to complete each sentence.

1 We've looked **everywhere** / **everything** but we can't find the car keys.
2 Is there **everything** / **anything** about the job that you don't like?
3 I didn't listen to **everything** / **everywhere** the manager said.
4 They are looking for **anyone** / **someone** who can cook and clean.
5 My mum's new office is **somewhere** / **anywhere** in the city centre.
6 There's **something** / **anything** I need to ask my boss today.

2 Complete the sentences with the words in the box.

anything | anywhere | everyone
everywhere | someone | something

1 ___________ who visits the office must speak to the receptionist.
2 Is there ___________ I can do to help?
3 They have customers ___________ in the country, in all the towns and cities.
4 ___________ in the office is going to be the next manager.
5 I can't find my mobile phone and diary ___________ .
6 There's ___________ I need to do before I leave today, so don't wait for me.

3 Complete the text. Choose the best word (A, B or C) for each gap.

PLAN ahead

News | Home

In all schools and colleges, students (**1**) ____ in the UK, have a chance to do work experience before they finish school. This means they spend one or two weeks working to learn what it's like to have a job. Of course, (**2**) ____ has different experiences, and two weeks isn't long enough to learn (**3**) ____ there is to know about a job. But most students say they definitely learnt (**4**) ____ while they were on work experience, and there was always (**5**) ____ there to help them.

However, there is a school in London that wants to make work experience even better for its students. Lister Community School uses technology called the *Life Skills Pod* to help students choose work experience. Inside the *pod* (a room with a large screen), students choose (**6**) ____ they want to work, for example a factory or a hotel. Then they have to answer questions, which could be about (**7**) ____ that's connected to the place and job they've chosen. Students who use the *Life Skills Pod* usually find it helps them to decide where to work and it also helps to make sure they don't go (**8**) ____ they won't enjoy.

	A	B	C
1	**A** everything	**B** everywhere	**C** everyone
2	**A** everyone	**B** anyone	**C** someone
3	**A** anything	**B** everything	**C** something
4	**A** somewhere	**B** something	**C** someone
5	**A** anyone	**B** someone	**C** everyone
6	**A** something	**B** somewhere	**C** someone
7	**A** somewhere	**B** everyone	**C** anything
8	**A** anywhere	**B** something	**C** everyone

SAY IT RIGHT

Resource centre: Unit 11
/θ/

THINK | RESEARCH | CULTURE | LEARN | ME

How do young people in your country learn about and get ready for the world of work?

Words connected with *work and jobs*

1 3.19 **Match the jobs in the box to the descriptions. Listen and check.**

actor | cleaner | engineer | firefighter | journalist | pilot | police officer | shop assistant

1 someone who writes articles for a newspaper ____________
2 someone who flies planes ____________
3 someone who cleans an office or a home ____________
4 someone who is a member of the police ____________
5 someone who works in a theatre or in films ____________
6 someone who helps you in a shop ____________
7 someone who stops fires ____________
8 someone who designs or builds things such as roads, bridges or machines ____________

2 3.20 **Complete the text with the words in the box. Listen and check.**

career | companies | customer | earn | managers | meetings | social media officer | staff | worker

Thousands of us love using social networking. But have you ever thought of it as a (**1**) ____________? There are jobs for young people in most of the big social media (**2**) ____________. As a new (**3**) ____________, you might be a (**4**) ____________, for example – working with some of the social media (**5**) ____________, working on the website and going to (**6**) ____________. And if you're good at what you do, you'll get the chance to do different jobs and (**7**) ____________ more money. So instead of being a social media (**8**) ____________, why not think about becoming a member of (**9**) ____________?

Words with *-ian* / *-ress* / *-ist* / *-er* / *-r*

3 3.21 **Write the word stems in the correct column to make the names of jobs. Some words can go in more than one column.**

art | chem | clean | dent | drive | engine | explore | farm | football | journal | manage | music | photograph | reception | wait | write

-ian	-ress	-ist	-er	-r

4 **Complete the sentences using the jobs from Exercise 3.**

1 Jo's a ____________. She looks after animals and grows vegetables.
2 Phil's an excellent ____________. He plays the piano, guitar and violin.
3 The ____________ answers the phone and helps visitors when they arrive at the office.
4 The ____________ made a mistake. I didn't order a chicken salad.
5 When I have toothache, I usually visit my ____________.
6 If you are late to work, the ____________ won't be happy.

Words + prepositions

5 3.22 **Complete the sentences. Choose the correct preposition (A, B or C) for each gap. Listen and check.**

1 Alex is the manager ____ a clothes shop in the city centre.
A of **B** on **C** with
2 Charlie hopes to get a diploma ____ music from a college in London.
A from **B** in **C** to
3 Steph is a receptionist and she works ____ a company that makes computers.
A with **B** for **C** to
4 Judy is the singer ____ a local rock band.
A at **B** on **C** in
5 Michael is a writer ____ children's books.
A in **B** to **C** of
6 We have an important meeting today ____ the manager.
A of **B** with **C** to

▶ **Vocabulary reference,** page 168 ▶ **Workbook Unit 11:** Vocabulary, pages 86–87, exercises 1, 2, 3

11 LISTENING | Gap fill

1 Work in pairs and answer the questions.

1 Think about things you like doing in your free time. Could you start a business doing any of these things?
2 If you could start a business, what would you do?

EXAM SKILL

Taking notes

- Don't write down everything you hear, just write the important words.
- Be careful with spelling, especially when the word is spelled out for you.

2 3.23 Listen to the names of people and places being spelled out and write them down.

1 ____________ 4 ____________
2 ____________ 5 ____________
3 ____________

3 3.24 Listen to Ed talking about his business idea and correct the notes.

The concert

When?	1 in *June*
Where?	2 in Dan's large *house*
Number of people:	3 *18 people and six bands played*
Best band:	4 *Jaybeeland*
Earned:	5 *£220*

OPTIMISE YOUR EXAM

Gap fill

- Sometimes you need to write more than one word as the answer.
- Remember to write the exact words you hear. You don't need to change them.

4 3.25 Listen to an interview with a teenager who has started a business. Complete the information.

Zi Yang's Business

Name:	Our Daily *Fruit*
Sells to:	1 local factories ....
Works with:	2 his..
Place:	3 .... , in Bolton
Number of customers:	4
Won:	5 Business Teen of ....

THINK | **RESEARCH** | CULTURE | LEARN | ME

Find out about a young business person from your country who has earned a lot of money. What was their idea? How did they make money?

 ▶ **Workbook Unit 11:** Listening, page 88, exercises 1, 2

GRAMMAR 2 | Relative clauses: *who, which, that*

Grammar in context

Look at these sentences from the audio in the listening lesson and do the task below.

1 *This afternoon I'm talking to someone* ***who*** *studies hard at ...*

2 *So, my dad works in a big factory* ***which*** *is in the city centre.*

3 *And you've just won a competition* ***that*** *was for young business people.*

Choose the correct word.

a) In sentence 1, *who* is about the person ***talking / studying hard***.

b) In sentence 2, *which* is about ***dad / the factory***.

c) In sentence 3, *that* is about ***people / a competition***.

REMEMBER

- Relative clauses give us more information about someone or something we have already mentioned earlier in a sentence.
- We use relative pronouns (*who, which, that*) at the beginning of relative clauses.
- We use the relative pronoun *who* to talk about a person or people, and *that* or *which* to talk about a thing or things: *Henry's the man* ***who*** *works in the new offices in town. Reading is something* ***that/which*** *I like doing in my spare time.*

▶ **See Grammar reference, Unit 11,** page 160

1 Choose the correct words to complete the sentences.

1 It's a question **which** / **who** no-one has the answer to.

2 The secretary **who** / **which** works in our office is away today.

3 Kelly has got a job **that** / **who** she is enjoying a lot.

4 The message **who** / **which** you sent yesterday hasn't arrived yet.

5 I want to get a job in the new office building **who** / **which** has just been built.

6 Is that the mechanic **who** / **which** repaired your car last week?

7 One of the men **which** / **who** works in our London office is coming to visit us today.

8 Where's the shop assistant **which** / **who** works in the food department?

2 Make one sentence from these two sentences using *who, which* or *that* to replace the underlined words.

1 Alex is a manager. He works in my dad's office.
Alex is a manager who works in my dad's office.

2 There is a factory near here. It makes cars.
____

3 Fred is the waiter. He took our order.
____

4 I would like a desk. It is near the window.
____

5 They had a meeting. It was with the new manager.
____

3 Complete the article with *who, which* or *that*.

I'm a firefighter (**1**) __________ works in a large city in the north-east of England. I love my job, but it's really hard work. We work in teams (**2**) ________ are called watches, and there are eight of us in each team. I've known the people (**3**) __________ are in my team for a long time.

The hours (**4**) __________ I work are not the same every day. Today I started work at 8 am and will finish at 6 pm, but next week I will work through the night. Every day, we need to check everything at the fire station is working. It's an important job (**5**) __________ usually takes about an hour.

At any time, we can get a call from someone (**6**) __________ needs help. This morning we went to a hotel (**7**) __________ was on fire. There were over 100 guests there and a lot of them were very afraid. Inside the hotel, there was fire everywhere. It was really hot and very dangerous, but we helped all the people (**8**) __________ were there to get outside safely. It's all in a day's work!

11 SPEAKING | Interview

Flipped classroom

1 **Watch the *Talk2Me* video and answer the questions.**

1 Whose birthday is it soon?
2 Where is the party going to be?
3 How many people can go to the party?

2 **Watch the video again. Match the phrases in the *Phrase expert* box to who said them.**

PHRASE EXPERT

I have (two) brothers and (two) sisters.
I'm an only child, but I have three (cousins).
In my family there are (five) people.
My dad/mum is a (job) …

3 **Work in pairs. Follow the instructions.**

1 Write down as many jobs as you can in one minute.
2 Write down as many family members as you can in one minute.
3 Tell your partner about the jobs people in your family do.
Example: *My uncle is a builder.*

4 3.26 **Listen to a student talking about her family. Are the sentences true (T) or false (F)? Correct the false ones.**

1 She's got two brothers and a sister. **T / F**
2 Her older brother is an actor. **T / F**
3 Matthew works in an office. **T / F**
4 Her dad works in Manchester. **T / F**
5 Her mum is a lawyer. **T / F**

EXAM SKILL

Talking about jobs

- We say *I work for* + company; *I work as a/an* + occupation; *I work in* + place.
- Remember to use the present simple to talk about someone's daily routines, e.g. *She checks her emails in the morning.*
- When we talk about situations that last for a short time, we also use the present continuous, e.g. *He usually works in London, but this week he's working in Bristol.*

5 3.26 **Choose the correct form to complete each sentence. Listen and check.**

1 Marta **works** / **is working** in a theatre. She's worked there for ten years.
2 Matthew often **meets** / **is meeting** his manager in the morning.
3 Anna **cooks** / **is cooking** lunch at the moment.
4 Jane usually works in an office, but this month she **visits** / **'s visiting** customers.

OPTIMISE YOUR EXAM

Interview

- In this part of the test, the examiner may ask you about your family.
- Practise talking about your family and learn how to describe your parents' jobs.
- Answer the questions in full sentences, or use short answers and then add more information.

6 **Work in pairs. Take turns asking and answering the questions. Make notes of your partner's answers.**

1 What jobs do people in your family do?
____

2 Where do they work?
____

3 What job would you like to do when you finish school or university?
____

4 Would you prefer to work in a big or small company? Why?
____

5 What is more important to you – earning lots of money or helping people? Why?
____

 ▶ **Workbook Unit 11:** Speaking, pages 88, exercises 1, 2, 3

1 **Work in pairs. Look at the photo in Exercise 4 and answer the questions.**

1 What job do you think the woman in the photo opposite is doing?

2 What do you think are the good and bad things about doing a job like this? Make a list then discuss with your partner.

EXAM SKILL

Understanding the type of word that is missing

- It is important in the open cloze exercise that you understand what type of word is missing.
- Possible words that might be missing are a noun, a pronoun, a determiner, a preposition, a linking word, a verb or auxiliary verb.

2 **Read the sentences and choose the type of word (a, b or c) that goes in each gap.**

1 Linda ____ like working at weekends.
a) noun **b)** adjective **c)** auxiliary verb

2 My cousin works ____ a company in Paris.
a) preposition **b)** verb **c)** adverb

3 He is the journalist ____ asked me a lot of questions.
a) noun **b)** preposition **c)** pronoun

4 Ethan is looking for a new ____ because he wants to work with animals.
a) verb **b)** noun **c)** adjective

5 I would like ____ job that is exciting and interesting.
a) article **b)** pronoun **c)** preposition

3 **Now choose the correct words below to complete the sentences in Exercise 2.**

1 **a)** is **b)** not **c)** doesn't
2 **a)** to **b)** on **c)** for
3 **a)** which **b)** where **c)** who
4 **a)** work **b)** job **c)** staff
5 **a)** the **b)** some **c)** a

OPTIMISE YOUR EXAM

Open cloze

- Remember to read the whole text first.
- When you write the words, check you have spelled the words correctly.
- Read through each sentence and check the word you have written makes sense.

4 **Complete the article about the explorer. Write one word in each gap.**

The world at my feet

I'm Sara. I'm 38 years old, and I'm **Example:** _an_ explorer. I work **(1)** ____________ an international travel magazine. I write stories and articles about places **(2)** ____________ most people don't visit. I have travelled to some of **(3)** ____________ most beautiful countries in the world. My job is exciting and I love it, **(4)** ____________ it isn't easy.

First of all, I **(5)** ____________ lots of research about different places in the world before I choose where to go. Then I think **(6)** ____________ how I'm going to get there, how I'm going to travel when I'm there, and how safe it is. As an explorer, I often go to places **(7)** ____________ are dangerous and far away from our safe modern world.

Last year, I went to Borneo, **(8)** ____________ large island in south-east Asia. I wanted to visit the people **(9)** ____________ live in the forests and learn about their natural medicine. I was there for six months. It was amazing.

Being an explorer isn't a job for everyone. You don't earn **(10)** ____________ money, you are away from home for a long time, you have to be very fit, brave and also a little bit crazy!

THINK | RESEARCH | CULTURE | LEARN | ME

Which country in the world would you most like to work in? Why?

1 **In pairs or as a group, look at the adverts below. What do you think you have to do in each job? Which job would you prefer to do? Why?**

Dog walkers needed!
We're looking for people who love dogs ... and exercise!
Interested? Call us on 06295 332131

DELIVER NEWSPAPERS IN DUNSTON
Minimum age 14
Two mornings a week
Email p.morton@myemail.com

Babysitter wanted
Tuesday and Friday 5pm – 7pm
£8 per hour
Phone for details: 022 435 8181

EXAM SKILL

Negative phrases and opposites

- In this part of the exam, look for negative phrases that have the same or nearly the same meaning as positive phrases. For example, *We* ***usually finish*** *work* ***early***. and *We* ***don't often finish*** *work* ***late***.
- Learn opposite adjectives and adverbs to help you.

2 **Match the words (a–f) to the words with the opposite meaning (1–6).**

1 difficult	____	a) boring
2 alone	____	b) dangerous
3 safe	____	c) open
4 last	____	d) first
5 interesting	____	e) easy
6 closed	____	f) together

3 **Complete the sentences using words from Exercise 2.**

1 Our staff never work alone. They always work ____________ in teams.
2 The meeting was really boring. No-one said anything ____________ .
3 Please don't leave the office door open. Keep it ____________ so it doesn't get cold inside.
4 It can sometimes be dangerous. It isn't very ____________ .
5 It's a difficult place to work. It isn't ____________ working here.
6 We weren't the first company to do this and we won't be the ____________ .

4 **Read texts 1 and 2 below. Then correct Simon's notes.**

1

Cosmos supermarket
Temporary shop assistants needed
Over 16 years old

Hours: Monday–Saturday 8:00 to 16:00
Pay: £8.50 per hour (16–18-year-olds)
£9.50 per hour (18+ year-olds)
Come in now and be the first to apply!

2

From: Daniela **To**: Simon

Good news! We can apply for holiday jobs as shop assistants now.

The pay is good and it's really close to your house. It may be boring, so it would be better to do it together.

It's your birthday soon then we'll both be 16.

Can you pick up some forms and give one to me at school? We can fill them in together.

3

Simon's notes

Holiday Job

Place:	*Cosmos Supermarket*
Job:	1 *cleaner*
Pay:	2 £ *9.50* per hour
Hours:	3 Monday to Saturday *9:00 - 17:00*
Where:	4 near *my school*
Need to:	5 get *a book*

OPTIMISE YOUR EXAM

Information transfer

- This part of the exam tests reading and writing.
- You may need to write a word or a phrase to complete the notes.
- Check that you spell your answers correctly.

5 Plan

You are going to complete Hannah's notes. Tick the things you need to do before you start writing.

1 Read both texts. ____
2 Find the mistakes in Tim's email. ____
3 Make sure I know exactly what information I need to complete Hannah's notes. ____

JOB INFORMATION DAY

At Queen's Road Library
Friday 16 June

9.30 am–11.00 am
(science and computer companies)

11.00 am–12.30 pm
(banks and finance companies)

No entry without a ticket

Hannah's notes

Job Information Day – 16th June

Where:	1	
Start?	2	
Remember:	3	Need a to get in
Tim wants:	4	about work experience
Later:	5	Lunch at at 1 pm

From: Tim **To:** Hannah

Hi Hannah,

Are you going to the Job Information Day at the library next Friday? Lots of local companies are going to be there.

I can't go, so can you get me some information about work experience with HiCCo, the computer company, please?

Can we meet for lunch at Palace Café at 1 pm?

6 Write

Write the information to complete Hannah's notes. Check your spelling and use of capital letters.

7 Check

Before you hand in your notes, complete this checklist.

Checklist

- ◯ I've carefully read both texts.
- ◯ I've looked carefully for negative phrases and opposites.
- ◯ I've completed all the answers on the form.
- ◯ I've checked my spelling.
- ◯ I've checked my use of capital letters.

Extra writing

8 You're Hannah. You're going to write a short reply to Tim's email in Exercise 5. First answer questions 1–3.

1 What is happening at the library next Friday? ____________________
2 What does Tim want you to get? ____________________
3 Where is Tim suggesting you meet? ____________________

Now write your email in 25–35 words.

12 Home time

READING | Multiple-choice cloze | An online article

1 **In pairs or as a group, answer the questions.**

1 What do you like most about the area where you live?

2 Is there anything in your home that you couldn't live without?

2 **Read the online article on page 125 quickly and find out who Joe Durling lives with.**

____

3 **Read the article on page 125 quickly again and answer the questions.**

1 What is Tinker's Bubble?

____

2 When did Tinker's Bubble start?

____

3 How many people live at Tinker's Bubble?

____

4 What have the houses at Tinker's Bubble **not** got?

____

5 Which rooms are shared?

____

6 Where do most of the people at Tinker's Bubble work?

____

EXAM SKILL

Possessive adjectives

- We use *my, your, his, her, our* and *their* before a noun to talk about the person who owns it, e.g. *His book is on the table.*
- We usually use *them* for people we talked about earlier in the text.

4 **Find these sentences in the article. Write down who or what the underlined words refer to.**

1 Their houses are made from wood … (paragraph 2) ______________

2 The cooking and the washing-up is also shared between them. (paragraph 2) ______________

3 He lives with his mum, Mary. (paragraph 3) ______________

4 And the light from the sun is used to make electricity for their radio … (paragraph 3) ______________

5 Most of the people at Tinker's Bubble work on its small farm. (paragraph 4) ______________

Living with Nature

Have you ever wanted to live somewhere far away from the town or city? Would you like to wake up to the sounds of birds and the wind in the trees?

1 Well, if you could also live without your own bathroom and **Example:** _C_ all your meals outside, then you might be interested in living in a place called Tinker's Bubble.

2 Tinker's Bubble is a small village in the middle of a forest in the south-west of England. It was started in 1994 by a group of people (**1**) ____ didn't want to live in towns or cities anymore. It is home to 10 adults and two young children. Their houses are made from wood. They (**2**) ____ quite small and they haven't got bathrooms. There is a bathroom and kitchen which is shared by everyone who (**3**) ____ there. The cooking and the washing-up is also shared between them.

3 Joe Durling has grown up in Tinker's Bubble. He lives with his mum, Mary. (**4**) ____ house only has one room, but it has everything they need. There isn't a sofa, but there is a table, some shelves, some chairs and beds with lots of blankets. (**5**) ____ it's cold, the house is heated by a fire and stays nice and warm in the winter. And the light from the sun is used to make electricity for their radio and lamp.

4 Most of the people at Tinker's Bubble work on its small farm. They work on the land with horses and they grow (**6**) ____ of fruit and vegetables. Some of the fruit is sold in the local market. The money they earn is shared between everyone.

5 Life in Tinker's Bubble isn't for everyone. (**7**) ____ if you want to live close to nature and don't need to turn on the TV or use a laptop every time you're bored, it might be for you.

OPTIMISE YOUR EXAM

Multiple-choice cloze

- Remember to read the text quickly first and look carefully at the words before and after each gap.
- Answer every question. You won't lose marks for wrong answers.

5 3.27 **Read the article about people who live in a forest. For questions 1–7, choose the best answer (A, B or C) to fill each gap.**

Example:

	A	B	C
	A cooks	**B** cooked	(**C**) cook
1	**A** who	**B** which	**C** they
2	**A** be	**B** are	**C** is
3	**A** lived	**B** lives	**C** live
4	**A** Theirs	**B** Their	**C** Our
5	**A** What	**B** Why	**C** When
6	**A** much	**B** many	**C** lots
7	**A** And	**B** But	**C** For

6 **The underlined words are highlighted in the article above. Find them and choose the correct word or phrase to complete each sentence.**

1 There are **a lot of** / **few** shops and offices in the middle of a city.
2 Wood comes from **trees** / **flowers**.
3 We shared the cake so **everyone** / **no-one** got a piece.
4 We usually put the sofa in the **garden** / **living room**.
5 I keep my **farms** / **books** on shelves.
6 If you're **hot** / **cold**, you can have some blankets.
7 Our living room is heated by **a fire** / **the refrigerator**.
8 Many years ago, people **cooked** / **slept** on a fire.

THINK | **RESEARCH** | CULTURE | LEARN | ME

Find out about a group of people who choose to live somewhere different in your country. Make a poster about them which answers these questions:

- Where do they live and who lives there?
- Where do they get their food?

▶ **Workbook Unit 12:** Reading, pages 92–93, exercises 1, 2, 3, 4

Grammar in context

Look at these three passive sentences from the text on page 125 then answer the question.

Their houses ***are made*** *from wood.* (paragraph 2)

... the house ***is heated*** *by a fire ...* (paragraph 3)

And the light from the sun ***is used*** *to make electricity for their radio ...* (paragraph 3)

Some of the fruit ***is sold*** *in the local market.* (paragraph 4)

Are these sentences right (R) or wrong (W)?

a) We can only use the passive if we know who does the action. ____

b) In passive sentences, we don't have to say who does the action. ____

c) We can use the passive when it is not important who does the action. ____

REMEMBER

- We use the present simple form of the verb *be* and the past participle of the main verb to make the present simple passive.
- We use the passive when the action is more important than who does the action.

▶ **See Grammar reference, Unit 12,** page 161

1 Choose the correct verb form to complete these active and passive sentences.

1 We **grow** / **are grown** lots of flowers in the garden.
2 These carpets **make** / **are made** in Turkey.
3 The rooms **clean** / **are cleaned** by the hotel staff.
4 The children sometimes **stay** / **are stayed** at their grandparents' house.

2 Put these words into the correct order to make present simple passive sentences.

1 is / month / The / cut / grass / every

____

2 made / houses / from / are / wood / The

____

3 every / This / week / is / kitchen / cleaned

____

3 Complete the present simple passive sentences about a house using the correct form of the verbs in brackets.

1 Meals ______________ (**cook**) in the kitchen.
2 The car ______________ (**keep**) in the garage.
3 The front door ______________ (**open**) with a key.
4 The garden ______________ (**not use**) very often in the winter.
5 These fridges ______________ (**make**) in Germany.
6 The heating ______________ (**not turn on**) in the summer.

4 Complete the article using the present simple passive form of the verbs in brackets.

MOVING HOUSES

Have you ever moved house? It can be very tiring. Before the move, all your things (**1**) ______________ (**pack**) into boxes. Next, everything (**2**) ______________ (**carry**) out of your house and put into a big lorry. Then someone drives everything to your new home.

But in some countries, when people say they are going to move house, they mean it. Their whole house (**3**) ______________ (**move**) to a different place!

In the villages in Indonesia, the houses (**4**) ______________ (**make**) from wood. Sometimes there is a lot of rain, which makes it difficult to live in some areas. When this happens, the houses (**5**) ______________ (**pick up**) and moved away from the rainy areas.

In the USA, people usually leave one house to go and live in another one. But sometimes 'old' houses (**6**) ______________ (**take**) to new places. If the people who want to do this are Amish and they don't believe in using modern technology, they might do it by hand. This (**7**) ______________ (**not do**) very often, because it is very difficult and can be dangerous. But it is amazing to watch when it does happen.

THINK | RESEARCH | **CULTURE** | LEARN | ME

Find out how many people in your class have moved house. Ask ...

- where did they move from and to?
- how did they move?
- how long did it take?

Words connected with *houses and homes*

1 3.28 **Write the words on the correct lines. Some words can go on more than one line. Listen and check.**

armchair | bath | bed | blanket
bookcase | chair | cooker | fridge
lamp | pillow | shower | sink
sofa | table | toilet | towel

kitchen: ____________________

living room: ____________________

bathroom: ____________________

bedroom: ____________________

2 **Work in pairs. Decide which is the odd one out in each group (1–5) and why.**

1 bath | sink | sofa | towel ________
2 pillow | lamp | blanket | fridge ________
3 sofa | bookcase | cooker | armchair ________
4 sink | table | chair | bed ________
5 blanket | cooker | fridge | sink ________

Phrasal verbs

3 3.29 **Complete the sentences. Choose the best word (A, B, or C) for each gap. Listen and check.**

1 My dad grew ____ in a small wooden house in a village.
A up **B** out **C** down

2 In the evenings, I often lie ____ on my bed and read a book.
A in **B** down **C** to

3 If you go ____ tonight, take a front door key.
A in **B** out **C** up

4 My bed is really comfortable so I find it very difficult to get ____ in the morning.
A on **B** up **C** in

5 Please tidy the dining room and wash ____ your things in the sink before you leave.
A off **B** in **C** up

6 Can you find ____ how much those new flats cost?
A of **B** for **C** out

4 **Complete the text about Albert Parker with the correct form of some of the phrasal verbs you completed in Exercise 3.**

I **(1)** ______________ in Liverpool in the 1930s. Our family didn't have much money. My mum worked in the kitchen of a restaurant. She had to **(2)** ______________ hundreds of dishes every day. My dad **(3)** ______________ early every morning and sold newspapers. I went to school and studied hard. After doing my homework, I used to **(4)** ______________ on my bed for a rest. I often fell asleep and so never **(5)** ______________ with my friends during the week as I was always tired.

Collocations with verbs

5 3.30 **Match the nouns (a–f) to the verbs (1–6) to make things you do at home. Listen and check.**

1 wash ____ **a)** house
2 tidy ____ **b)** my bed
3 make ____ **c)** the washing-up
4 do ____ **d)** your room
5 have ____ **e)** the floor
6 move ____ **f)** a shower

6 **Complete the sentences with the correct form of the collocations from Exercise 5.**

1 My mum doesn't like leaving dirty dishes around so we always ______________ after dinner.
2 My sister always listens to music in the bathroom when she ______________ in the morning.
3 Can you ______________ before you go out? There are clothes and books everywhere.
4 If you go into the kitchen with dirty shoes on, you'll have to ______________.
5 Next year, we're going to ______________ because we want to live somewhere bigger.
6 Mum sometimes ______________ for me.

▶ Vocabulary reference, page 168 ▶ Workbook Unit 12: Vocabulary, pages 94–95, exercises 1, 2, 3

12 LISTENING | Multiple choice

1 **Work in pairs and answer the question.**

Would you like to live on a boat?
Why / Why not?

EXAM SKILL

Checking your answers

- The speakers may talk about all the possible answers but only one is correct.
- When you listen the second time, check that the possible answers you didn't choose aren't correct.

2 3.31 **Read the question and possible answers. Then listen and choose the best answer. Listen and check.**

Where does Gabriel live now?

a) on a boat **b)** in an apartment **c)** in a house

3 3.31 **Work in pairs and discuss the following question: What does Gabriel say about the other answers in Exercise 2? Listen again and check.**

4 **Read the questions (1–5) in Exercise 5 and match them to the ideas below (a–e).**

a) the room that isn't on the boat ____
b) the thing that Heidi doesn't like on the boat ____
c) the type of people who like living on a boat ____
d) something Heidi really likes on the boat ____
e) how long Heidi has lived on a boat ____

OPTIMISE YOUR EXAM

Multiple choice

- Read the questions and all the possible answers carefully.
- The first time you listen, make a note of the words you hear that are in the possible answers.
- When you listen again, think carefully about what the speakers are saying about those words.

5 3.32 **Listen to Heidi talking to her friend Jed about living on a boat and choose the correct answers.**

1 Heidi has lived on a boat
A for two years.
B for four years.
C all her life.

2 On the boat, there isn't
A a kitchen.
B a bathroom.
C a dining room.

3 Heidi's favourite thing about the boat
A is the fire.
B is her bedroom.
C are the views.

4 She doesn't like
A the heating.
B that there isn't a washing machine.
C where the boat is.

5 She says that life on a boat is for
A people who don't like noise.
B everyone.
C people who want lots of space.

SAY IT RIGHT

Resource centre: Unit 12
/b/ and /v/

▶ **Workbook Unit 12:** Listening, page 96, exercises 1, 2, 3

GRAMMAR 2 | Past simple passive and *by*

Grammar in context

Look at these sentences from the audio in the listening lesson and answer the questions.

*But four years ago, when I was ten, my parents **were given** a boat **by their cousins**. It **was built** about 30 years ago, but it **wasn't finished**, ...*

a) Did Heidi's parents buy the boat? ____

b) Do we know who gave her parents the boat? ____

c) Do we know who built the boat? ____

REMEMBER

- We use the past simple form of the verb *be* and the past participle of the main verb to make the past simple passive.
- When we want to say who did something, we use *by*: *The house was built **by** my grandfather.*

▶ **See Grammar reference, Unit 12,** page 161

1 Underline who did the action in these past simple passive sentences.

1 The pictures were given to me by my grandmother.
2 The man was interviewed for the waiter's job by the manager.
3 The essays were written by the pupils in Year 8.
4 The children were taught English by my mother.
5 The furniture was made by a man from Scotland.
6 The house was moved by a team of 30 men.

2 Look at the sentences in Exercise 1 again and circle the passive verbs.

3 Put these words into the correct order to make past simple passive sentences.

1 bought / my father / The fruit trees / by / were

____

2 driven / a taxi driver / home / were / My parents / by

____

3 made / The / were / by / every / beds / morning / the hotel staff

____

4 designed / a man called Jasper / was / new house / Our / by

____

5 weren't / The English tests / teacher / our / by / marked

____

4 Complete the article about a teenager who built a house, using the correct past or present passive form of the verbs in brackets.

BUILD YOUR OWN HOME

When he was 15, and most of his friends were playing video games, Austin Hay was building his own house!

Austin first became interested in house building at school, but he (1) ____________ (**not give**) the chance to build a house there, so he decided to build one at home. He wanted to build a tree house, but when he (2) ____________ (**tell**) that he could build a house on wheels, that seemed like a better idea. He bought a trailer, which is a metal floor on wheels, for $2,000 and started building.

Austin (3) ____________ (**help**) by his dad and his friends. Lots of pieces of wood and glass (4) ____________ (**give**) to him by friends and family, and they (5) ____________ (**use**) for different parts of the house.

Inside the house there is a kitchen, shower and toilet, a very small living room, and a bed. There is also electricity. A total of about $12,000 (6) ____________ (**spend**) on the house. After the house (7) ____________ (**finish**), Austin became quite famous and a documentary (8) ____________ (**make**) about him by the journalist, Kirsten Dirksen. Quite often, Austin (9) ____________ (**ask**) by local schools to help with their building projects, and in his town the house (10) ____________ (**know**) as the house built by a boy.

5 Look at the highlighted examples of *by* in the text and answer the questions.

1 Who helped Austin build his house?
2 Who gave him some glass and wood?
3 Who made the documentary about him?
4 Who does Austin help with their building projects today?

THINK | RESEARCH | CULTURE | LEARN | **ME**

Design your own small home on wheels. Draw a plan of your home and include different rooms.

Talk2Me
How much is … ?

Flipped classroom

1 Watch the *Talk2Me* video and answer the questions.

1 What is Evie asked to buy?
2 Who was the picture in Jojo's room painted by?
3 Who was the lemon cake made by?

2 Watch the video again. Underline the phrases in the *Phrase expert* box that you hear on the video.

> **PHRASE EXPERT**
> (Adult) tickets are … and (student) tickets are … | How much is (it / a ticket)? | It costs …
> It's free. | There's a free car park.
> There's no charge.

3 Work in pairs and answer the questions.

1 What is your favourite room in your house? Why?
2 Look at the photo. What do you think the person who owns this bedroom is like?

EXAM SKILL

Talking about money

- This part of the exam will often include information about money.
- Practise asking and answering questions about how much things cost: *How much is … ? What does … cost? It's fifteen pounds. A student ticket costs five pounds.*

4 3.33 Look at the question prompts and number them in the order you hear the questions.

- time / open ? ____
- what / see ? ____
- what / buy ? ____
- student ticket ? £ ? ____
- car park ? £ ? ____

5 3.33 Listen to the questions and answers again and correct the mistakes in the advert below.

____
____
____

> **FAMILY HOME SHOW**
> Saturday and Sunday 9am – 4pm
> More than 50 room designs
> Furniture and decoration for sale
> Large free car park
> Tickets: Adults £10.00
> Students £5.00

OPTIMISE YOUR EXAM

Collaborative task

- You can ask the questions in any order. Sometimes it is useful to ask simple questions first, to give you time to think of the vocabulary or grammar to ask other questions.
- Before you finish, check you have asked all five questions.

6 3.34 Listen to five speakers. Complete the sentences with one word in each gap.

1 I'm ____________ , I didn't understand. Can you say that again, please?
2 Was ____________ 429 or 492?
3 I'm sorry, I didn't hear that. Can you speak a bit ____________ , please?
4 Can you ____________ that, please?
5 Sorry, did you ____________ 16 or 60?

7 In pairs (Student A and Student B), do the exam task.

Student A: turn to page 138 and look at the information about a furniture shop. Answer Student B's questions about it.
Student B: look at the question prompts on page 141. Ask Student A your questions.
Student B: turn to page 141 and look at the information about the Flat for Sale. Answer Student A's questions about it.
Student A: look at the question prompts on page 138. Ask Student B your questions.

 ▶ **Workbook Unit 12:** Speaking, pages 96–97, exercises 1, 2, 3

LANGUAGE IN USE | Multiple-choice sentences

1 **Work in pairs. Tell your partner about all the different homes you know, e.g. your house, your grandparents' house, your friend's house, etc.**

EXAM SKILL

Learning vocabulary

- In this part of the test you read and identify appropriate vocabulary.
- It is important to know the difference in meaning and use between similar words.
- Learn collocations and phrases rather than individual words, e.g. verb + infinitive / *-ing* form; verb + noun; adjective + noun; adjective + preposition.

2 **Choose the correct words to complete the sentences.**

1 Does Ellie **want** / **like** to go to France on holiday next year?
2 I think I **made** / **did** a mistake when I painted the kitchen purple.
3 It's nice and warm inside the house but there's a **strong** / **large** wind outside.
4 Harry doesn't **want** / **mind** living in a small village.
5 Mum hasn't **made** / **done** the shopping yet.
6 Are you **worried** / **interested** in moving to a new place and starting a new school?

3 **Complete the sentences with the words in the box. There are two extra words you do not need.**

arrived | came | corner | good
opposite | tired | went

1 Moving house has been really ____________ for us. We're much happier in our new home.
2 They are very interested in old museums, so they ____________ to visit Italy.
3 My grandad was ____________ of living in the city centre, so he moved to a village.
4 They were hungry and ready for dinner when they ____________ at the hotel.
5 They bought a new house on the ____________ of my street.

OPTIMISE YOUR EXAM

Multiple-choice sentences

- There are five sentences about the same subject.
- Read each sentence carefully and look at the words before and after the gap.
- If you don't know the answer, read the sentence with each possible answer in it and choose the one that sounds best.

4 **Read the sentences about Emily's home. For questions 1–5, choose the best answer (A, B or C) to fill each gap.**

Example:
I __*B*__ up in a small house by a river in the south of England.
A lived (**B**) grew **C** came

1 Last year, my family ____ house and now we live near the Scottish mountains.
A changed **B** left **C** moved
2 My dad is really ____ in climbing, which is one reason why we came here.
A interested **B** keen **C** good
3 There are four bedrooms, a large garden and the house has a ____ of the mountains.
A look **B** view **C** picture
4 I love my new bedroom and I ____ it every Saturday so it always looks nice.
A move **B** wash **C** tidy
5 In the kitchen, there's a large table, a ____ for washing-up and a very old cooker.
A towel **B** sink **C** curtain

THINK | RESEARCH | CULTURE | **LEARN** | ME

Writing your own sentences is a great way to learn vocabulary. Try writing six sentences describing your own house, using some of the words and ideas from this lesson.

1 **In pairs or as a group, look at the photo and answer the questions.**

1 Would you like to live in a place like this?
2 What would be the good and bad things about living in this village?
3 Would you prefer to live in a village or a city? Why?

EXAM SKILL

Using adjectives

- When you write a postcard, you often need to describe a feeling, place or an event.
- Use adjectives ending in *-ed* to describe how you feel, and adjectives ending in *-ing* to describe what something is like.

2 **Write the adjectives in the correct list.**

attractive	awful	boring	comfortable
exciting	horrible	popular	terrible

1 Positive adjectives: ____________ , ____________ , ____________ , ____________
2 Negative adjectives: ____________ , ____________ , ____________ , ____________

3 **Choose the correct adjective to complete each sentence.**

1 It was an **amazed** / **amazing** day. I won't forget it for a long time.
2 I was really **bored** / **boring** because I had nothing to do at home all day.
3 Joe is very **interested** / **interesting** in old furniture.
4 There are lots of **excited** / **exciting** things to do near my house in the holidays.
5 They were **tired** / **tiring** after cleaning the house.

4 **Read the postcard from George. What three questions does he ask? Write them below.**

Post Card

Hi Ella,
Here's a postcard of my village. Please send me a postcard of your town or village. Where is your house? What can you see from your bedroom window? What do you like about your home?
George

____
____
____

5 **Work in pairs. Read the two replies to George, below. Which reply is better? Why?**

A

Post Card

Hi George,
I live in a small house with two bedrooms. I can see a park and café from my window. I like it here. There are lots of things to do.
Best wishes,
Ella

B

Post Card

Hi George,
My apartment is in a quiet road near the centre. I can see a beautiful park from my window.
I love our living room because it's large and the view is amazing.
Best wishes,
Ella

6 **Read the exam task and underline the three questions Frazer asks.**

Read the postcard from your English friend, Frazer.

Post Card

Hi,
Here's a postcard of Newcastle. We live in an apartment. It's quite noisy. Please send me a postcard of your city. Where do you live? How long have you lived there? What's near your home?
Frazer

Write a postcard to Frazer and answer the questions.
Write **25–35** words.

OPTIMISE YOUR EXAM

A postcard

- The three questions in your friend's postcard will help you plan your answer.
- You also need to add detail and description to make your writing more interesting.
- Remember to check the spelling and punctuation in your answer.

7 **Plan** **Plan your postcard. Use the chart to help you.**

	Detail	Useful language	My notes and answers
First line		*Hello …,* *Hi …,* *Dear …,*	
Question 1		*We live …* *It's …*	
Question 2		*I've lived here for/since …*	
Question 3		*There's / There are …* *At the end of the road, …* *About 50 metres away, …*	
Last line		*See you soon,* *Love,* *Best wishes,*	

8 **Write** **Write your postcard to Frazer in an appropriate style. Write 25–35 words.**

9 **Check** **Before you hand in your postcard, complete this checklist.**

Checklist

- ◯ I've followed my writing plan.
- ◯ I've started and ended my postcard in the right way.
- ◯ I've answered the three questions.
- ◯ I've used a good range of adjectives.
- ◯ I've written 25–35 words.
- ◯ I've checked my spelling, punctuation and grammar.

▶ **Writing reference,** page 169 ▶ **Workbook Unit 12:** Writing, page 98, exercises 1, 2, 3, 4, 5 and Progress check 12, page 99

PROGRESS CHECK # UNITS 11–12

GRAMMAR AND VOCABULARY

1 Write the job each person does.

1 I fly planes all over the world. I'm a ______________ .
2 I write articles for a local newspaper. I'm a ______________ .
3 I grow vegetables and keep cows and pigs. I'm a ______________ .
4 I serve customers in a shop. I'm a ______________ .
5 I repair engines and machines. I'm an ______________ .
6 I look after people's teeth. I'm a ______________ .
7 I help when there is a fire. I'm a ______________ .
8 I serve people meals in a restaurant. I'm a ______________ .
9 I clean the floors in an office. I'm a ______________ .
10 I talk to people when they come into the office, and answer the phone. I'm a ______________ .

__/10

2 Read the descriptions. What is the word for each one? The first letter is given.

1 We can bake cakes in this. c__ __ __ __ __
2 We keep food and drink cold in this. f__ __ __ __ __
3 We do the washing-up in this. s__ __ __
4 We can use this to read in the dark. l__ __ __
5 We put our heads on this in bed. p__ __ __ __ __
6 We eat dinner sitting around it. t__ __ __ __
7 We sit and relax on this. a__ __ __ __ __ __ __ __
8 We can fill this with water and sit in it. b__ __ __
9 We keep dishes, cups and food in this. c__ __ __ __ __ __ __ __
10 We can put this on our bed to keep warm. b__ __ __ __ __ __

__/10

3 Choose the correct word to fill each gap.

I'm the manager (**1**) __________ a famous pop group. I travel (**2**) __________ with them. It's a job (**3**) __________ I've done for years. The main thing I do is to make sure that they have (**4**) __________ they need. I work with boys (**5**) __________ are great singers. But they don't enjoy talking on TV, so I talk for them. When (**6**) __________ goes wrong, I have to help. Once there wasn't (**7**) __________ to eat after a concert. So I had to cook dinner for (**8**) __________ . It's all in a day's work!

	A	B	C
1	**A** of	**B** in	**C** to
2	**A** somewhere	**B** everything	**C** everywhere
3	**A** what	**B** where	**C** which
4	**A** something	**B** everything	**C** everywhere
5	**A** who	**B** that	**C** where
6	**A** everything	**B** something	**C** someone
7	**A** anything	**B** everything	**C** something
8	**A** someone	**B** anyone	**C** everyone

__/8

4 **Complete the sentences using the correct passive or active form of the verbs in brackets.**

1 The swimming pool ______________ (**close**) by the manager last week.
2 Last year, Camilla ______________ (**give**) a job in a large company that makes computers.
3 My parents ______________ (**buy**) the house when they first moved to England.
4 Teenagers ______________ (**not teach**) enough about healthy eating.
5 The engineer ______________ (**not repair**) the fridge very well and it stopped working again.
6 The woman's bag ______________ (**take**) while she was talking to the receptionist.
7 The workers ______________ (**not tell**) that the factory was closed.
8 Everyone ______________ (**move**) their picnic tables and chairs closer to the river.
9 Uniforms ______________ (**wear**) by all the staff while they are working.
10 Everyone ______________ (**pay**) more money after the company did very well.
11 He ______________ (**write**) the book while living in France for a year.
12 Most of the clothes we buy ______________ (**make**) in Asia.

__/12

5 **Complete the blog post about Domenico's home with one word in each gap.**

I live in a small town (**1**) ___________ is about 20 km from Naples. We have a large house and a garden (**2**) ___________ is full of flowers. I share a bedroom with my brother, (**3**) ___________ is two years older than me. My parents work in Naples. My dad is the manager (**4**) ___________ a shoe shop and my mum works (**5**) ___________ a company that sells holiday apartments. My grandparents help around the house. My grandmother is always cooking and my grandfather does the gardening. My brother and I have (**6**) ___________ make our beds each morning and wash (**7**) ___________ after dinner every night.

I grew up (**8**) ___________ the town. I often go out to a café (**9**) ___________ my two best friends. My favourite café has the best ice cream. It (**10**) ___________ made with fresh fruit and tastes amazing!

__/10

Total score __/50

EXAM SKILLS

Tick the statements that true for you. Review the skills in the unit if you need more help.

I can …	**Unit/page**
☐ understand the reason for / purpose of a text.	Unit 11 p114
☐ take notes when I listen.	Unit 11 p118
☐ talk about jobs people do.	Unit 11 p120
☐ understand the type of word that is missing from a text.	Unit 11 p121
☐ understand negative phrases and opposites.	Unit 11 p122
☐ understand who owns something from words like *my*, *your*, etc.	Unit 12 p124
☐ check my answers.	Unit 12 p128
☐ check that I understand what I need to know.	Unit 12 p130
☐ use the correct adjectives and prepositions.	Unit 12 p131
☐ use different adjectives in my writing.	Unit 12 p132

PROMPT CARDS

Unit 2 page 20

Student A – your answers

Answer Student B's questions using the information below.

Hip hop, rock and dance music

Weekly on Fridays @ 7–10 pm

Brilliant music, friendly people

Over 14s only

Student tickets €5

Free wi-fi

Unit 4 page 42

Student A – your answers

Answer Student B's questions using the information below.

TRAVEL PHOTOGRAPHY
EXHIBITION

Photographs by teenage travellers

14 Market Street

Come and meet these young adventurers

5 pm–10 pm Friday–Sunday

£3 entry

Visit our website for more information

Unit 2 page 20

Student A – your questions

Ask Student B your questions using the prompts below.

FILM FESTIVAL

- what / see?
- open / Mondays?
- student ticket? £?
- buy / drink?
- telephone number?

Unit 4 page 42

Student A – your questions

Ask Student B your questions using the prompts below.

MOTOR SHOW

- what / see?
- open / weekend?
- student ticket? £?
- buy / cars?
- buy / food?

Unit 6 page 64

Student A – your answers

Answer Student B's questions using the information below.

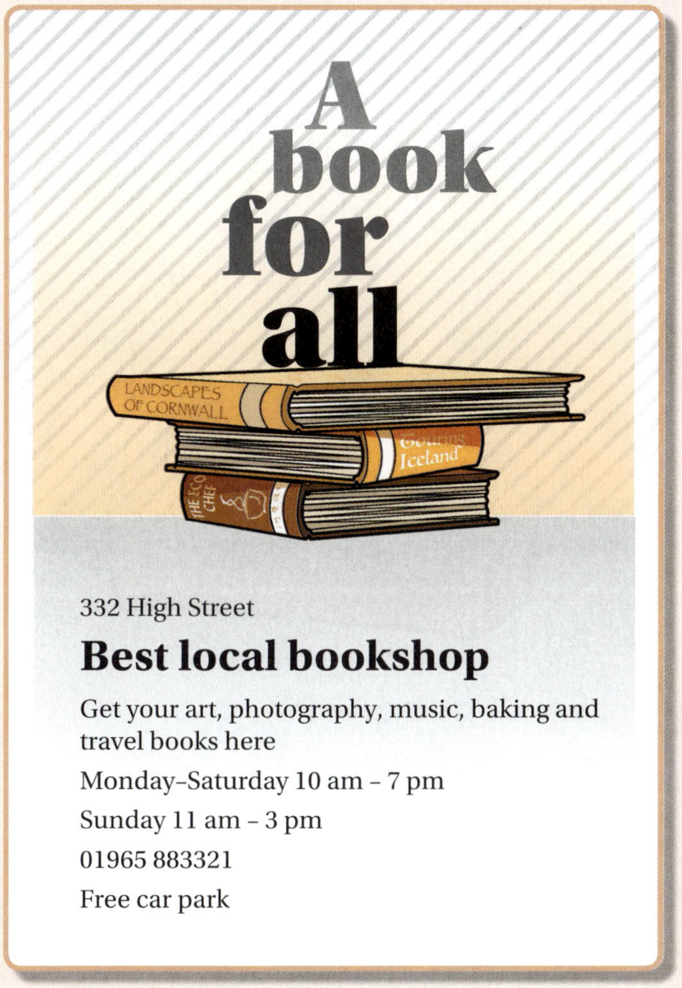

Unit 8 page 86

Student A – your answers

Answer Student B's questions using the information below.

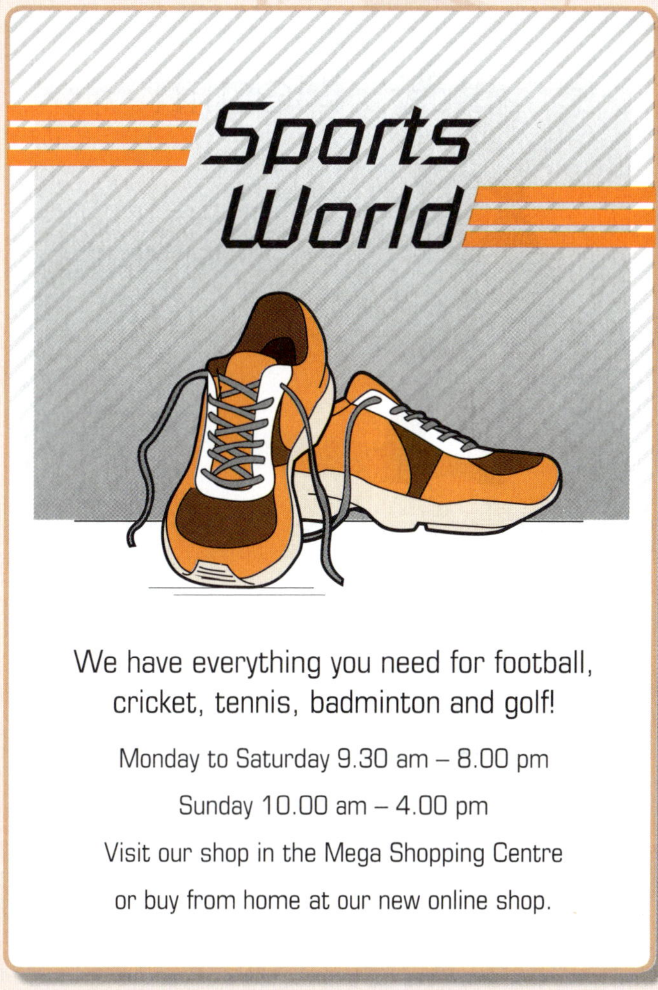

Unit 6 page 64

Student A – your questions

Ask Student B your questions using the prompts below.

FASHION STORE

- what / buy?
- address?
- closed / Mondays?
- cheap / expensive?
- telephone number?

Unit 8 page 86

Student A – your questions

Ask Student B your questions using the prompts below.

CRICKET LESSONS

- when?
- for children?
- price?
- need a bat?
- telephone number?

PROMPT CARDS

Unit 10 page 108

Student A – your questions

Answer Student B's questions using the information below.

Health and wellbeing lessons

Learn how to keep healthy through sensible eating and regular exercise

Classes

14–16 year olds Mondays and Thursdays 7–8 pm

16+ Mondays and Thursdays 8–9 pm

£4 per class

Contact Mrs Jones on 01856 449720

Unit 12 page 130

Student A – your answers

Answer Student B's questions using the information below.

BEAUTIFUL FURNITURE

Small but special

Beautiful selection of tables, chairs and sofas to see in shop

Tel: 0203 667 5434

Monday – Sunday 10.00 am – 6.00 pm

Unit 10 page 108

Student A – your answers

Ask Student B your questions using the prompts below.

FOOD SHOP

- address?
- what / sell?
- big / small?
- closed / Sundays?
- telephone number?

Unit 12 page 130

Student A – your questions

Ask Student B your questions using the prompts below.

FOR SALE

- what / sale?
- big / small?
- have / dining room?
- when / see?
- email?

Unit 2 page 20

Student B – your questions

Ask Student A your questions using the prompts below.

DISCO

- what / music?
- time / start?
- on / Saturdays?
- student ticket? £?
- wi-fi?

Unit 4 page 42

Student B – your questions

Ask Student A your questions using the prompts below.

PHOTOGRAPHY EXHIBITION

- what / see?
- address?
- open / Wednesdays?
- ticket? £?
- more information?

Unit 2 page 20

Student B – your answers

Answer Student A's questions using the information below.

Student
Film
Festival

Come and watch amazing short films on a big screen before the makers become famous!

Saturday & Sunday 1–6 pm

Tickets: €10 / €8 for students

Café open for snacks and drinks between films

Tel: 881390

Unit 4 page 42

Student B – your answers

Answer Student A's questions using the information below.

ARDEN
MOTOR SHOW

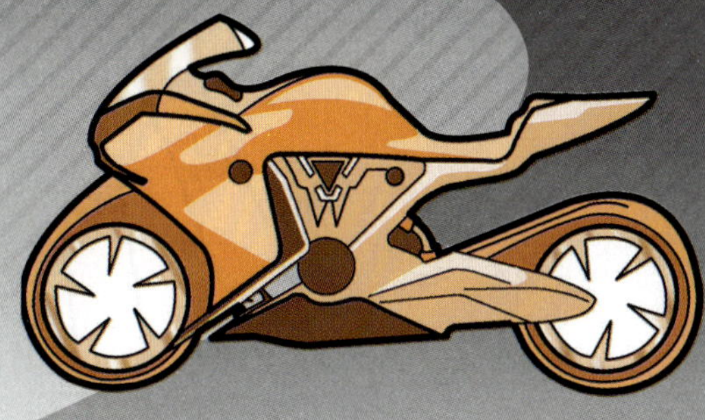

Come and see these incredible new cars and motorbikes

Saturday & Sunday 8 am–10 pm

Tickets: €30 adults / €20 for students

Cars and motorbikes not for sale

Snacks and drinks available all day

PROMPT CARDS

Unit 6 page 64

Student B – your questions

Ask Student A your questions using the prompts below.

BOOK SHOP

- address?
- sell / music books?
- closed / Sundays?
- telephone number?
- car park?

Unit 8 page 86

Student B – your questions

Ask Student A your questions using the pro mpts below.

SPORTS SHOP

- name?
- where?
- open Sunday evening?
- sell / tennis rackets?
- buy online?

Unit 6 page 64

Student B – your answers

Answer Student A's questions using the information below.

16 North Bridge Street

Buy the latest fashions at the lowest prices

New shop opens 10 am–6 pm, Monday–Saturday

Closed Sundays

021 789 6533

Unit 8 page 86

Student B – your answers

Answer Student A's questions using the information below

Cricket lessons

Learn to play cricket this summer

Lessons for 8–18 years old

Only £6 a lesson

We have everything you need to start playing!

Every Wednesday evening 6–8 pm

Call 0723 8971 for more information.

Unit 10 page 108

Student B – your questions

Ask Student A your questions using the prompts below.

HEALTH AND WELLBEING

- what / learn?
- when / classes for 14 year olds?
- class / £?
- telephone number?
- who / contact?

Unit 12 page 130

Student B – your questions

Ask Student A your questions using the prompts below.

FURNITURE SHOP

- what / see?
- big or small?
- bookshelves?
- telephone number?
- closed / Sundays?

Unit 10 page 108

Student B – your answers

Answer Student A's questions using the information below.

54 Green Street

For all your health food needs

Largest health food shop in the area

Monday – Saturday 8.00 am – 5.00 pm

Sunday 11.00 am – 4.00 pm

Tel: 0102 4567882

Unit 12 page 130

Student B – your answers

Answer Student A's questions using the information below.

Large flat with amazing views

Lounge, dining room, kitchen, 2 bedrooms and 2 bathrooms

Come to see – Thursday 2.00 – 4.00 pm

Email: flatforsale@sellme.com

OPTIMISE YOUR EXAMS | Reading and Writing

OPTIMISE

In **Part 1**, you read five sentences and match them to eight signs and notices.

Read the example and cross out the notice it matches, so you don't choose it again.

Underline the important words in the sentences and then find words in the notices that mean the same.

To help you do this, think where you may see the notices and who they are from.

1 Read sentences 1–5 and underline the important words. Match the sentences to the signs and notices on page 5 of the Student's Book.

1 This place is closed this afternoon. ____
2 You can try this activity tomorrow morning. ____
3 You can't go through this door. ____
4 This place is never closed. ____
5 You can't use your mobile phone here. ____

OPTIMISE

In **Part 2**, you read five sentences about the same topic and choose the correct word for the gap in each sentence. There is an example to help you.

Look carefully at the words before and after the gap.

Read the sentences with all three answers so you can choose the correct one.

This part of the exam often tests topic vocabulary and collocations.

2 Read the sentences, looking carefully at the words before and after each gap. Choose the correct word to complete each sentence. Then look at Exercise 4 on page 131 to check your answers.

1 Last year, my family moved house and now we ____________ near the Scottish mountains.
A lived **B** living **C** live

2 My dad is really interested ____________ climbing, which is one reason why we came here.
A in **B** at **C** from

3 There ____________ four bedrooms, a large garden and the house has a view of the mountains.
A have **B** are **C** got

4 I love my new bedroom and I tidy it ____________ Saturday so it always looks nice.
A once **B** every **C** often

5 In the kitchen, ____________ a large table, a sink for washing-up and a very old cooker.
A it's **B** they're **C** there's

OPTIMISE

In the first part of **Part 3**, you read five short conversations and choose the best response (A, B or C) for each one. There is an example to help you.

First think of your own ideas for the second speaker's responses. Then read the answer options.

If an option is like yours, it may be the correct answer.

3 Read questions 1–5 and write what you think the answers might be. Then look at Exercise 5 on page 55 to see how similar your answers are.

1 What are you downloading?
____
2 Which website is it on?
____
3 Did you talk to them on the phone?
____
4 Please could you answer the phone?
____
5 Who called just now?
____

OPTIMISE

In the second part of **Part 3**, you read a longer conversation between two speakers, with five of the second speaker's responses missing. You choose the missing answers from eight options.

Read the example and cross out the option it uses, so you don't choose it again.

Read the conversation and all the options carefully. Think about the function of each sentence (e.g. Is it inviting someone to go somewhere?) before you choose the best answer.

4 Read the conversation again in Exercise 4 on page 65 and cover the answers (A–H) with a piece of paper. Complete the conversation. Then look to see how similar your answers are to the ones in your Student's Book.

OPTIMISE

In **Part 4**, you read a text and answer seven questions. The questions may be multiple-choice comprehension questions or you may be asked if the sentences are right or wrong, or if it doesn't say in the text. There is an example to help you.

Read the text quickly then read the questions. The questions are in the same order as the text.

Remember that 'Wrong' means that the sentence isn't true according to the information in the text. Choose 'Doesn't say' when there isn't enough information in the text to choose 'Right' or 'Wrong'.

5 **Read the text about a teenage snowboarder. Are sentences 1–7 'Right' (A) or 'Wrong' (B)? If there is not enough information to answer 'Right' (A) or 'Wrong' (B), choose 'Doesn't say' (C).**

Chloe Kim is a 16-year-old snowboarder who lives in California, USA. She has already won three gold medals at the X-Games and she dreams of winning gold at the Winter Olympics in Pyeongchang in 2018. She was too young to take part in the 2014 games in Sochi, but she is as good as some Olympic gold winners.

Her parents Jong and Boran came from Korea, but Chloe is American. Her dad first took her snowboarding when she was four. At first, she wasn't keen on doing it, but she soon became very good at it. She can now do the most difficult jumps and has taken part in competitions since she was six years old.

She speaks French as well as English because she lived with her aunt in Switzerland for two years when she was at primary school. Her parents visited her in the school breaks and took her snowboarding in France.

Chloe is well known in the USA, both for her snowboarding talent and also for her hair. She often changes her hair colour, and she likes to colour it pink for competitions.

1 Chloe is a teenage snowboarder.
A Right **B** Wrong **C** Doesn't say

2 She has never won a silver medal.
A Right **B** Wrong **C** Doesn't say

3 She won a gold medal at the 2014 Olympics.
A Right **B** Wrong **C** Doesn't say

4 She is Korean.
A Right **B** Wrong **C** Doesn't say

5 She learnt to snowboard when she was four.
A Right **B** Wrong **C** Doesn't say

6 She speaks two languages.
A Right **B** Wrong **C** Doesn't say

7 She wants to become a hairdresser.
A Right **B** Wrong **C** Doesn't say

OPTIMISE

In **Part 5**, you read a short text with eight gaps. You choose the correct word (A, B or C) for each gap. There is an example to help you.

As you read the text, ask yourself what it is about. This part of the exam tests you on grammar.

After choosing your answers, read the whole sentence with the two options you didn't choose, to check they don't fit.

6 **Read the article about a famous stone circle. For questions 1–8, choose the best answer (A, B or C) to fill each gap.**

A famous stone circle

Stonehenge is _B_ the south of England. It is the **(1)** ____ famous stone circle in Europe. Historians think **(2)** ____ is between five thousand and three-and-a-half thousand years old. They think that people used machines **(3)** ____ move the stones.

No-one **(4)** ____ 100% sure why Stone Age people built Stonehenge. Some people think it was a type of clock **(5)** ____ people used to tell the longest and shortest days of the year. The shortest day is called **(6)** ____ winter solstice and it takes place on the 21st of December each year.

Some of the stones came **(7)** ____ Wales. Historians think that it **(8)** ____ 31 million man hours to build the stone circle we can see today!

Example:

	A	B	C
	A on	**B** in	**C** at
1	**A** much	**B** many	**C** most
2	**A** it	**B** they	**C** he
3	**A** for	**B** to	**C** off
4	**A** is	**B** isn't	**C** aren't
5	**A** who	**B** what	**C** which
6	**A** a	**B** some	**C** the
7	**A** from	**B** of	**C** to
8	**A** take	**B** taking	**C** took

OPTIMISE

In **Part 6**, you have to produce five words about a topic and spell them correctly. There is an example to help you.

The first letter and the number of letters in the words are given.

Check your spelling carefully.

7 **Read the descriptions of some words about jobs and work. Complete the words. Then ask your teacher to check your answers.**

This person uses a camera to do their job. **p***hotographer*

1 This job involves looking after animals and growing food.
f __ __ __ __ __

2 A person who writes for a newspaper or magazine.
j __ __ __ __ __ __ __ __ __

3 All the people who work for a company are called this.
s __ __ __ __

4 If you buy something in a shop or online, you are this.
c __ __ __ __ __ __ __

5 In hotels and offices, this is the person who welcomes you.
r __ __ __ __ __ __ __ __ __ __ __

OPTIMISE

In **Part 7**, you complete a text that has ten gaps by writing one word in each gap. There is an example to help you.

First read the whole text to make sure you understand it. Complete the gaps that you find easy first, then look again at the more difficult ones.

Check your spelling and read everything to check that the words you have written make sense.

8 **Complete the article about a TV cookery programme with one word in each gap.**

Junior Masterchef is **Example:** *a* TV cookery competition for children. You can watch it **(1)** ________ the children's channel of the BBC, CBBC. The competition is **(2)** ________ nine- to twelve-year-olds. In the UK, the programme was on television for five years **(3)** ________ the 1990s and then it started again in 2010.

(4) ________ were over 2,000 children who applied to be in the first competition. From these, 30 children **(5)** ________ successful and competed in the 'heats', **(6)** ________ were the first stage of the competition. The winner of each heat went to the quarter-final, then **(7)** ________ best two cooks from each quarter-final went to the semi-final. In the semi-final, the children **(8)** ________ to cook food for people from a TV programme and then for a famous boy band, JLS.

In the final, four children took **(9)** ________ in the competition. They made a meal for the presenters and then the presenters **(10)** ________ the winner – Georgia Bradford.

OPTIMISE

In **Part 8**, you use information from two short texts to complete five missing pieces of information in some notes. There is an example to help you.

Remember to read both texts carefully.

You may need to write a word or a phrase to complete the notes. Check that you spell your answers correctly.

9 **Read the texts A and B, below. Underline the times in text A. Match the words or phrases in text B that say the same thing.**

A

LEARN TO DANCE SALSA

Join us to learn salsa in these free weekly classes at Green's Leisure Centre

Thursday 3:45–5.45 pm
Room 16B

Extra beginners' classes
Saturday 2–4 pm
Room 24

B

To: Sam,

Would you like to come along to salsa classes with me?

We haven't done it before, so let's try the beginners' classes.

Shall we meet at 1.30 so we can travel together?

We don't have to pay for the classes, so we don't need any money, but I'm going to take something to drink.

Gina

10 **Read Sam's notes below. Then look at the texts in Exercise 9 again and write the answers.**

SAM'S NOTES – SALSA CLASSES

Place:	*Green's Leisure Centre*
Class:	1
Day:	2
Meeting time:	3
Room number:	4
Take:	5

OPTIMISE

In **Part 9**, you read a short text from a friend (email, note or postcard) then write a reply (25–35 words).

Underline the important words and think of different ways to say the same things.

Use the questions in your friend's text to plan your answer.

11 **Read the exam task below. How many questions does Tom ask? Underline the important word(s) in each one.**

Read the note from your brother, Tom.

Post C

Mum said you want to go the cinema tonight.
What film do you want to watch?
What time is it on?
Can my friend come?
Tom

Write a note to Tom. Answer his questions.

Write **25–35** words

OPTIMISE YOUR EXAMS | Listening

1 3.35 **Listen to the five conversations. There is one question for each conversation. For each conversation, choose the correct answer (A, B or C).**

1 Where is Kara's bag?

A ☐

B ☐

C ☐

2 What time does the film start?

A ☐

B ☐

C ☐

3 Where are Kevin and his sister going at the weekend?

A ☐

B ☐

C ☐

4 What is Dad going to buy Mum for her birthday?

A ☐

B ☐

C ☐

5 What's the weather going to be like tomorrow?

A ☐

B ☐

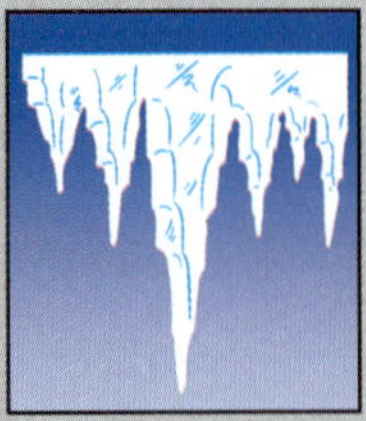
C ☐

OPTIMISE

In **Part 1**, you listen to five short conversations. Each one has a question and you choose the correct picture (A, B or C) to answer the question. There is an example to help you.

Read the questions first and underline the important words. When you listen to the audio, listen for words with a similar meaning to your underlined words.

OPTIMISE

In **Part 2**, you listen to a conversation and match two lists of items, using key information from the audio. There is an example to help you.

Read the example and cross out the answer it matches, so you don't choose it again.

Cross out other answers as you hear them.

Check that the answers you didn't use are not needed.

Focus on meaning. Just hearing one of the answer words on the audio doesn't mean it is a correct answer.

2 3.36 **Listen to Fiona talking about what she did on her holiday last week. For each day, choose a place she went to (A–H). There are three extra letters which you do not need to use.**

1 Monday ☐
2 Tuesday ☐
3 Thursday ☐
4 Friday ☐
5 Saturday ☐

A the beach
B the park
C a farm
D the mountains
E the river
F a waterfall
G the forest
H the cinema

OPTIMISE

In **Part 3**, you listen to a conversation and answer five multiple-choice (A, B or C) questions. There is an example to help you.

Make notes of words in the possible answers the first time you listen.

Check the answer options you didn't choose.

3 **Read the sentences and options A–C in Exercise 4. Underline the important words. Write short notes predicting what you will hear.**

4 3.37 **Listen to Matt talking to his friend Joe about going to a concert and choose the correct answers.**

1 Matt and Joe are going to the concert with
A Tim. ☐
B Peter. ☐
C Jill. ☐

2 What time does the concert start?
A 6.30 ☐
B 7.15 ☐
C 7.30 ☐

3 The Birds' latest song is
A *Time After Time*. ☐
B *Time to Dance*. ☐
C *Time to Sing*. ☐

4 Matt and Joe are going to the concert
A by bus. ☐
B by train. ☐
C by car. ☐

5 How much did the tickets cost each?
A £15 ☐
B £25 ☐
C £45 ☐

OPTIMISE

In **Parts 4 and 5**, you identify specific information (e.g. days, dates, numbers) and use the information to complete notes. There is an example in each part to help you.

Read the questions and think about what sort of words you might hear. Sometimes the answers are more than one word.

Think about what the missing information might be (days, dates, numbers, prices, etc).

5 3.38 **Listen to a boy, Adam, telling his mum about a school trip to the theatre. Complete the information.**

SCHOOL TRIP – THEATRE	
Student's name:	*Adam Field*
Day:	1
Bus leaves at:	2
Play:	3
Theatre:	4
Price of tickets:	5 £..........

6 3.38 **Listen again and check your answers.**

7 3.39 **Listen to Kay talking about a charity event she organised. Complete the information.**

Brother's name:	*Ben*
Charity:	1 .... *for the blind*
Brother's dog:	2
Kay organised:	3 .... *morning*
Money made:	4
Phone number:	5 *01926*..........

OPTIMISE YOUR EXAMS | Speaking

The Speaking test **OPTIMISE**

You are going to see a video of two students, Oscar and Giovanni, doing the Cambridge Key English for Schools Speaking test.

To prepare for this test, practise asking and answering questions about yourself and about a situation your teacher gives you.

OPTIMISE

In **Part 1**, the examiner asks you personal questions.

Be ready to talk about things like your family, your hobbies and your likes and dislikes (giving reasons).

Ask the examiner to repeat the question if you don't understand it and give full answers. Try to avoid answering with only 'Yes' or 'No'.

1 **Read the statements about the Speaking test and decide if they are true (T) or false (F). Write the correct answers then watch the video and check.**

Example:
There are three examiners. *F - There are two examiners.*

1 One examiner just listens. ______
2 Candidates hand over their mark sheets at the end of the test. ______
3 The examiner asks the candidates exactly the same personal questions. ______
4 It is better to say nothing than say something grammatically incorrect. ______
5 You should give full answers in Part 2 of the test. ______

2 **Watch Part 1 of the video and tick the questions you hear. Then watch the video again and make notes on Oscar and Giovanni's answers. Compare your answers with a partner.**

What's your name?	☐	What sports do you like doing?	☐
What's your surname?	☐	What other things do you do in your free time?	☐
How do you spell it?	☐	How often do you go to the cinema with friends?	☐
Where do you live?	☐	When's your birthday?	☐
Do you study maths at school?	☐	What will you do on your next birthday?	☐
What other subjects do you study?	☐	What presents did you get for your last birthday?	☐
Tell me something about where you live.	☐	Tell me about the food your mother cooks.	☐
Do you live in a city or a town?	☐	Do you like the food in this country?	☐

3 **Work in pairs. Use the prompts, and then take turns asking and answering the questions.**

What / name?	What / usually / at weekend?
How spell / surname?	How / people / family?
Where / come from?	Who / best / friend?
What / hobbies?	What / do / together?
What / things / like / do?	What / subjects / study?

OPTIMISE

In **Part 2,** you ask and answer questions with a partner, using prompt cards.
Make sure you know the correct word order for questions.
It's OK to say things like 'Let me think.' while you think of your answer.
It's OK to correct yourself if you make a mistake.

4 **Watch the first half of Part 2 and circle each question you hear Oscar ask. Tick the questions that are correct English.**

1	When the school party starts?	☐	When does the school party start?	☐
2	Is the school party for all students?	☐	The party is for all students?	☐
3	Where is the school party?	☐	What is the address of the school party?	☐
4	What are we going to do there?	☐	What we are going to do there?	☐
5	Do you have any more information?	☐	There is more information?	☐

5 **Look at the prompts and make questions. Watch the second half of Part 2. Does Giovanni ask the same questions?**

1	What / see? ____
2	When / open? ____
3	How much / ticket for a student? ____
4	car park? ____
5	What / website? ____

6 **Work in pairs – Student A and B. Student A, look at the information below. Student B, look at the list of prompts below.**

Student A

Radley school party
All students welcome!
at City Hall
77 Western Street
25th June
7.00 pm–10.00 pm
Dance, sing and have fun!
Contact Mrs Cook, science teacher for more information

Student B

School party

- when/school party?
- for all students?
- address?
- what/do?
- more information?

Student B, look at the information below. Student A, look at the list of prompts below.

Student B

Natural Science Museum
OPEN WEEKDAYS AND SATURDAYS
9.30am-6.30pm
Sundays closed
See more than 50 different types of dinosaurs!
Visit our shop for souvenirs and presents.
Free parking before 10.30am
Tickets: Adults £10 Students £8
Website: www.sciencemuseum.com

Student A

Science Museum

- what/see?
- when/open?
- student ticket? £?
- car park?
- website?

GRAMMAR REFERENCE

GRAMMAR REFERENCE | Unit 1 | Present simple, adverbs of frequency, imperatives

Present simple

FORM:

Positive
I/You/We/They ***live*** *here.*
He/She/It ***lives*** *here.*
Negative
I/You/We/They ***do not live / don't live*** *here.*
He/She/It ***does not live / doesn't live*** *here.*
Questions
Do *I/you/we/they* ***live*** *here?*
Does *he/she/it* ***live*** *here?*
Short answers
Yes, I/you/we/they ***do****.* *No, I/you/we/they* ***don't****.*
Yes, he/she/it ***does****.* *No, he/she/it* ***doesn't****.*

Spelling patterns for the present simple after *he*, *she* or *it*

- We add *-s* to most verbs: ***I wear → he wears***
- We add *-es* to verbs that end with *o*: ***they go → she goes, I do → he does***
- If the verb ends in *-s, -sh,-ch, -x* or *-z* we add *-es*: ***you finish → it finishes***
- If the verb ends in a consonant + *-y*, the *-y* changes to *-ies*: ***we study → he studies***
- If the verb ends in a vowel + *-y*, the *-y* does not change: ***I play → she plays***

Common irregular verbs

- *Have* is irregular: *I/you/we/they* ***have*** *→ he/she/it* ***has***
- *Be* is irregular: *I* ***am*** *→ you/we/they* ***are*** *→ he/she/it* ***is***

USE: to talk about: **1** habits or things we do often, and **2** things that are usually or always true:

1	*I* ***walk*** *to school.*
2	*She* ***lives*** *in Spain. It* ***rains*** *in winter.*

Adverbs of frequency

We use adverbs of frequency to say how often something happens:

never *sometimes* *often* *usually* *always*

0% ________________________________ 100%

FORM: Adverbs of frequency usually come before the main verb:

I ***usually play*** *tennis on Saturday.*

I ***don't often eat*** *pizza.*

She ***never listens*** *to the radio.*

! Adverbs of frequency come after *be* when it is used as a main verb:

It ***is usually*** *very hot in August.*

I ***am never*** *late for school.*

Sometimes can also come at the beginning or end of a sentence:

Sometimes *I make dinner. / I make dinner* ***sometimes****.*

Time expressions

every day
every week
twice a week
three times a week

We use time expressions to show when we do things:

He rides his bike ***every day****.*
She plays tennis ***twice a week****.*

Imperatives

FORM: Imperatives use the bare infinitive of a verb. The verb doesn't change when you are talking to one person or more than one person:

Find *a club to join.* ***Wait*** *there children!*

For negative imperatives, we use *don't*:

Don't do *that!* ***Don't worry****.*

USE: to give instructions or orders, or to make a strong suggestion:

Open *your book.* ***Write*** *your name.*

Try *a new sport …*

! We don't have to use the subject (e.g. *you*) with imperatives:

Come *here!* ***Look*** *at that!*

! We can use *please* with imperatives to be more polite:

Please be *quiet. /* ***Be*** *quiet,* ***please****.*

! We can also use *never* and *always* with imperatives for general instructions or orders:

Never eat *or* ***drink*** *in class.*
Always listen *to your teacher.*

GRAMMAR REFERENCE | Unit 1 | Possessive 's, prepositions of time and place

Possessive 's

FORM: Add 's to a singular noun:

*I like to play games on **Paul's** computer.*

*I sometimes ride my **friend's** bike.*

Add 's to irregular plural nouns:

***Children's** toys are expensive here.*

*Are these **men's** shoes?*

Add ' to plural nouns ending in *-s*:

*This is my **parents'** car.*

*Those are **girls'** clothes.*

USE: to show possession (who something belongs to / who owns something):

*Jack has a football. It's **Jack's** football.*
*The book belongs to **Ellie**. It's **Ellie's** book.*

! If we use possessive 's in an answer, we don't have to repeat the noun:

Whose bike is this?	*It's Jan's bike. / It's **Jan's**.*
Whose phone is this?	*It's my brother's phone. / It's my **brother's**.*

Prepositions of time and place

FORM: Prepositions of time or place go before nouns or pronouns:

***at** 7 pm / **in** summer / **on** the floor/ **in** her garden*

USE: to tell us when something happens, or where something or someone is:

*When do you ride your bike? I ride it **at** the weekend.*

*Where's Kim? She's **in** the house.*

GRAMMAR REFERENCE | Unit 2 | Present simple and present continuous

Present simple

See Grammar reference, Unit 1, page 150 for information about the form and use of the present simple.

Present continuous

FORM:

am/is/are + verb + *-ing*

Positive
*I **am/'m playing**.*
*He/She/It **is/'s playing**.*
*You/We/They **are/'re playing**.*
Negative
*I **am/'m not playing**.*
*He/She/It **is not / isn't playing**.*
*You/We/They **are not / aren't playing**.*
Questions
***Am** I **playing**?*
***Is** he/she/it **playing**?*
***Are** you/we/ they **playing**?*
Short answers
*Yes, I **am**.* *No, I'**m not**.*
*Yes, he/she/it **is**.* *No, he/she/it **isn't**.*
*Yes, you/we/they **are**.* *No, you/we/they **aren't**.*

USE: to talk about: **1** things that are happening at the moment, **2** actions happening around now, **3** temporary or changing situations, and **4** descriptions of pictures:

1	*I'**m enjoying** this food.*
2	*Where **are** you **living** these days?*
3	*I'**m staying** at my aunt's house this week.*
4	*All the people in the picture **are looking** at their phones.*

Spelling patterns for the present continuous

- We add *-ing* to the bare infinitive of most verbs: ***start** → **starting***
- If the verb ends in *-e*, we take away the *-e* before adding *-ing*: ***make** → **making***
- If the verb ends in *-ie*, we change the *-ie* to *-y* before adding *-ing*: ***lie** → **lying***
- If the verb has one or two syllables and ends in a vowel + a consonant, we double the consonant before adding *-ing*: ***stop** → **stopping**, **begin** → **beginning**, **travel** → **travelling***

! There are some verbs, called stative verbs, which we usually only use in the present simple form. These include:

- verbs about thinking, e.g. *know, believe, understand*

✔ *I **understand** this book.*

✘ *I'**m understanding** this book.*

- verbs connected with likes/dislikes, e.g. *like, love, hate*

✔ *I **love** that film.*

✘ *I'**m loving** that film.*

- verbs connected with possession, e.g. *belong to, have, own, possess*

✔ *I **have** shoes like that.*

✘ *I'**m having** shoes like that.*

! We don't use contracted forms (*I'm, they're, she's*, etc.) in positive short answers:

Are you reading a book?

✔ *Yes, I am.*

✘ *Yes, I'm.*

Present simple and present continuous

- It is possible to have verbs in both the present simple and the present continuous in the same sentence. The present simple talks about a habit or something we do often, and the present continuous talks about an action happening now or around now, or a temporary situation:

*I usually **walk** to school but this week **I'm going** by bus.*

GRAMMAR REFERENCE | Unit 2 | Present continuous for future use

USE: to talk about future plans and arrangements:

*We're **watching** a new film later.*

*I'm **meeting** Jess at the library tomorrow morning.*

! We usually use the present continuous to talk about future plans and arrangements that are already agreed/ planned. We usually give a time, day, etc. in present continuous sentences that talk about the future:

*They're **travelling** to London tomorrow.*

*Mum **isn't working** next weekend.*

! We can also use the present simple to talk about the future, when we're talking about timetables or programmed events:

*The exam **starts** at 10:30 am.*

GRAMMAR REFERENCE | Unit 3 | Past simple: regular verbs, *Wh-* words

Past simple, regular verbs (positive)

FORM: verb + *-ed*

Positive
I/You/He/She/It/We/They **worked** yesterday.

See Grammar reference, Unit 3, page 153, for information about the negative, question and short answer forms of the past simple.

USE: to talk about: **1** something that happened once in the past, **2** something that happened again and again in the past, and **3** something that was true for some time in the past:

1	*I **played** basketball at the weekend.*
2	*She always **visited** her grandmother in the summer holidays.*
3	*Katy **helped** her mum prepare all the family meals.*

Spelling patterns for the past simple of regular verbs

- We add *-ed* to the bare infinitive of most verbs: ***work** → **worked**, **start** → **started***
- If the verb ends in *-e*, we add *-d*: ***live** → **lived**, **love** → **loved***
- If the verb has one syllable and ends in a vowel and a consonant, we double the consonant: ***stop** → **stopped**, **plan** → **planned**, **travel** → **travelled***
- With verbs that end in a consonant + *-y*, we change the *-y* to *-ied*: ***try** → **tried**, **study** → **studied***

! We often use time expressions with the past simple:

in: *in 2027, in the 1990s, in winter/summer, in the morning/afternoon/evening, in October*

last: *last week/month/year, last December, last night*

this: *this morning, this week*

on: *on Saturday, on Monday night, on 29th March*

at: *at eight o'clock, at weekends, at night*

Wh- words

FORM:

*Wh-*question word + verb + subject

***What** is your name?*

USE: to start many questions. *Wh-* words are used to get more information than *yes/no* questions, e.g. ***Did** you live abroad? Yes, I did.*

***Where** did you live? I lived in Oxford, a city in England.*

! *What, which,* and *whose* can be followed by a noun:

***What music** do you like? **Which bag** is yours? **Whose phone** is this?*

What can be used if there are many possible answers:

***What** do you want to eat?*

Which can be used if there are a few possible answers:

***Which** do you prefer, apples or pears?*

How can be followed by an adjective or adverb:

***How old** is your brother? **How fast** is the internet connection?*

How can also be followed by *much* and *many*:

***How many** times have you played this game?*
***How much** cheese do you want?*

GRAMMAR REFERENCE | Unit 3 | Past simple: irregular verbs

FORM:

Negative
I/You/He/She/It/We/They ***did not / didn't come*** *yesterday.*
Questions
Did *I/you/he/she/it/we/they* ***come*** *yesterday?*
Short answers
Yes, I/you/he/she/it/we/they ***did****.* *No, I/you/he/she/it/we/they* ***didn't****.*

! Both regular and irregular verbs follow the same pattern in the past simple for negatives, questions and answers. However, irregular verbs do not follow a pattern for the positive form in the past simple. You need to learn the past simple positive form of irregular verbs.

Some common irregular verbs

be → *was/were*
buy → *bought*
choose → *chose*
come → *came*
do → *did*
drink → *drank*
eat → *ate*
get → *got*
go → *went*
have → *had*
meet → *met*
see → *saw*
teach → *taught*
think → *thought*

See the *Irregular verbs reference,* page 175, for a full list of irregular verbs used in the A2 Student's Book.

GRAMMAR REFERENCE | Unit 4 | Past continuous, linking words

Past continuous

FORM:

was/were + verb + *-ing*

Positive
I/He/She/It **was eating**. You/We/They **were eating**.
Negative
I/He/She/It **was not / wasn't eating**. You/We/They **were not / weren't eating**.
Questions
Was I/he/she/it **eating**? **Were** you/we/they **eating**?
Short answers
Yes, I/he/she/it **was**. No, I/he/she/it **wasn't**.
Yes, you/we/they **were**. No, you/we/they **weren't**.

USE: to talk about: **1** something that was happening over a period of time at a specific time in the past, **2** background information or description in a story, **3** an action in progress in the past when another thing happened (possibly interrupting it or stopping it), **4** two actions in progress at the same time, and **5** a temporary situation in the past:

1	*At four o'clock yesterday afternoon, I* ***was playing*** *online games.*
2	*I looked out of the window. Rain* ***was falling*** *heavily.*
3	*He* ***was watching*** *TV when his phone rang.*
4	*When I arrived, Katy* ***was reading*** *and Ellie* ***was sleeping****.*
5	*I* ***was using*** *his phone because I couldn't find mine.*

! The past continuous is not used to talk about repeated actions in the past:

✔ *I* ***checked*** *my emails ten times yesterday.*

✘ *I* ***was checking*** *my emails ten times yesterday.*

Linking words

USE: we use linking words (*and, because, but, or, when*) to link phrases, clauses and sentences.

We use *and* to link phrases and clauses:
She swims in the mornings ***and*** *she goes jogging in the evenings.*

We use *because* for a reason:
We walked ***because*** *it was a sunny day.*

We use *but* to link two different ideas:
I like apples ***but*** *I hate oranges.*

We use *or* to link alternatives:
Would you like a hot ***or*** *cold drink?*

We use *when* to link clauses with time:
I liked school ***when*** *I was eight.*

! We can use *because* and *when* at the beginning and in the middle of a sentence:

I went to bed ***because*** *I was feeling tired.*

Because *I was feeling tired, I went to bed.*

GRAMMAR REFERENCE | Unit 4 | Past simple and past continuous

Past simple

See Grammar reference, Unit 3, pages 152 and 153 for information about the form and use of the past simple.

Past continuous

See Grammar reference, Unit 4, page 153, for information about the form and use of the past continuous.

! It is possible to have verbs in both the past simple and the past continuous in the same sentence. The past continuous talks about what was happening when another shorter action happened. We use the past simple for the shorter action that happened:

*I **was listening** to music in my room when Mum **walked** in.*

! In stories or descriptions, we use the past continuous to describe the situation or to give background information, and we use the past simple to talk about events and actions:

*It **was raining** outside so we **stayed** in and **played** a game.*

! In questions, we can use the past continuous to ask about what was happening before an action or event, and we can use the past simple to ask about what happened after an action or event:

*What **were** you **doing** when it **started** to snow? We **were walking** in the woods.*

*What **did** you **do** when it started to snow? We **went** home.*

GRAMMAR REFERENCE | Unit 5 | Quantifiers with countable and uncountable nouns

Countable and uncountable nouns

Countable nouns can be counted and have a singular and plural form, e.g. *one book, three books, one child, five children*.

Uncountable nouns are often ideas (e.g. *information*), materials (e.g. *water, wood*) or groups of similar things (*furniture, luggage, money,* etc.). After uncountable nouns, we use a verb in the singular, even if we are talking about more than one object:

*All the furniture **was** old.*

*Their luggage **is** heavy.*

! To talk about one part of something that we usually refer to as a group of things, we can use words like *piece, slice, glass*, etc. We usually use *of* after these words, and we can use plural verbs with these words, where appropriate:

***Are** two **pieces of** cake enough?*

*There **are** two **slices of** meat left on the plate.*

! Some nouns are both countable and uncountable, e.g.

Uncountable: *The **glass** in the window is broken.*

Countable: *Put the **glasses** of juice on the table.* (**glasses** = things to drink from)

Uncountable: *I need more **paper** to write on.*

Countable: *Dad reads the **papers** every morning.* (**papers** = newspapers)

Uncountable: *I love **chocolate**!*

Countable: *Let's buy Mum some **chocolates**.* (**chocolates** = small sweets in a box/bag)

Quantifiers

USE:

much/many

We use *much* with uncountable nouns in questions and negatives:

***How much water** do you drink every day?*

*He doesn't want **much cake**.*

We use *many* with countable nouns in questions and negatives:

***How many books** have you got?*

*There weren't **many people** at the party.*

! *Too much* and *Too many* have a negative meaning. We use them to mean *more than the right amount*:

*There are **too many** people here. Let's go somewhere quieter.*

some/any

We use *some* when we don't know, or don't want to say, the exact number of something:

*I think **some** people are coming.* (I don't know how many.)

We use *some* in positive sentences and in questions when we think the answer will be yes:

*Do you want **some** milk to drink?*

We use *any* before countable and uncountable nouns in negative sentences to mean a zero amount:

*There isn't **any** time to call her now.*
*There aren't **any** free apps that I like.*

We use *any* in questions when we don't know if the answer will be *yes* or *no*:

*Do you need **any** help?*

! *No* means the same as *not any*:

*There is**n't any** money in my bag. /*
*There's **no** money in my bag.*

a few / a lot of

A few means *a small number of*. We use it in positive sentences with countable nouns:

*I bought **a few** T-shirts.*

We use *few* in sentences with a negative meaning:

*There are **few** shops open today.*

Both *a lot of* and *lots of* mean *a large number or quantity*. We use both phrases with countable and uncountable nouns:

Lots of / A lot of *people play computer games every day.*

A little means *a small number or quantity*. We use it in positive sentences with uncountable nouns:

I ate ***a little*** *soup and felt better.*

We use *little* in sentences with a negative meaning:

There's ***little*** *point in phoning him. He never answers.*

GRAMMAR REFERENCE | Unit 5 | Comparatives and superlatives

FORM:

Type of adjective	Adjective	Comparative	Superlative
Adjective (one syllable)	*old*	+ *-er* ***older***	+ *-est* ***oldest***
Adjective (one/ two syllables) ending in *-e*	*wide*	+ *-r* ***wider***	+ *-st* ***widest***
Adjective (one syllable) ending in a vowel + consonant	*big*	double the final letter + *-er* ***bigger***	double the final letter + *-est* ***biggest***
Adjective (two syllables) ending in *-y*	*happy*	replace *-y* with *-ier* ***happier***	replace *-y* with *-iest* ***happiest***
Other adjective (two or more syllables)	*beautiful*	*more* + adjective ***more beautiful***	*most* + adjective ***most beautiful***
Irregular adjectives	***good bad far little many/much***	***better worse farther/ further less more***	***best worst farthest/ furthest least most***

USE: we use the comparative form of adjectives + *than* to compare two people, things, etc:

This game is ***newer than*** *the others.*

we use *the* + the superlative form of adjectives to compare more than two people, things, etc.:

This is ***the most interesting*** *website ever!*

! We don't always use *than* with comparatives when we are comparing something which is obvious:

This is my ***older*** *sister. (= older than me)*

In the winter, the weather is usually ***worse***. *(= worse than at other times)*

! We don't always use *the* with superlatives. We replace *the* with a possessive adjective:

This is ***my*** *best score so far.*

! We can use *even* and *much* with comparatives to make them stronger:

My design is good, but Sasha's design is ***even/much*** *better!*

GRAMMAR REFERENCE | Unit 6 | Present perfect simple with *ever* and *never*

FORM:

have/has + the past participle of the main verb

Positive
I/You/We/They ***have/'ve played*** *football.*
He/She/It ***has/'s played*** *football.*
Negative
I/You/We/They ***have not / haven't played*** *football.*
He/She/It ***has not / hasn't played*** *football.*
Questions
Have *I/you/we/they (ever)* ***played*** *football?*
Has *he/she/it (ever)* ***played*** *football?*
Short answers
Yes, I/you/we/they ***have***. *No, I/you/we/they* ***haven't***.
Yes, he/she/it ***has***. *No, he/she/it* ***hasn't***.

! The past participles of regular verbs end in *-ed*.

See the *Irregular verbs reference*, page 175, for the past participle of irregular verbs.

! We don't use contracted forms (*I've, they've, she's*, etc.) in positive short answers:

Have you lived here long?

✔ *Yes, I have.*

✘ *Yes, I've.*

USE: to talk about: **1** past actions when the time they happened isn't important or isn't known, **2** to talk about experiences, **3** with *ever*, in questions asking about experiences up to now, and **4** with *never*, in sentences to talk about experiences that have not happened up to now:

1	***I've bought*** *lots of pairs of shoes.*
2	*They**'ve lived*** *all over the world.*
3	***Have*** *you* ***ever seen*** *one of these?*
4	***I've never eaten*** *food like this before.*

GRAMMAR REFERENCE | Unit 6 | Present perfect simple and past simple

Present perfect simple and past simple

USE: we use the present perfect simple: **1** to talk about a finished action in the past that is still linked to the present, **2** to report information or news, and **3** for a situation which has gone on up to the present:

1	*Anna **has bought** her train ticket.*
2	*I**'ve bought** a new phone.*
3	*We**'ve lived** here for four years.*

We use the past simple: **1** to talk about finished actions in the past; we usually know when the action happened, **2** to give details or explanations, and **3** for a situation in the past which has now finished:

1	*Anna **bought** her train ticket last week.*
2	*I **bought** a new phone at the shopping centre last week.*
3	*We **studied** there for four years.*

GRAMMAR REFERENCE | Unit 7 | *going to*

FORM:

be + *going to* + bare infinitive

Positive
*I **am/'m going to** play.*
*You/We/They **are/'re going to** play.*
*He/She/It **is/'s going to** play.*
Negative
*I **am/'m not going to** play.* *You/ We/They **are/'re not going to** play.* *He/She/It **is not / isn't going to** play.*
Questions
***Am** I **going to** play?*
***Are** you/we/they **going to** play?*
***Is** he/she/it **going to** play?*

Short answers
*Yes, I **am**.* *No, I**'m not**.*
*Yes, you/we/they **are**.* *No, you/we/they **aren't**.*
*Yes, he/she/it **is**.* *No, he/she/it **isn't**.*

USE: **we use** *going to* to: **1** talk about future plans, and **2** to predict something because of what see or know now:

1	*We**'re going to visit** my grandparents next month.* *What **are** you **going to do** at the weekend?*
2	*He's very near the goal. I think he**'s going to score**.* *Who **is going to win** the race?*

! When we have already made an arrangement with someone else, we can also use the present continuous:

*I'm **playing** tennis with Nina this evening.*

GRAMMAR REFERENCE | Unit 7 | *will* and *going to*

See Grammar reference, Unit 7, above, for information about the form and use of *going to*.

FORM:

will + bare infinitive

Positive
*I/You/ He/She/It/We/They **will play**.*
Negative
*I/You/He/She/It/We/They **will not / won't play**.*
Questions
***Will** I/you/he/she/it/we/they **play**?*
Short answers
*Yes, I/you/he/she/it/we/they **will**.* *No, I/you/he/she/it/we/they **won't**.*

USE: we use *will*: **1** when we decide to do something at that moment, **2** to say what we think or guess what will happen, and **3** to make offers or requests:

1	*I'm cold. I**'ll close** the window.*
2	*I don't think the test **will be** difficult.* *Do you think everyone in the class **will pass**? Yes, I think they **will**.*
3	***Will** you **help** me with my homework?* *I**'ll get** you a drink if you're thirsty.*

! Sometimes *will* and *going to* are both correct. We usually use *going to* when we speak:

*Do you think the teacher **will** give us any homework?*
*'Do you think the teacher **is going to** give us any homework?'*

GRAMMAR REFERENCE | Unit 8 | Modals (1): ability, necessity, obligation, possibility

FORM:

Modals have only one form and are usually followed by the bare infinitive of the main verb.

Positive
I/You/He/She/It/We/They ***may/can/must***, etc. ***go***.
Negative
I/You/He/She/It/We/They ***may not / can't/mustn't***, etc. ***go***.
Questions
May/Can/Must, etc. *I/you/he/she/it/we/they* ***go****?*
Short answers
Yes, I/you/he/she/it/we/they ***may/can/must***, etc. *No, I/you/he/she/it/we/they* ***may not / can't/mustn't***, etc.

! *Need* and *have to* change form like a regular verb:

✔ *She **needs** to go.*

✘ *She **need** to go.*

✔ *It **has to** go.*

✘ *It **have to** go.*

! We use *don't need to* or *needn't* with the bare infinitive.

*We **don't need to** finish our homework tonight.*

*We **needn't** finish our homework tonight.*

! We don't use *can* as an infinitive. We use *be able to*:

✔ *I'd like to **be able to** run a marathon.*

✘ *I'd like to **can** run a marathon.*

USE: to talk about ability, possibility, and obligation.

Ability – *can/could*

To talk about ability in the present, we use *can*:

*Tom **can** speak three languages.*

*Linda **can't** swim.*

! We don't use *can* to talk about ability in the future. We use *will be able to*.

✔ ***I'll be able to** speak Spanish well in a few years' time.*

✘ *I **can** speak Spanish well in a few years' time.*

To talk about general ability in the past, we use could:

*Andrea **could** play the piano when she was six.*

*Sam **couldn't** read when he was four.*

! We don't use *could* for specific ability in the past. We use *was/were able to*:

✔ *I **was able to** finish my homework in one hour last night.*

✘ *I **could** finish my homework in one hour last night.*

Necessity – *need/needn't*

To say that something is necessary in order to achieve something else, we use *need*:

*I **need to** pass the exam to go to university.*

*You **need to** go to bed early because you've got an exam tomorrow.*

To say that something isn't necessary, we use *needn't*:

*You **needn't** shout. I can hear you!*

*You **needn't** answer both questions. You can just choose one.*

Obligation – *have to / must*

When something is necessary, we use *have to*:

*I **have to** arrive at school before 9:00 every morning.*

*My dad **has to** go to work on Saturdays.*

When something isn't necessary, we use *don't have to*:

*We **don't have to** go to school on Sundays.*

*My sister **doesn't have to** wear a uniform to school.*

! We often use *have to* to talk about something that someone else says is necessary:

*We **have to** stand up when our teacher comes in the classroom.*

! To talk about obligation in the past, we usually use *had to*:

✔ *I **had to** go to school yesterday.*

✘ *I **must** go to school yesterday.*

To talk about things that are essential or necessary to do, because other people say so or because the person doing the action believes so, we use *must/mustn't*:

*You **must** go to school.*

*We **mustn't** be late.*

! *Must* is not common in the question form. We usually use *have to*:

***Do** you **have to** wear a school uniform?*

Possibility – *may/might*

To say that something is possibly true or not true, or will possibly happen or not happen, we use *may/might*:

*I **may** need some help to finish my homework.*

*It **might not** be the correct answer. I'm not sure.*

GRAMMAR REFERENCE | Unit 8 | Modals (2): advice, permission, polite requests, prohibition

FORM: *modal verb* + bare infinitive

Positive
*I/You/He/She/It/We/They (**should**) leave.*
Negative
*I/You/He/She/It/We/They (**should not / shouldn't**) leave.*
Questions
*(**Should**) I/you/he/she/it/we/they leave?*
Short answers
*Yes, I/you/he/she/it/we/they (**should**).* *No, I/you/he/she/it/we/they (**shouldn't**).*

USE: to talk about advice, permission, polite requests, prohibition.

Advice – *should*

We also use *should* when we want to ask for and give advice:

***Should** I buy this shirt?*

*You **should** eat a lot of fruit and vegetables.*

When we want to say something is a good or bad idea but not necessary, we use *should* or *shouldn't*:

*Everyone **should** learn how to swim.*

*You **shouldn't** play video games late at night.*

Permission – *can*

To ask for, give and refuse permission now, in the future, or generally, we use *can*:

***Can** I watch TV?*

*I **can** go out with my friends at the weekend.* (Mum has already given me permission.)

*We **can't** eat or drink in class.* (The teacher never gives us permission to do this.)

! To talk about permission in the past, we don't use *could*. We often use *be allowed to*:

✔ *I **wasn't allowed to** play video games when I was young.*

✘ *I **couldn't** watch video games when I was young.*

Polite requests – *could*

To make a polite request, we use *could*:

***Could** you open the window, please?*

***Could** I ask a question?*

Prohibition – *mustn't*

To talk about something that is not allowed, we use *mustn't*:

*You **mustn't** copy your friend's homework.*

*You **mustn't** use your phone in class.*

GRAMMAR REFERENCE | Unit 9 | Zero conditional, first conditional

Zero conditional

FORM:

If + present simple, present simple

*If you **push** the button, the door **opens**.*

! The *if* clause can be at the beginning or the end of the sentence. If it is at the beginning, it has a comma after it:

***If** the weather is good, we play in the park.*

*We play in the park **if** the weather is good.*

***If** you have a headache, what do you do?*

*What do you do **if** you have a headache?*

USE: to talk about things that are always or usually true, and facts:

*If it's sunny, our cat usually **spends** the day in the garden.*

*Water **turns** to ice if the temperature **falls** to zero degrees.*

! We can use *when* or *if*. The meaning is the same:

***If** I don't feel well, I usually stay at home.*

***When** I don't feel well, I usually stay at home.*

First conditional

FORM:

If + present simple, *will/won't* + bare infinitive

*If it's cold this evening, **I'll turn on** the heating.*

*If it **rains** this afternoon, I **won't go** outside.*

USE: to talk about possible events/actions now or in the future, and the results of those events/actions:

*If the internet **doesn't work**, **we'll play** some board games.*

*If it **doesn't snow** this winter, we **won't go** skiing.*

***You'll get wet** if you **don't take** an umbrella.*

GRAMMAR REFERENCE | Unit 9 | Second conditional

Second conditional

FORM:

If + past simple, *would/wouldn't* + bare infinitive

*If I **had** a helicopter, I **would fly** to school every day.*

! The contracted form of *would* is *'d*:

*If I **had** a helicopter, **I'd fly** to school every day.*

USE: to talk about events/actions that are impossible or unlikely now or in the future, and what the results of the events/actions would be if they did happen:

*If you **were** much taller, you**'d be** the best basketball player at school.*

*You **wouldn't speak** Spanish if you **lived** in France.*

! We can also use other modal verbs.

*If my sister **spoke** English, she **could help** me with my homework.*

! We can use both *was* and *were* with *I, he, she* and *it*, in second conditional sentences.

*If **I was** a scientist, I'd help to protect plants and animals.*

*If **I were** a scientist, I'd help to protect plants and animals.*

GRAMMAR REFERENCE | Unit 10 | Present perfect simple: *for, since, already, just, yet*

See Grammar reference, Unit 6, pages 155 and 156, for information about the form and use of the present perfect simple.

USE:

There are some words we can use with the present perfect simple tense which help to tell us more about when something happened.

for and *since*

When we use the present perfect simple tense to talk about something that began in the past and is still true, we can use *for* and *since* to give more information.

We use *for* to talk about a period of time and *since* to talk about the time something started:

*I've been a waiter **for** eight years.*

*I've been a waiter **since** 2010.*

already, just and *yet*

When we use the present perfect simple tense to talk about a finished action in the past that is still linked to the present, we can use *already, just* or *yet* to give more information.

We use *already* when something happened before now:

*I've **already** brushed my teeth.* (I did it earlier.)

We use *just* when we want to say something happened a very short time ago:

*The match has **just** finished.* (The players are still on the field.)

We use *yet* with negative sentences and questions:

*The doctor hasn't arrived **yet**.* (We are waiting for him/her.)

*Has the doctor arrived **yet**?* (Is the doctor here now?)

GRAMMAR REFERENCE | Unit 10 | Verb patterns: verb + infinitive / *-ing*

Verb + infinitive / *-ing*

FORM:

Sometimes we use one verb followed by another verb. The second verb can be in the infinitive or the *-ing* form:

verb + infinitive form of the second verb

verb + *-ing* form of the second verb

*She **wants to give** me a present.*

*He **enjoys reading** about animals.*

Verbs or phrases usually followed by the full infinitive (+ *to*)
be able, agree, ask, choose, decide, forget, hope, learn, need, offer, plan, prepare, promise, tell, wait, want, would like *Gemma **decided to go** skateboarding.* *We **didn't wait to see** the end of the film.*

Verb or phrases usually followed by the *–ing* form of a verb
dislike, enjoy, finish, hate, keep, like, love, (don't) mind, miss, practise, understand *He **enjoyed playing** the new video game.* *They **practised speaking** in English.*
Verb followed by the full infinitive or *-ing* form of the verb, with no change in meaning
begin, continue, hate, love, start *They **began to watch** a film. / They **began watching** a film.* *Ethan **loves to go** climbing. / Ethan **loves going** climbing.*
Verb followed by the full infinitive or *-ing* form of the verb, with a change in meaning
forget, go on, like, mean, remember, stop, try ***I remember buying** this book for Mum.* (I remember when I bought it.) ***I remembered to buy** a book for Mum.* (I didn't forget to buy the book I wanted to get for Mum.)

GRAMMAR REFERENCE | Unit 11 | Indefinite pronouns

FORM:

	People	Places	Things
every-	*everyone*	*everywhere*	*everything*
some-	*someone*	*somewhere*	*something*
any-	*anyone*	*anywhere*	*anything*

USE: to talk about people, places or things without saying exactly who or what they are.

We use pronouns ending in *-body* or *-one* for people, pronouns ending in *-thing* for things and pronouns ending in *-where* for places:

*I think there is **someone** in the garden.*
(We don't know who it is.)

*I like **everything** about this house.*
(the bedrooms, the kitchen, the garden, the view, etc.)

*Is there **anywhere** you'd like to go?*
(This could be any place.)

! We use the *he/she/it* form of a verb after indefinite pronouns:

*Everyone **wants** to go to the party.*

*Tell me when something **happens**.*

When we want to talk about all of the people, places or things without saying exactly what they are, we use *everyone, everywhere* or *everything*:

***Everyone** I know likes this TV programme.*

*I've looked **everywhere** for my keys, but I can't find them.*

***Everything** he said to me is true.*

When we want to talk about a person, place or thing that we don't know or that isn't important, we use *someone, somewhere* or *something*:

***Someone** phoned earlier but they didn't leave a message.*

*I left my bicycle **somewhere** near here.*

*I'm sure I have forgotten **something** important.*

! We don't usually use *someone, somewhere* or *something* in negative sentences:

✔ *I haven't got **anything** in my bag.*

✘ *I haven't got **something** in my bag.*

In questions and negative sentences, we use *anyone, anything* and *anywhere*:

*Did **anyone** visit while I was at the shops?*

*Is there **anything** we need to do before we go on holiday?*
*We didn't go **anywhere** at the weekend.*

! We can also use *anyone, anything* and *anywhere* in positive sentences:

*You can have **anything** you'd like in the shop.*

*We can go **anywhere** you want on holiday.*

! We can add possessive *'s* to indefinite pronouns:

*We found somebody**'s** phone in the park.*

*Is this anybody**'s** bag?*

GRAMMAR REFERENCE | Unit 11 | Relative clauses: *who, which, that*

FORM:

Pronoun	Use	Example
who or *that*	for people	*He's the man **who** lives next door.*
that or *which*	for things	*I work for a company **that** sells computers.* *Dad works in a factory **which** makes cars.*

USE: we use **relative clauses** to say exactly who or what we are talking about:

*Mr Ackmann is the man **who checks the money**.*
(It tells us exactly who Mr Ackmann is.)

*This is the card **that opens the office door**.*
(It tells us what the card does.)

We use *who* to talk about people (and sometimes animals):

*I think he's the boy **who** broke my phone!*

We use *which* to talk about things (and sometimes animals):

*Is this the book **which** the teacher was talking about yesterday?*

We use *that* for people or animals and things:

*Is she the girl **that** you were telling me about?*

! We can use *that* instead of *who* or *which*.

*I think he's the boy **that** broke my phone!*

*Is this the book **that** the teacher was talking about yesterday?*

GRAMMAR REFERENCE | Unit 12 | Present simple passive

FORM: *be* + past participle

Positive
*I **am/'m taught** English every day.*
*You/We/They **are/'re taught** English every day.*
*He/She/It **is/'s taught** English every day.*
Negative
*I **am/'m not taught** English every day.*
*You/We/They **are not / aren't taught** English every day.*
*He/She/It **is not / isn't taught** English every day.*
Questions
***Am** I **taught** English every day?*
***Are** you/we/they **taught** English every day?*
***Is** he/she/it **taught** English every day?*
Short answers
*Yes, I **am**.* *No, I **am/'m not**.*
*Yes, you/we/they **are**.* *No, you/we/they **are not / aren't**.*
*Yes, he/she/it **is**.* *No, he/she/it **is not / isn't**.*

USE: we use the present simple passive when: **1** we don't know who does the action, **2** it isn't important who does the action, and **3** when everyone knows who does the action:

1	*The window **is broken**.* (We don't know who broke the window.) *Bicycles **are** often **stolen** outside the railway station.* (We don't know who steals them.)
2	*The best tomatoes **are grown** in Romania.* (We aren't interested in the person who grows them.) *The building **is painted** once a year.* (It isn't important who paints the building.)
3	*We **are given** homework every day.* (Everyone knows the teacher gives us homework.) *Lunch **is served** every day from 12–2 pm in the restaurant.* (We know that the waiters serve lunch.)

GRAMMAR REFERENCE | Unit 12 | Past simple passive and *by*

FORM: *was/were* + past participle

Positive
*I/He/She/It **was hurt** during the game.*
*You/We/They **were hurt** during the game.*
Negative
*I/He/She/It **was not / wasn't hurt** during the game.*
*You/We/They **were not / weren't hurt** during the game.*
Questions
***Was** I/he/she/it **hurt** during the game?*
***Were** you/we/they **hurt** during the game?*
Short answers
*Yes, I/he/she/it **was**.* *No, I/he/she/it **was not / wasn't**.*
*Yes, you/we/they **were**.* *No, you/we/they **were not / weren't**.*

USE: we use the past simple passive when: **1** we don't know who did the action, **2** it isn't important who did the action, and **3** when everyone knows who did the action:

1	*This car **was made** in Spain.* (We don't know which people made the car.)
2	*The dogs **weren't taken** for a walk last night.* (The person who didn't take the dog for a walk is not important.)
3	***Were** the students **given** a test yesterday.* (We know tests are given by teachers.)

! When we want to say who or what does the action, we can use *by*:

*The garden is looked after **by** my father.*

*Dinner is usually cooked **by** my grandmother.*

We use *by* when it is important to say who or what did the action:

*We were given this picture **by** a local artist.*

*This book was written **by** Roald Dahl.*

! We always put *by* before the person or thing that did the action:

✔ *They were sent this postcard **by** their friends in Brazil.*

✘ *They were sent **by** this postcard their friends in Brazil.*

! We don't use *by* when we don't know who did the action or it isn't important:

This fridge was made ~~by people in a factory~~ in Germany.

The lights were turned on ~~by someone~~ before we arrived.

VOCABULARY REFERENCE

Introduction

This *Vocabulary reference* contains all the target vocabulary from *Optimise A2* Student's Book. The words and phrases are grouped in unit order, so you can look at them as you work on the vocabulary lessons throughout the book. You can also use these pages for revision when you're preparing for a test or an exam.

The target vocabulary has been divided into five groups:

Topic vocabulary

The **Topic vocabulary** sections focus on words connected to the unit topic. Learning these words and being able to use them correctly will help you in your exams. Having a wide vocabulary is important for Reading and Writing and Speaking exams.

Word formation

The **Word formation** sections give you all the different parts of speech – verbs, adjectives, nouns and adverbs – that come from root words that appear in *Optimise A2* Student's Book. Exams often test you on word formation, so learning all the forms of a word is a good way to make sure you are prepared for your exam.

Collocations

Collocations are phrases with two or more words which go together in English. Learning collocations will help you in some exam tasks. It will also improve your English in Speaking and Writing exams.

Word patterns

Word patterns are phrases which use a range of grammatical structures, for example, phrases with prepositions (*good at, interested in*) or nouns that go together (*car park, petrol station*).

Phrasal verbs

Phrasal verbs are made of a verb (*take, come, look,* etc.) plus a word called a particle. The particle can be an adverb (*up, down,* etc.) or a preposition (*in, on,* etc.). Remember that some phrasal verbs have more than one meaning; in the tables, the meaning given for the phrasal verb always matches the one used in the unit.

These are the main types of phrasal verbs:

Type 1: the verb is transitive (has an object).

When the object is a noun, we can put the particle before or after the noun:

*I'll **pick** Jo **up** at six. / I'll **pick up** Joe at six.*

When the object is a pronoun, the pronoun must separate the two parts of the phrasal verb:

✔ *I'll **pick** her **up**.*

✘ *I'll **pick up** her.*

Type 2: the verb is intransitive (does not have an object) and you cannot separate the two parts of the verb:

✔ *Please **come in** and get warm.*

✘ *Please **come** and get warm **in**.*

! Some phrasal verbs may have different meanings when they are used transitively or intransitively:

*The plane **took off** at ten thirty. (= leave the ground and go into the sky) I'll **take** my jacket **off** when I feel warmer. (= remove clothing)*

Type 3: the verb is transitive (has an object) but you cannot separate the two parts of the verb:

✔ *Can you **look after** the cat while I'm away?*

✘ *Can you **look** my cat **after** while I'm away?*

Throughout the *Vocabulary reference*, you will see different abbreviations. This key explains what they all mean.

KEY: adj = adjective; adv = adverb; n = noun; sth = something; v = verb

UNIT 1

TOPIC VOCABULARY | Words connected with *hobbies*

Word	Example sentence
cycling (n)	My history teacher goes cycling every summer.
horse-riding (n)	Elly sometimes goes horse-riding in Wales with her school.
painting (n)	I don't enjoy drawing with a pencil, but I like painting.
playing computer games (n)	Mark loves playing his favourite computer games at the weekend.
reading (n)	Liam loves reading, so he buys lots of books.
rock climbing (n)	Helen often hurts her knee when she goes rock climbing.
skateboarding (n)	I never go skateboarding! It looks dangerous.
swimming (n)	She says that swimming is her favourite sport.
barbecue (n)	We sometimes have a barbecue in our garden during the summer.
beach (n)	Do you ever play volleyball on the beach?
collect (v)	Jamie collects old comics – he's got more than two hundred!
magazine (n)	His picture looks great in the magazine.
photograph (n)	Lizzie has about 200 photographs for her school project.
tent (n)	I don't like sleeping in a tent because I get cold.

WORD FORMATION | Nouns/verbs

Core word	Derivatives
guitar (n)	guitarist (n), play the guitar (v)
music (n)	musician (n), musical (adj), make/play music (v)
paint (n)	painting (n), painter (n), paint (v)
photograph (n)	photographer (n), photography (n), photograph / take photographs (v)
video (n)	video (v), video gamer (n), play video games (v)

PHRASAL VERBS

Phrasal verb	Meaning	Example sentence
come in (type 2)	enter	It's cold outside! Come in and get warm.
come round (type 2)	visit	Rebecca comes round for dinner on Fridays.
get back (type 2)	return after going somewhere	When did you get back from Ireland?
get off (type 2)	leave a bus or train	We get off the train at Hallwood station then walk home.
look after (type 3)	take care of something	Tom always looks after our dog when we go on holiday.
turn off (type 1)	stop a machine	Turn off the alarm clock! It's Sunday!
turn on (type 1)	start a machine	Turn on the TV please, the news is on.

UNIT 2

TOPIC VOCABULARY | Words connected with *entertainment*

Word	Example sentence
art gallery (n)	Mary loves the paintings of famous people in the art gallery.
concert hall (n)	My aunt plays the piano in a concert hall once a month.
gaming café (n)	I enjoy going to the gaming café to meet my friends.
museum (n)	Bridget's looking at the old cars in the museum.
opera house (n)	I sometimes go to the opera house with my class and listen to famous singers.
theatre (n)	Do you like going to see plays at the theatre?

WORD PATTERNS | Words + prepositions

Core word	Example sentence
act in	Matt sometimes acts in school plays.
dance with	Amber danced with her sister at the concert in the park.
go out	Do you usually go out with your friends on Saturdays?
listen to	Please listen to me when I'm talking to you.
look at (sth)	What are you looking at?
play with	Do you play with your classmates after school?
stay in	We usually stay in when there is a bad storm.
try (sth) **on**	I always try shoes on before I buy them.

COLLOCATIONS | Collocations with nouns

Collocation	Example sentence
board game	This board game is boring – can we play *Cluedo* instead?
cinema screen	Dan doesn't wear his glasses when he watches films on a cinema screen.
DVD player	We watch films on the computer, so we don't use our DVD player now.
newspaper article	She reads newspaper articles about sport every morning.
TV programme	What is your favourite TV programme? I think *Friends* is great!

UNIT 3

TOPIC VOCABULARY | Words connected with *food*	
Word	**Example sentence**
apple (n), **banana** (n)	Apples and bananas are my favourite fruits.
beans (n)	Dad grows beans in the garden, so we often eat them with our meals.
beef (n)	We're having beef for dinner.
bread (n)	My mum bakes very nice bread. I love it with honey on it.
carrots (n), **cereal** (n)	My favourite food is carrots, but Ellie's is cereal.
cheese (n)	I am having a cheese sandwich for lunch.
chicken (n)	We often have chicken salad for dinner.
honey (n)	Do you like honey with yoghurt?
lettuce (n)	Ryan doesn't like salad, so he never eats lettuce!
milk (n)	My dad buys milk every week from the supermarket.
oil (n)	Mum usually cooks the potatoes in the oven – she puts oil on them.
onions (n)	Do you usually eat onions with your steak?
oranges (n)	We always have oranges in the house. Mum likes us to eat an apple or an orange every day.
pasta (n)	You can make a nice meal with pasta and tomatoes.
potatoes (n), **rice** (n)	Do you prefer potatoes or rice with your beef?
salt (n)	Tim never puts salt on his food, but I do.
steak (n)	I never eat meat, but my brother's favourite meat is steak.
strawberries (n)	We love eating strawberries and ice cream in the summer.
tomatoes (n)	Mum prepared a tomato salad for us to have with the chicken.
vinegar (n)	Do you put vinegar on fish and chips?
yoghurt (n)	Adam eats yoghurt on his cereal for breakfast.

WORD FORMATION | Verbs/adjectives	
Core word	**Derivatives**
bake (v)	baked (adj), baker (n)
boil (v)	boiled (adj), boiler (n)
fry (v)	fried (adj), fryer (n)
grill (v)	grilled (adj), grill (n)
roast (v)	roasted (adj), roast (n)

COLLOCATIONS | Collocations with verbs	
Collocation	**Example sentence**
bake bread	Colin learnt to bake bread because he wants to be a baker one day.
do homework	Do you prefer doing homework at home or in the library?
have lunch	Can we have lunch in a restaurant on my birthday?
make breakfast	Who makes breakfast in your house?
take an exam	All the students are taking an exam at the moment.

UNIT 4

TOPIC VOCABULARY | Words connected with *travel*	
Word	**Example sentence**
bridge (n)	The Golden Gate Bridge in San Francisco is very big!
bus stop (n)	Matt is waiting for you at the bus stop.
delayed (adj)	Flights are often delayed at Christmas time.
miss (v)	Be quick! I don't want to miss the bus.
railway station (n)	The railway station is near my house.
roundabout (n)	You need to stop at the roundabout!
traffic (n)	There's always a lot of traffic in the city centre.
traffic lights (n)	Cars stop when the traffic lights are red.

WORD PATTERNS | Compound nouns	
Core word	**Example sentence**
car park	He is trying to find a space in the car park.
driving licence	You can get a driving licence in England when you're 17.
helicopter ride	She is going on a helicopter ride and she's very excited about it.
petrol station	There is a petrol station at the end of my road.
sailing boat	Dad is planning a holiday on a sailing boat next summer.
ticket machine	The ticket machine isn't working so we can't buy our train tickets here.
tour guide	Ed wants to be a tour guide when he's older.
traffic news	My grandpa always checks the traffic news before he leaves the house.

PHRASAL VERBS		
Phrasal verb	**Meaning**	**Example sentence**
come in (type 2)	what somebody says to invite you into a place	Come in and have a drink of juice.
go in (type 3)	to enter a place	Let's go in the house – it's snowing!
pick up (type 1)	to collect something or somebody, often in a car	Rachel is picking me up at three o'clock.
set off (type 2)	to start a journey	Henry is setting off now to go to the skateboarding competition.
take off (type 2)	to leave the ground and go into the sky	How do you feel when the plane takes off?
turn off (type 1)	to leave a main road	Turn off at the next exit. That's the road to Edinburgh.

UNIT 5

TOPIC VOCABULARY | Words connected with *communication and technology*

Word	Example sentence
camera (n)	Harry often uses his dad's new camera to take pictures at the weekend.
keyboard (n)	My grandma can use a keyboard, but she's a bit slow.
laptop (n)	Danielle sometimes takes her laptop to school.
mouse (n)	My computer works well, but the mouse isn't very good, so I want a new one.
printer (n)	This printer only prints in black and white!
screen (n)	That screen is broken, so I can't see the picture.
blogging (v)	Vespa's new hobby is blogging about school. She often posts photos as well.
download (v)	I want to download Rihanna's song onto my phone.
graphics (n)	The graphics in his last film are amazing!
online (adj)	Did you find all the information for your project online?
software (n)	It's important to have good computer software because it means you can do more things.
stream (v)	I am thinking of streaming the *Harry Potter* films on my computer.

WORD PATTERNS | Compound nouns

Core word	Example sentence
CD player	Not many people use CD players these days.
cell phone	In America, they call mobile phones cell phones.
computer software	Some people spend a lot of money on new computer software.
laptop computer	Do the pupils in your school use laptop computers in class?
web page	Our school has its own web page.

COLLOCATIONS | Collocations with verbs

Collocation	Example sentence
download a piece of software	Do you want me to download that piece of software for you?
make a phone call	I need to make a phone call to my grandma now.
open a file	Did you open the correct file?
send a text message	Jed sent me a text message to say what time he wanted to meet.
start a conversation	He started a conversation with me about blogs and blogging.
take a photograph	Lisa says she wants to take a photograph of our school from a helicopter!
watch a DVD	Darren wanted to watch a DVD, but he decided to read a book instead.

UNIT 6

TOPIC VOCABULARY | Words connected with *fashion, clothes and shopping*

Word	Example sentence
bill (n)	Don't forget to ask the waiter for the bill.
buy (v)	Are you buying those shoes?
cash (n)	Robert lost his backpack, but luckily he keeps his cash in his pocket.
change (n)	Here's your £2 change.
cheque (n)	I never pay for anything by cheque.
cost (v)	How much does that jacket cost?
credit card (n)	I'm going to use my credit card to pay to join the gym.
customer (n)	It's my job to ask customers what they want.
department store (n)	They sell lots of different things in that department store.
market (n)	All the fruit in the market looks lovely.
receipt (n)	Liz got a receipt for the clothes she bought.
shop assistant (n)	Let's ask the shop assistant if he has these shoes in a bigger size.
shopper (n)	There aren't many shoppers here today because the weather is so bad.
shopping centre (n)	There are always a lot of people in the shopping centre on Saturdays.
spend (v)	Do you spend a lot of money going horse-riding every month?
supermarket (n)	Grant, will you go to the supermarket and get some bread, please?

WORD PATTERNS | Verbs + prepositions

Core word	Example sentence
pay for	I will pay for your new tennis racket.
pay in	Is Sam paying in cash for the cinema tickets?
put on	Put your coat on – it's cold outside.
take back	Seth didn't like the jeans so he took them back to the shop and changed them.
take off	Please take your dirty trainers off before you come in.
write down	Mum always writes down what she wants before she goes shopping for food.

COLLOCATIONS | Collocations with verbs

Collocation	Example sentence
catch a/the bus	Do you catch the bus to school or do you walk?
do the shopping	Mum does the shopping every Saturday.
for sale	There are some trainers for sale in *Sporty Shoes* today.
go shopping	My friend and I go shopping together.
keep the change	That's nine pounds, fifty, please. Here's ten pounds – keep the change.
save money	Bez is saving money because he wants to buy a new laptop.

UNIT 7

TOPIC VOCABULARY | Words connected with *school and studying*

Word	Example sentence
biology (n)	I'm not going to study biology at university. I'm not interested in plants and animals.
board (n)	My English teacher writes new words on the board.
bookshelf (n)	Did you have a bookshelf in your old room?
desk (n)	Elinor has got a lot of books on her desk.
dictionary (n)	We can use our dictionaries in English lessons.
eraser (n)	Can I borrow your eraser, please?
geography (n)	I enjoy geography because I like learning about different countries.
history (n)	We learnt about Henry VIII in history today.
learn (v)	Nadine thought she would learn a lot during her acting course.
maths (n)	I heard that Albert Einstein wasn't good at maths when he was at school.
music (n)	Do you sing in your music lessons, or do you just play the piano?
physics (n)	We did an experiment in physics today.
practise (v)	It's good to practise speaking English every day.
remember (v)	Did you remember to do your homework?
study (v)	Hugo is studying very hard because he wants to become a doctor.
teach (v)	Can you teach me how to play the violin?

WORD PATTERNS | Words + prepositions

Core word	Example sentence
arrive at	We need to arrive at the airport by 12:00 a.m.
at work	What did you do at work today?
borrow (sth) **from**	Can I borrow a pencil from you, Harriet?
help with	She said she needed help with preparing dinner.
learn about	We learn about pronunciation in English lessons.
learn from	I learnt a lot from the teachers in my old school.

COLLOCATIONS | Collocations with verbs

Collocation	Example sentence
do homework	I need to do homework before we go out.
draw a picture	Can you draw a picture of me with my cat?
go to university	My brother is going to go to university in September.
learn a foreign language	My mum wants to learn a foreign language – French.
leave school	He left school early because he didn't feel well.
take a course	I'm going to take a photography course.

UNIT 8

TOPIC VOCABULARY | Words connected with *sport*

Word	Example sentence
badminton (n)	Badminton is the best sport I have ever played!
cricket (n)	My grandpa is very good at cricket and plays every weekend in the summer.
kit (n)	Mum, where's my kit? I'm going to play football.
pool (n)	The pool near my school is busy on Saturdays because lots of children go swimming at the weekend.
skiing (n)	She loves skiing, but it doesn't snow very often where she lives.
stadium (n)	We enjoyed going to the stadium to watch the rugby match.
table tennis (n)	Will you teach me to play table tennis?
winner (n)	And Will is the winner of the competition!

WORD FORMATION | Verbs/nouns

Core word	Derivatives
play (v)	player (n)
run (v)	running (n), runner (n)
surf (v)	surfing (n), surfer (n)
swim (v)	swimming (n), swimmer (n)
win (v)	winning (n), winner (n)

COLLOCATIONS | Collocations with verbs

Collocation	Example sentence
climb a mountain	She is going to climb a mountain in March.
enter a competition	He entered the competition, but he hasn't started training yet.
go swimming	I am going to go swimming every week next term.
play cricket	Playing cricket looks easy, but it's not.
throw a ball	Are you going to throw the ball to me or not?
win a race	And Bolt wins the race again!

UNIT 9

TOPIC VOCABULARY | Words connected with *weather and nature*

Word	Example sentence
cloudy (adj)	It's cloudy, but the planes are still taking off.
fog (n)	We couldn't see the lake because of all the fog.
foggy (adj)	It is dangerous to drive when it's foggy.
ice (n)	There was ice on the road so we decided to go back to the hotel.
rainy (adj)	We don't go camping when it's very rainy.
snow (n)	When I woke up and looked outside, the garden was covered in snow.
sun (n)	Let's go out and play – the sun's shining now.
sunny (adj)	It's so sunny today! I am going to stay inside.
thunderstorm (n)	We aren't taking the dog for a walk in this thunderstorm!
windy (adj)	Don't wear a hat – it's too windy!
beach (n)	He could go to the beach if he is bored.
forest (n)	Can we take the dog for a walk in the forest?
hill (n)	You can see our house from the top of that hill.
mountain (n)	Look! There's snow on the top of the mountain.
river (n)	Can we go for a boat trip on the river?
sky (n)	It isn't cloudy so we can see a lot of stars in the sky tonight!

WORD PATTERNS | Words + prepositions

Core word	Example sentence
do experiments	It's interesting to do experiments and learn about why things happen.
good at	Suzi is good at singing and playing the guitar.
important to	It's important to study hard for your exams.
learn about (sth) **by**	I learnt about cooking by watching a video on YouTube!
the best time for/to	What is the best time of the year to visit your country?
want to	We all want to do well in the English test.

WORD FORMATION | Nouns/adjectives

Core word	Derivatives
cloud (n)	cloudy (adj)
fog (n)	foggy (adj)
ice (n)	icy (adj)
rain (n)	rainy (adj), rain (v)
snow (n)	snowy (adj), snow (v)
sun (n)	sunny (adj)

UNIT 10

TOPIC VOCABULARY | Words connected with *health*

Word	Example sentence
ankle (n)	When did you hurt your ankle? Were you running at the time?
arm (n)	I broke my arm so I can't write at the moment.
back (n)	You can get back problems if you sit at the computer for too long.
brain (n)	Is it true that your brain remembers everything you've ever done?
ear (n)	My grandma had her ears checked last month because she can't hear well.
eye (n)	Some people have one blue eye and one green eye.
face (n)	He looked at his face in the mirror and then brushed his hair.
finger (n)	My finger hurts because my brother shut the door on it!
foot (n)	These trainers don't fit well – I think I've got one foot bigger than the other.
hand (n)	Luke held his mum's hand while they walked across the busy road.
heart (n)	Running makes your heart go faster.
knee (n)	Lots of people hurt their ankles or their knees when they try skateboarding for the first time.
leg (n)	Jack had never been in an ambulance before he broke his leg.
neck (n)	She had a beautiful scarf round her neck.
nose (n)	The football hit Fred on the nose and broke it!
stomach (n)	Cows have four stomachs!
throat (n)	Your throat's going to hurt if you keep singing!

WORD PATTERNS | Words + prepositions

Core word	Example sentence
appointment with	I need to make an appointment with Doctor Jones, please.
course in	I took that course in English last year.
danger to	If you eat too much fast food, it could be a danger to your health.
hospital for	This is a hospital for people with back problems.
matter with	What is the matter with Dan? He looks worried.
medicine for	Keri has to take medicine for her sore throat.
pain in	I've got a pain in my leg. I hurt it climbing.
problem with	Sophie's got a problem with her ear, so she's seeing the doctor later.

COLLOCATIONS | Collocations with verbs

Collocation	Example sentence
break your leg	Amy broke her leg when she went skiing last year.
brush your teeth	Do you brush your teeth twice a day?
catch a cold	I think I've caught a cold. I feel hot and my throat hurts.
feel ill/better	Fed is feeling much better since he took his medicine.
make an appointment	Millie is feeling ill so we need to make an appointment with the doctor.
take your temperature	Does your mum take your temperature when you're not feeling well?

UNIT 11

TOPIC VOCABULARY | Words connected with *work and jobs*

Word	Example sentence
actor (n)	She's wanted to be an actor since she was five years old.
cleaner (n)	Have you seen the cleaner who looks after our offices?
engineer (n)	You have to go to study if you want to be an engineer.
firefighter (n)	The firefighters helped everyone to leave the building before the fire got too big.
journalist (n)	Ned is a journalist and he writes for a car magazine.
pilot (n)	The pilot managed to land the plane safely on a river!
police officer (n)	The police officer asked us questions about the robbery.
shop assistant (n)	The shop assistant helped me to find the right shoes.
career (n)	Mari has a good career as an actress in a new TV programme.
company (n)	Some young people have started their own companies.
customer (n)	All the customers love the new pizza restaurant.
earn (v)	Vicky is saving the money she earns to buy a new car.
manager (n)	If there's a problem, we speak to the manager.
meeting (n)	I have meetings all day today; I hope I have time for lunch.
social media officer (n)	Why do you want to work as a social media officer?
staff (n)	The manager is meeting the new staff today.
worker (n)	All the workers enjoy working for this company.

WORD FORMATION | Words with *–ian / -ress / -ist / -er / -r*

Core word	Derivatives
art (n)	artist (n), artistic (adj)
chemist (n)	chemistry (n)
clean (n/v)	cleaner (n)
dentist (n)	dentistry (n)
drive (v)	driving (n), driver (n)
engine (n)	engineer (n), engineering (n)
explore (v)	explorer (n)
farm (n)	farmer (n)
football (n)	footballer (n)
journal (n)	journalist (n)
manage (v)	manager (n)
music (n)	musical (adj), musician (n)
photograph (n)	photographer (n), photography (n)
reception (n)	receptionist (n)
wait (v)	waiter/waitress (n)
write (v)	writing (n), written (adj), writer (n)

WORD PATTERNS | Words + prepositions

Core word	Example sentence
diploma in	She just got a diploma in engineering.
manager of	He is the manager of a famous football team.
meeting with	I have an important meeting with my manager later today.
singer in	Sanjay is a singer in a local rock band.
works for	Beth works for a big company.
writer of	She is famous as a writer of children's stories.

UNIT 12

TOPIC VOCABULARY | Words connected with *houses and homes*

Word	Example sentence
armchair (n)	My grandma loves sitting in her comfortable armchair.
bath (n)	I usually have a shower in the mornings, but sometimes I lie in the bath and listen to music.
bed (n)	The bed in the hotel wasn't comfortable.
blanket (n)	Can you give me a blanket please? I'm a bit cold.
bookcase (n)	Seb's bought a new bookcase for all his books.
chair (n)	Let's take the chairs outside and sit in the sun.
cooker (n)	Mum's standing by the cooker, preparing dinner.
fridge (n)	Can you get the cheese out of the fridge, please?
lamp (n)	I have a lamp so I can read in bed.
pillow (n)	I put my head on the pillow and fell asleep immediately.
shower (n)	It takes me five minutes to have a shower.
sink (n)	Please wash those dishes in the sink before you leave.
sofa (n)	Let's sit together on the sofa and watch TV.
table (n)	Put the food on the table please while I bring the water.
toilet (n)	Please may I go to the toilet?
towel (n)	You're wet! Here's a towel for you.

PHRASAL VERBS

Phrasal verb	Meaning	Example sentence
find out (type 3)	to discover	She finally found out who the present was from.
get up (type 2)	to get out of bed after sleeping	Please get up! You'll be late for school.
go out (type 2)	leave home and go somewhere else	Can we go out somewhere tomorrow, Dad?
grow up (type 2)	to become older	Where did you grow up?
lie down (type 2)	to place your body in a flat position, e.g. on a bed	I need to lie down for a minute because I'm so tired!
wash up (type 1)	to wash plates, spoons, etc. after a meal	Can you start washing up for me, please?

COLLOCATIONS | Collocations with verbs

Collocation	Example sentence
do the washing-up	She does the washing-up to help her mum.
have a shower	I want to have a shower before we go out.
make my bed	I make my bed every morning, as soon as I get up.
move house	Have you and your family ever moved house or have you always lived here?
tidy your room	I tidy my room every Saturday morning before I go out to meet my friends.
wash the floor	Harry walked in with dirty trainers on so Mum had to wash the floor.

WRITING REFERENCE

AN INFORMAL EMAIL | Example task

Read the email from your English friend, Ethan.

> Hi Jake!
>
> Thanks for your email. I went to the cinema at the weekend with my friends and played tennis with my brother. Do you play tennis?
>
> What are your hobbies? Do you have the same hobbies as your friends and family?
>
> Email soon!
>
> Ethan

Write an email to Ethan and answer his questions.

Write 100 words.

To: Ethan Wallace ‹ewallace@fastmail.com›
Subject: My Hobbies

Hi Ethan! — *Use* Hi *or* Hello *and your friend's first name.*

Thanks for your email. I like hearing about your weekend. Did you and your friends enjoy the film? I like films, too, but I don't like tennis! — *Thank your friend for their email.* / *Respond to what your friend said in their email. Ask some questions about what they said.* / *Answer your friend's first question.*

You asked about my hobbies. Well, I don't have a lot of free time, but I like playing computer games. I play with friends online. I have friends all over the world and we enjoy playing together. — *Answer your friend's second question.*

I also really like collecting coins. My uncle gave me a coin from China last year. I've got ten coins from different countries! — *Answer your friend's third question.* / *Use short forms.* / *Use exclamation marks to show excitement or surprise.*

Write soon, and send me some photos of your family. — *At the end of the email say* Write soon, Write back, Email back. *You can also use* Take care, Love *or* I look forward to hearing from you *to end an informal email.*

Jake — *Write your first name at the end.*

Read the email from your English friend, Ella.

> Hi!
>
> Thanks for your email. I went out with my friends for dinner at the weekend. We ate Chinese food.
>
> What food do you like eating? What was the last meal you cooked? Do you have any interesting food in your country?
>
> Write back soon!
>
> Ella

Write an email to Ella and answer her questions.

Write 100 words.

A STORY | Example task

Your English teacher wants you to write a story with the title *'A cat – and my cousin – in a tree!'*.

Write your story in 100 words.

Give your story an interesting title.

In the first paragraph, answer the questions When?/Where?/Who?/What were you/they (doing/playing/eating, *etc.*)?

A CAT – AND MY COUSIN – IN A TREE!

Last summer, my cousin Ed came to stay. One Saturday morning, we were playing in the garden when we heard someone shout 'Help!' in the street.

We ran into the street and saw Mrs Taylor, our neighbour. She was pointing at the top of a big tree. 'What's the problem, Mrs Taylor?' I asked.

'My cat, Fluffy, is in the tree and she can't get down.'

'Don't worry, Mrs Taylor,' said Ed. 'I'm good at climbing trees. I'll get her.'

Ed climbed the tree. It was difficult but after twenty minutes, he shouted, 'I'm at the top! And I can see Fluffy! She's fine!'

Then, a minute later, he shouted loudly, 'Oh, no! I can't move! Help!'

I went to find Dad.

In the end, Fluffy climbed down the tree. She was fine and Mrs Taylor was very happy. My dad climbed the tree and helped Ed. He finally came down with a red face. We thought it was really funny!

Use the past simple for main events in a story.

In paragraph 2, say what happened next.

If different people speak, start each person's speech on a new line.

Say what happened next. Use words/phrases such as then, after that *and* next.

Use the past continuous to show a situation in progress when something else happened.

Use quote marks to show the exact words people say.

Adverbs such as loudly *and adjectives such as* difficult *make the story more interesting.*

In the last paragraph, say what happened at the end of the story. Use phrases such as in the end, finally *or* at last.

Your English teacher wants you to write a story.

The story must begin with the sentence *'I was surprised when I heard a knock at the door …'*.

Write 100 words.

A LETTER GIVING ADVICE | Example task

Read the letter from your friend, Rupert. Write a letter to him giving advice.

Write 100 words.

> Hi Joanne,
>
> How are you? I passed my cycling test last week. I'm so happy!
>
> But now I have to do a project and it's really difficult. I have to write about an English king or queen from history. I don't know who to write about! Can you help me with some ideas?
>
> Write back soon,
>
> Rupert

Write Dear *or* Hi, *+ first name only. Remember to put a comma or exclamation mark after the name.*

Thank your friend for their letter. Talk about something in their letter (but not the project yet).

Hi Rupert,

Thanks for your letter. I'm glad you passed your cycling test.

So, you've got to do a history project? Maybe you should choose a king in a Shakespeare play, like Richard III or Henry VIII (he had six wives!). Or, why not choose a famous queen? The other students will probably choose men. What about Queen Victoria or Elizabeth I?

I've got one more idea! How about choosing someone who was only a king or queen for a very short time? For example, Lady Jane Grey. She was queen for only nine days!

I hope you like my ideas. Write back and let me know who you choose!

Bye for now!

Joanne

Some short forms are acceptable in an informal letter.

We can use should, why don't you, how about, why not *and* what about *to make suggestions.*

Talk about the project. Make your first suggestion.

Make another suggestion.

Make another suggestion.

You don't need to write complete sentences in an informal letter.

Use exclamation marks to show excitement or surprise.

Say goodbye (and express your love if you want to). You can use other phrases such as Cheers, Thanks a lot, Write back soon *to end an informal letter.*

Write your first name.

This is a part of a letter you receive from an English friend.

> I'm visiting your city in the summer! Can you give me some advice on things to do? What places should I visit? What things should I bring with me?

Write a letter answering your friend's questions.

Write 100 words.

A MAGAZINE ARTICLE | Example task

Write an article for a magazine about how school life is different now from in the past.

Write 100 words.

Give your article an interesting title.

School life then and now

Introduce the topic and say a few general things.

Ask questions to attract your readers' attention.

Everyone goes to school when they are young. But have you ever thought about how schools have changed? In the past, school life was very different from today.

Make your first main point, e.g. describe what things were like in the past.

When our parents were at school, they didn't have so much technology. There was no internet, no mobile phones and very few computers. They did all their work on paper.

Use we, us *and* our *to get close to your reader.*

Make your next main point, e.g. describe what things are like now.

Today, we have computers and the internet to find things out. We still have books, but they often have a link to download more material.

Summarise your opinion and conclude. Use words and phrases such as In summary …, So …, So you can see …

So in summary, school life today is very different from our parents' school life. However, education is just as important today as it was then.

Use however *and* but *to make contrasting points.*

You have been asked by the editor of your school magazine to write an article on the following topic.

Today's television programmes are worse than programmes ten years ago.

Write 100 words.

AN ESSAY | Example task

Your teacher has asked you to write an essay on the following question.

Has technology made our lives better or worse?

Write 100–140 words.

Technology makes our lives better and easier in many ways, but I believe it has made our lives worse and more complicated in more ways.

Write a strong first sentence, stating your opinion.

Use words such as firstly *and* first *to introduce your first point.*

Firstly, we don't spend as much time speaking to our friends and family. Talking to people is important and sometimes you can misunderstand things that are written in an email or online. Before technology, people talked to each other more and I think they were less lonely.

Write about the opposite view. Then say why you disagree.

Use words such as however, *and* but *to make contrasting points.*

Use phrases such as for example *and* for instance *to introduce examples.*

Use phrases such as in addition *to give extra information.*

Technology has made some things much faster. However, it has also made life more complicated in other ways. For example, if your computer breaks, you need time and money to fix it. In addition, it can be expensive to buy and repair computers and smartphones.

Write your final point.

Finally, technology has made it possible for us to travel more quickly and cheaply than before, but this isn't necessarily a good thing as it is bad for the environment.

Write a short conclusion. Use phrases such as In conclusion, To sum up, In summary *or* To conclude.

In conclusion, there are lots of positive effects of technology, but I think there have been more negative consequences.

Your teacher has asked you to write an essay on the following topic.

Big cities have lots of environmental problems. How do you think these problems can be solved?

Write 100–140 words.

A FORMAL LETTER OF COMPLAINT | Example task

You recently had a bad experience in a restaurant. Write a formal letter of complaint to the restaurant manager, explaining the problems and what you want him/her to do.

Write 100–140 words.

Start formal letters with Dear. *Use* Sir/Madam *if you don't know the name of the person you're writing to. Use* Mr/Mrs + surname *if you know the name of the person you are writing to.*

Give basic details of your complaint.

Use the first sentence to say why you are writing. Use phrases such as I'm writing to complain about …

Dear Sir/Madam,

I am writing to complain about a recent experience at your restaurant. I visited the restaurant with a friend on 5th December in the evening.

Give further details of your complaint.

When we arrived it took a long time for the waiter to notice us. He then said we needed to wait for another half an hour. We booked a table for 7:30 pm, but we didn't sit at our table until 8:30 pm. Then, when our food finally came, some of it was cold and some of it was very spicy. I couldn't eat any of it. I told the waiter but he didn't apologise, so we left.

Say specifically what you want from the recipient of the letter. Use phrases such as I would like a refund / a free meal / an apology.

I would like you to refund us 30 euros for the meal or to offer us a free meal at your restaurant.

I look forward to your reply.

Use a phrase such as I look forward to hearing from you / your reply *to end the letter.*

Yours faithfully,

End formal letters with Yours faithfully, *if you don't know the name of the person you're writing to and* Yours sincerely, *if you know the name.*

Jamie Morris

Sign off with your full name.

You bought some boots online, but when they arrived they were the wrong colour and style.

Write a formal letter of complaint to the seller.

Write 100–140 words.

IRREGULAR VERBS REFERENCE

Bare infinitive	Past simple	Past participle
be	was/were	been
become	became	become
begin	began	begun
break	broke	broken
bring	brought	brought
build	built	built
buy	bought	bought
catch	caught	caught
choose	chose	chosen
come	came	come
cost	cost	cost
cut	cut	cut
draw	drew	drawn
do	did	done
drink	drank	drunk
drive	drove	driven
eat	ate	eaten
fall	fell	fallen
feel	felt	felt
find	found	found
fly	flew	flown
forget	forgot	forgotten
get	got	got
give	gave	given
go	went	been/gone
grow	grew	grown
have	had	had
hear	heard	heard
hit	hit	hit
hold	held	held
hurt	hurt	hurt
keep	kept	kept
know	knew	known
leave	left	left
let	let	let
lie	lay	lain

Bare infinitive	Past simple	Past participle
lose	lost	lost
make	made	made
mean	meant	meant
meet	met	met
pay	paid	paid
put	put	put
read	read	read
ride	rode	ridden
ring	rang	rung
run	ran	run
say	said	said
see	saw	seen
sell	sold	sold
send	sent	sent
set	set	set
shine	shone	shone
show	showed	shown
sing	sang	sung
sit	sat	sat
sleep	slept	slept
speak	spoke	spoken
spend	spent	spent
stand	stood	stood
steal	stole	stolen
swim	swam	swum
take	took	taken
teach	taught	taught
tell	told	told
think	thought	thought
throw	threw	thrown
try	tried	tried
understand	understood	understood
wake	woke	woken
wear	wore	worn
win	won	won
write	wrote	written

Macmillan Education
4 Crinan Street
London N1 9XW
A division of Macmillan Publishers Limited

Companies and representatives throughout the world

ISBN 978-0-230-48826-7

Written by Jeremy Bowell and Richard Storton

The authors have asserted their right to be identified as the authors of this work in accordance with the Copyright, Designs and Patents Act 1988.

First published 2017

Designed by Designers Collective
Illustrated by David Belmonte, Dani Geremia, Andrew Painter and Red Giraffe.
Cover design by Designers Collective
Cover photograph by **Getty Images**/Echo; **Shutterstock**/ProStockStudio and Shutterstock/phototy (background)
Picture research by Penelope Bowden, Proudfoot Pictures

Authors' acknowledgements
Jeremy and Richard would like to thank the team at Macmillan and all the many teachers and students around the world who helped make this wonderful project possible.

The publishers would like to thank the course consultants Malcolm Mann and Steve Taylore-Knowles.

The authors and publishers would like to thank the following for permission to reproduce their photographs:
Alamy/adrian arbib p103, Alamy/America p126(b), Alamy/Cultura RM p12(t), Alamy/Tim Gainey p92, Alamy/MANDY GODBEHEAR p14(inset tr), Alamy/Hemis p78, Alamy/Hero Images Inc. p53, Alamy/Friedrich von Hörsten p126(t), Alamy/Juice Images p100, Alamy/Lumi Images p11, Alamy/Mint Images Limited p58(cl), Alamy/Andrey Moisseyev p103(bl), Alamy/nagelestock.com p44, Alamy/Shotshop GmbH p7(4), Alamy/ Slik Pictures Ltd p84(inset tl), Alamy/travelstock44.de/Juergen Held p60: **BANANASTOCK** 1996-98 AccuSoft Inc., All right p143(r); **Barcroft Media** p75; BRANDX p114(lm); **By kind permission of Children's Railway** p115(tr,cl); **Classcraft** p77; **Comstock Images** p29; Dean Ryan p114(tr); **Johnny Cupcakes 279 Newbury Street Boston, MA USA** www.johnnycupcakes.com p59(boxes, store); **George Kaponay/ Réka Kaponay - Dreamtime Traveler** p43; **Getty** pp5(tr), 27(main), 63(background), 81(ball), p114(bm), 125(berries), p114(tc), Getty/ iStockphoto /Thinkstock/Jana BlaÅ…Â¡kovÃƒÂ¡ p49(background right), Getty/Caiaimage/Paul Bradbury p20(r), Getty/EyeEm Premium/Tom Chambers p19(background concert), Getty/imagestock p19(background t-shirts), Getty/iStockphoto/Martin-Kubik p125(owl), Getty/Blend Images/Jose Luis Pelaez Inc p98, Getty/Betsie Van Der Meer p49(iphone selfie), Getty/moodboard RF/moodboard p142, Getty/iStockphoto/ Thinkstock Images/mysondanube p115(background), Getty/Photodisc pp114(c, bl), Getty/iStockphoto/Thinkstock/Thomas Pullicino p145, Getty/iStockphoto/Thinkstock Images/Diana Taliun p125(carrots); **Getty Images**/Brian Bailey p121, Getty Images/Ben Pipe Photography p14(inset cm), Getty Images/TORSTEN BLACKWOOD/Staff p103(t), Getty Images/Clive Brunskill/Staff p81(l), Getty Images/Caiaimage/Robert Daly p50, Getty Images/DGLimages p85, Getty Images/Caiaimage/Tom Merton p7(7), Getty Images/CommerceandCultureAgency p71(tr), Getty Images/DrAfter123 p70, Getty Images/David Henderson p99, Getty Images/ChrisHepburn p37(background), Getty Images/lzf p110, Getty Images/Julian Finney/Staff p81(tc), Getty Images/EyeEm p26, Blend Images/John Fedele p54(b), Getty Images/Peter M. Fisher p63, Getty Images/Flashpop p124, Getty Images/fstop123 p52, Getty Images/ gbh007 p7(2), Getty Images/GoodLifeStudio p14(inset l), Getty Images/ Priscilla Gragg p55(3), Getty Images/Eric Hanson p41, Getty Images/ Hero Images p5(tr), Getty Images/Hill Street Studios p7(8), Getty Images/ Image Source p55(2), Getty Images/iStock/seb_ra p40, Getty Images/ Jupiterimages p58(r), Getty Images/kali9 p88, Getty Images/kasto80 p37(a), Getty Images/kevinruss p38, Getty Images/Andreas Kuehn p58(cr), Getty Images/Keystone/Stringer p82, Getty Images/Lucia Lambriex p84(inset bl), Getty Images/Rob Lewine p55(1), Getty Images/ Justin Lewis p4(l), Getty Images/mattricphoto p66, Getty Images/Tom Merton p80, Getty Images/michaeljung p76, Getty Images/Daniel Milchev p7(1), Getty Images/Robert Niedring p4(tr), Getty Images/ nycshooter p83(tennis player), Getty Images/PeopleImages p83(rugby), Getty Images/Brigita Rafanelli/EyeEm p58(l), Getty Images /Marc Romanelli p7(3), Getty Images/Rtimages p83(cricketer), Getty Images/ scisettialfio p59(bottles), Getty Images/Ariel Skelley pp4(rc), 118, Getty Images/stevecoleimages p119, Getty Images/STRDEL/Stringer p72, Getty Images/Syldavia p7(5), Getty Images/Topalov p74, Getty Images/ Vertigo3d p18, Getty Images/Westend61 pp4(tc), 27(chef), Getty Images/WIN-Initiative p7(6), Getty Images/Yalana p62; **Image Source**/Bill Miles p129(r), Image Source/Jasper White CM p19(background cinema); **iStock** p87; **Macmillan Australia** p27(chillis); **Macmillan Publishers Ltd** p125(cow); **Photodisc** p125(bird), PhotoDisc/ Getty Images p115(t), PhotoDisc/Getty Images/Lisa Zador p19(background dice); **Shutterstock** p114(cmr), Shutterstock/1000 words p128, Shutterstock/ Aaron Amat p114(br), Shutterstock/Ruth Black p28, Shutterstock/ chrisbrignell p114(tl), Shutterstock/Goran Bogicevic p34, Shutterstock/ Marie Charouzova p94(cow), Shutterstock/chirapbogdan p33, Shutterstock/Dimedrol68 p114(mr), Shutterstock/EFKS p83(background), Shutterstock/Peter Hermes Furian p71(cl), Shutterstock/Leszek Glasner p59(background), Shutterstock/ImageFlow p106, Shutterstock/ Brian A Jackson p102(tr), Shutterstock/JeniFoto p132, Shutterstock/ John Kasawa p114(bcr), Shutterstock/kikovic p30, Shutterstock/Kues p114(tcr), Shutterstock/Amy Laughinghouse p37(b), Shutterstock/ LTim p4(cm), Shutterstock/lolo1960 p109(a), Shutterstock/Cristi Lucaci p102(l), Shutterstock/macknimal p81(tennis green), Shutterstock/ maradon 333 p36, Shutterstock/matthi p37(c), Shutterstock/Minerva Studio p120, Shutterstock/Sergey Mironov p17(b), Shutterstock/ Monkey Business Images p14(inset cl), Shutterstock/morrowlight p19(b), Shutterstock/Sergey Novikov p84(main), Shutterstock/oneinchpunch p61, Shutterstock/onot p143(l), Shutterstock/Photographee. eu p130, Shutterstock/pikselstock p59(boy), Shutterstock/PKpix p12(b), Shutterstock/Rawpixel.com p54(a), Shutterstock/pinkomelet p114(girl), Shutterstock/Rawpixel.com p117, Shutterstock/Roman Rvachov p16, Shutterstock/Gino Santa Maria p83(female footballer), Shutterstock/sdecoret p48, Shutterstock/Syda Productions p109(b), Shutterstock/charles taylor p21, Shutterstock/TonyNg p22, Shutterstock/ TravnikovStudio p102(trb), Shutterstock/Varuna p104, Shutterstock/ wavebreakmedia p5(lc), Shutterstock/YanLev p14(main), Shutterstock/ Zonda p114(tcl); **SWNS** p15(t,cr); **123RF**/Dmitriy Shironosov p14(inset cr), 123RF/Olha Shtepa p19(a).

Printed and bound in Spain by Edelvives

2021 2020 2019 2018 2017
10 9 8 7 6 5 4 3 2 1